Encouraging Sustainable Behavior

Increasingly it is being recognized that consumer behavior may be a key trigger in the march toward sustainable development. Several lines of psychological theory and approaches have been developed relatively independently, each of which may provide major implications and action points on how consumers might be moved toward more sustainable behavior. This book is the first to bring together this variety of perspectives and theoretical angles around the common ambition of sustainable development.

The contributors are all leading social scientists in the field of consumer behavior who met the challenge to sketch out their theoretical perspectives, but also to go beyond their normal theorizing and to think out of the box in order to show how these theoretical perspectives might be made actionable in terms of key managerial and policy perspectives toward sustainable development. The result is a book that shows a wealth of information and approaches the question of how to encourage sustainable behavior from a myriad of divergent perspectives. This should stimulate scientists and policy-makers alike to find similarities, differences, and synergies between state-of-the-art psychological thinking about how to most effectively stimulate sustainable consumer behavior.

Hans C. M. van Trijp holds the Chair of Marketing and Consumer Behavior at Wageningen University and is part-time Lead Scientist in Consumer Behavior at Unilever R&D in the Netherlands. His scientific work focuses primarily on the extent to which consumer behavior theory can be exploited to inform marketing strategies to enhance sustainable consumer behavior. He was the Scientific Director within the Dutch innovation program Transforum in the area of mobilizing consumer demand for sustainable products and services. He has published extensively in the marketing, consumer psychology, and food domains. He is a member of the editorial boards of *International Journal of Research in Marketing* and *Food Quality and Preference* and chairs the Food and Consumer working group within the European Technology Platform Food for Life with the aim to leverage the research agendas between industry and governments across Europe.

Encouraging Sustainable Behavior

Psychology and the Environment

Edited by

Hans C. M. van Trijp

Psychology Press
Taylor & Francis Group

NEW YORK AND LONDON

First published 2014
by Psychology Press
711 Third Avenue, New York, NY 10017

Simultaneously published in the UK
by Psychology Press
27 Church Road, Hove, East Sussex BN3 2FA

Psychology Press is an imprint of the Taylor & Francis Group, an informa business

© 2014 Taylor & Francis

Library of Congress Cataloging in Publication Data
A catalog record for this book has been requested.

ISBN: 978-1-84872-988-9 (hbk)
ISBN: 978-1-84872-649-9 (pbk)
ISBN: 978-0-203-14118-2 (ebk)

Typeset in New Caledonia
by Taylor & Francis Books

Printed and bound in the United States of America by Publishers Graphics,
LLC on sustainably sourced paper.

Contents

SECTION 6   ENHANCING SUSTAINABLE BEHAVIOR IN PRACTICE

SECTION 7   CONCLUDING REMARKS

Contributors

Yana R. Avramova
University of Antwerp

Jillian C. Banfield
Yale University

Sheri L. Clark
State University of New York at Stony
Brook

Isaac M. Dinner
University of North Carolina

Janne van Doorn
Tilburg University

Bob M. Fennis
University of Groningen

Arnout R. H. Fischer
Wageningen University

Elizabeth S. Focella
University of Arizona

Antonio L. Freitas
State University of New York at Stony
Brook

Kentaro Fujita
The Ohio State University

Daniel G. Goldstein
Microsoft Research

Jennifer N. Gutsell
Brandeis University

Michael Inzlicht
University of Toronto Scarborough

Janneke de Jonge
Wageningen University

Aaron C. Kay
Duke University

Siegwart Lindenberg
University of Groningen and Tilburg
University

Marijn H. C. Meijers
University of Amsterdam

Geoffrey Miller
University of New Mexico and NYU
Stern School of Business

Thomas Morton
University of Exeter

Marret K. Noordewier
Leiden University

Tom Postmes
University of Groningen

Travis Proulx
Tilburg University

Anna Rabinovich
University of Exeter

Saskia A. Schwinghammer
Utrecht University of Applied Sciences

Steven Shepherd
Duke University

Paul Sparks
University of Sussex

Linda Steg
University of Groningen

Jeff Stone
University of Arizona

Hans C. M. van Trijp
Wageningen University

Kathleen D. Vohs
University of Minnesota

Marcel Zeelenberg
Tilburg University

Martijn van Zomeren
University of Groningen

Section 1

Introduction

1

Multiple Selves in Sustainable Consumption
An Introduction

YANA R. AVRAMOVA and HANS C.M. VAN TRIJP

S ustainable development is one of the key challenges that world economies are facing both in the commercial and in the public policy domain. The latest United Nations (UN) projections on population growth show that by the year 2050 the world population will likely have reached nine billion people with much of the growth taking place in developing and emerging countries. At the same time, the commitment to the UN Millennium Development Goals sets targets for increased social and environmental performance related to sustainable development worldwide. It is obvious that these ambitions cannot be achieved within the current consumption patterns or within the current marketing and production practices. There is a strong and global need to move consumption and production practices into the direction of more balanced and sustainable development.

Although technology in sourcing, manufacturing, and logistics can make an important contribution to sustainable development, it is increasingly recognized that consumer behavior also plays an important role in the advancement of sustainable development.

Creating consumer demand for sustainable products and services sets important challenges. To some extent, it can be portrayed as a classical social dilemma as the protection of the common good requires individuals to behave in ways that diverge from their traditional individual utility maximization. What is good for society in the long run is not necessarily the best option for the individual in the short term. Reassuringly, consumers seem to be increasingly concerned with sustainability and increasingly aware of the environmental impact of their individual purchase and consumption decisions. Unfortunately, for the majority of consumers these positive attitudes toward sustainable development still

3

translate only weakly into actual purchase and consumption behaviors. Thus, there is a discrepancy between what consumers say and what they actually do: Although they "talk green," they do not necessarily "walk green."

The discrepancy between good intentions and poor behavior has intrigued academic researchers from diverse scientific disciplines. It has been viewed as a particular instance of the traditional attitude–behavior discrepancy, or as a manifestation of the conflict between our different selves (angels vs. demons /citizens vs. consumers) and has even been related to the activity of distinct (more impulsive vs. more considerate) brain areas. These different theoretical perspectives have largely developed independently with cross-fertilization being virtually absent. This is unfortunate, as much can be learned from closer interaction and integration.

On November 18–19, 2010, we were in the fortunate position to facilitate such closer interaction and integration. Supported by Transforum, a Dutch innovation program on sustainable development, we organized a symposium on "Multiple Selves and Sustainable Development" in Amsterdam, the Netherlands. It enabled us to selectively invite some of the world's leading researchers, together with policy-makers and business representatives, to share their scientific and more applied perspectives. Each of the invited speakers was explicitly asked to present his or her scientific perspective on the issue, to link it to the specific application area of sustainable development, and to further reflect on how this particular perspective might inform intervention efforts of the commercial and policy sectors in promoting sustainable consumer behavior. This book reflects those perspectives from a range of different disciplines such as social psychology, evolutionary psychology, neuroscience, consumer behavior, and marketing.

In Chapter 2, de Jonge, Fischer, and van Trijp discuss the commercial challenges inherent in sustainable development from a social marketing perspective. As marketing is fundamentally grounded in the concept of value exchange, the social marketing approach suggests that sustainable behavior can be enhanced through the motivation, ability, and opportunity routes. In other words, a key challenge lies in positioning sustainable behavior as aligning with consumers' self-interest (motivation), thereby ensuring that this self-interest is recognized and understood (ability) and can be acted upon (opportunity). Along these lines, the social marketing perspective provides a transparent structure along which intervention strategies to promote sustainable development can be designed. For instance, self-interest can be enhanced if sustainable products also provide superior product quality (e.g., animal-friendly produced steaks with enhanced functionality in terms of tenderness), but perceived self-interest can also emerge from social distinctiveness or adherence to group norms. One implication of the social marketing perspective is that sustainable behavior is more likely to occur if barriers that withhold consumers from expressing their good intentions into behavior are removed. An effective strategy might be to make sustainable behavior options easily available and easily accessible, probably even the default option.

In Chapter 3, Geoffrey Miller takes on an evolutionary approach to understanding and promoting sustainable consumption. He argues that there is nothing in our evolutionary history and genetic disposition that would favor sustainable consumption for the sake of its sustainability. In his view, people use sustainable consumption as a means to display or "signal" their superiority to others. He argues that those engaging in conspicuous consumption of sustainable products probably do so to signal to potential mates, friends, and kin that they have the capacity to "handle it" (analogous to the male peacock's tail, which is a costly signaling device to attract mates and to deter rivals). Miller proposes that marketing efforts aimed at enhancing sustainable consumption should thus exploit our "trait signaling instincts," namely our tendency to signal to others that we possess highly valued traits, such as high intelligence, agreeableness, conscientiousness, etc. Miller's perspective suggests several routes to promoting sustainable consumption. For one thing, marketing efforts should not make "green" easily accessible, cheap, and popular, and certainly not the default. Rather, the "green" should be kept costly, elitist, and exclusive for the sake of preserving its signaling potential.

In Chapter 4, Lindenberg and Steg focus on the normative aspects of sustainable consumption. They argue that the normative goal to act pro-environmentally is relatively weak, and often much more abstract, as compared to the competing hedonic and gain goals (e.g., to have fun, to pay less). Thus, strategies for inducing sustainable behavior need to be backed up by consistent social support aimed at strengthening the normative goal. The authors argue that norm-guided behavior (i.e., compliance with the norm) can be stimulated by making the sustainability norm chronically more accessible and by making the gain and hedonic goals compatible with the normative goal. They further propose that self-regulation and pro-environmental behavior can be enhanced through providing consumers with customized comparative feedback (e.g., what similar others do), and by ensuring that descriptive norm information (e.g., traces in the environment indicating what is generally accepted and done) supports the norm.

In Chapter 5, Goldstein and Dinner elaborate on the potential of default-setting, well-established in many other domains, as an approach to promoting sustainable consumption. Defaults can be a powerful tool for guiding sustainable behavior, as consumers tend to perceive the default as indicative of majority preferences and as a cue for source recommendation and endorsement. Moreover, the otherwise high transaction costs of information search and switching to sustainable product options may be substantially reduced. That is, "green defaults" (e.g., factory-set configurations, smart consideration sets in household energy plans, customized feedback and reminders for appliance inspections, etc.) may "nudge" consumers to make more sustainable choices by ensuring that any extra time and effort—that often deter consumers from making greener choices—would be associated with opting out of (rather than with opting into) the pro-environmental default. Goldstein and Dinner provide some specific guidelines on default-setting that could help policy-makers and marketers to identify the most appropriate default configuration for a specific context (e.g., reverting, persistent, updating defaults). The critical variable here is the relative importance of the particular issue or policy at the individual and the societal level.

A complementary perspective is provided by Meijers, Noordewier, and Avramova in Chapter 6, which focuses on the *consequences* of behaving sustainably. Meijers and co-authors review evidence suggesting that although people may sometimes continue to behave sustainably after an initial sustainable act (carry-over effects), this is not always the case. In fact, engaging in sustainable behavior may sometimes lead to less sustainable behavior later on (balance effects)—a pattern that is in line with findings from the licensing and goal-pursuit literatures. That is, engaging in sustainable behavior makes people feel good about themselves, giving them a sense of having "done enough" in this domain, and thereby licensing them to behave unsustainably later. Similarly, achieving (rather than pursuing) the pre-set goal to behave sustainably pushes this goal into the background, thus decreasing the chances for subsequent goal-congruent behavior. Meijers et al. suggest that an important determinant of whether carry-over or balance effects ensue is self-view: When people have a sustainable self-view (or when such a view is temporarily activated), they are more likely to exhibit carry-over effects and thus consistently behave sustainably (i.e., be their sustainable selves). The authors further propose that the social labeling technique can be used to induce a sustainable self-view and thus elicit continued sustainable behavior, and that it can be efficiently incorporated in mass communication, package labeling, and product slogans.

In Chapter 7, Fujita, Clark, and Freitas build on construal level theory, arguing that the ways in which environmental issues are perceived and cognitively construed may affect the behaviors that people engage in. According to the construal level perspective, sustainability concerns are construed much more globally and abstractly than other, more immediate concerns and goals. The authors suggest that efforts promoting pro-environmental decisions and actions can benefit from either of two strategies. On the one hand, persuasive messages can be framed in such a way as to highlight the concrete features and benefits of sustainable options, thereby making distant and abstract concerns more immediate and relevant. Alternatively, persuasive communication may aim to induce a more abstract mindset, or a higher level of construal, in consumers, thereby promoting consideration of more global and abstract issues and ultimately leading to more environment-friendly decisions. Either way, the *fit* between consumers' level of construal and the persuasive message is crucial, with higher consistency yielding better results.

Chapter 8, by Travis Proulx, presents yet another approach inspired by theorizing and evidence from the field of social cognition. According to Proulx, the general level of concern for the environment is rather low, as compared to the concern raised by the ongoing economic crisis, since the latter is much more immediate, concrete, and *visibly* impactful. Taking an existentialist perspective, Proulx argues that people respond to threat, such as an impending environmental catastrophe, by reaffirming their core values and beliefs. Evidence from research in this tradition suggests that unexpected or threatening events challenge people's basic need for meaning, structure, and consistency, thus causing what Proulx calls "feeling of the absurd." As a consequence, people are more likely to stick to whatever is familiar and certain (even when it is not as positive), and to maintain the status quo. Along these lines, Proulx proposes that sustainability-oriented initiatives will be more successful if (1) environmental problems are perceived as more concrete, immediate, and economic, and if (2) there is a "sustainable status quo." In other words, people should be able to reaffirm their beliefs through engaging in sustainable (rather than unsustainable) behavior.

A closely related perspective is presented in Chapter 9 by Banfield, Shepherd, and Kay, who suggest that confronting people with global and massive, hardly comprehensible, environmental problems may be threatening and may thus cause people to maintain the status quo, thereby impeding behavior change. Banfield et al. review evidence from research on system justification and compensatory control, showing that when people feel helpless to solve environmental problems, they also avoid potentially useful (but still threatening) information regarding these problems. Moreover, the lack of personal control strengthens faith and trust in the system, as personified by God, the government, and other institutions. As a consequence, people feel a weaker sense of personal responsibility, which ultimately leads to less action and behavior change. According to Banfield et al., sustainability efforts should thus aim at providing people with a sense of agency and control, and at framing sustainable behavior as a means for satisfying this basic need by "imposing order on chaos." In addition, Banfield et al. suggest that environment-related information should be presented to the public in easily understandable formats, such as not to elicit a feeling of threat.

In Chapter 10, Vohs and Fennis provide a social-psychological perspective on how norms and social influence can be utilized in inducing sustainable behavior. Their research suggests that people who are low in self-control can be an easy target for various social influence techniques. Turning what could often be a *weakness* into a *strength*, the authors argue that social cues promoting sustainable behaviors will be more readily picked up and acted upon by people with lower self-control. The research shows that when self-regulatory resources are depleted, people become more compliant with salient social norms and persuasion tactics (e.g., reciprocity, celebrity endorsement). The major implication from this perspective for sustainability initiatives is that combining self-control depletion techniques (or targeting people with chronically low self-control) with social influence techniques seems to be an especially effective way to elicit sustainable behavior.

In Chapter 11, Gutsell and Inzlicht present a neuroscientific perspective focusing on the neural mechanisms underlying self-regulation. They show that setting a goal is only one step toward successful goal pursuit. Monitoring one's goal progress, as well as experiencing strong (negative) emotions after self-control failure (i.e., when the goal is not met) is also crucial. It is argued that from a neuroscientific perspective, motivating sustainable behavior through emphasizing pro-social values, such as empathy, may not be a very effective strategy. That is, since environmental issues are typically quite distant and abstract, it may be difficult to induce strong emotions toward the lot of anonymous people, remote places, or toward nature and the environment in general. Sustainable initiatives may thus be more successful if the environment is personalized and people feel connected to Nature (leading to stronger pro-environmental goals and stronger empathy); if sustainable goals are made more salient (e.g., through clear product labeling); and if violations of pro-environmental goals are made more "painful," such that stronger negative emotions are experienced after environmental transgressions (i.e., self-control failure). In addition, Gutsell and Inzlicht propose that sustainable behavior could be enhanced by treating it as an instance of the moral domain and stressing the sanctity and purity of nature.

In Chapter 12, Zeelenberg and van Doorn delve further into the importance of emotions in inducing sustainable behavior. Adopting a "feeling-is-for-doing" approach, which stresses the motivational function of emotions, the authors argue that different emotions may divergently influence consumers' decisions and choices. Empirical evidence is presented regarding the effects of envy, regret, shame, and guilt. The findings show, for instance, that feelings of benign envy might stimulate consumption (e.g., buying a product that someone who is better off also owns). Experiencing or anticipating regret, on the other hand, might drive one to switch to a different product, brand, or service provider, thus producing behavior change. Finally, guilt and shame can induce pro-social behavior (e.g., donating). It is suggested that the motivational power of emotions has practical implications for sustainability initiatives. Inducing feelings of regret and guilt, for example, can strengthen feelings of personal responsibility and thus motivate personal efforts toward sustainable behavior.

In Chapter 13, Paul Sparks addresses sustainable consumption from the perspective of attitude theories. Reviewing the general relationship between attitudes, intentions, and behavior, he questions the very notion of "multiple selves" and attitude–behavior discrepancies. In his view, the degree of incongruency between what people think and intend to do, on the one hand, and what they actually do, on the other, is largely a matter of measurement. That is, more accurate measures of attitudes and intentions—ones that are on the same level of generality as the behavior measures—would produce greater correspondence. Sparks suggests that a meaningful and fruitful framework of the multiple selves problem would be in terms of interpersonal and intergroup relations, rather than in intra-personal terms. Specifically, he argues that sustainable behavior is closely related to the domains of morality (as it concerns the welfare of others) and collective action (as it presents a social dilemma requiring cooperation between people).

In Chapter 14, Postmes, Rabinovich, Morton, and Van Zomeren provide a social identity perspective on the issue of sustainable consumption, suggesting that the "psychological disjuncture" between the individual and environmental problems stems from perceptions of these problems as distant and abstract. Specifically, the common view is that we have inherited the world as it is from the generations before us (hence, we are not responsible for causing the problems), and that any solutions we could possibly think of and implement will only affect generations after us (hence, we won't directly benefit from solving the problems). The authors note that using existing social identities to promote sustainability may actually backfire: Urging people to behave sustainably by eliciting in-group–out-group comparisons (e.g., *they* do it, but *you* don't) may actually decrease sustainable behavior.

According to Postmes et al., a better strategy would be to create novel, sustainable identities that extend the self-concept across time and space, thereby making responsibility for the existing problems, as well as actions toward solving them, more relevant and likely. It is suggested that the Social Identity Model of Collective Action (SIMCA) provides an appropriate theoretical framework for informing sustainability efforts. According to this model, moral convictions can be effectively used to create new sustainable identities, which are focused on the future, or what the authors term *becoming* (rather than on the current self, on *being*). As a result, environmental transgressions would be more salient, and the sense of injustice they trigger stronger. In sum, this chapter argues that collective pro-environmental action is triggered by the combination of several essential elements: moral convictions based on universal standards that transcend group boundaries; a sense of efficacy (sufficient followers and attainable targets); and emotions, such as anger, moral outrage, hope, and enthusiasm.

In Chapter 15, Focella and Stone approach the sustainability issue from the perspective of consistency theories, suggesting that hypocrisy can be used to induce sustainable behavior. Taking classic cognitive consistency theories as a point of departure, the authors argue that maintaining a coherent and consistent self, and striving for consistency between attitudes and behavior, is a basic motivator of human action. Making people aware of not *walking the talk* (e.g., by reminding them of their failure to follow up on an earlier stated intention to engage in a pro-environmental behavior) activates highly important cognitions that are strongly linked to the self-concept (e.g., I care for the environment). Realizing the discrepancy between the positive self-concept and actual behavior is likely to create psychological tension or cognitive dissonance, thus triggering sustainable behavior that can restore balance and consistency. The authors also introduce the notion of *vicarious hypocrisy*—the idea that one can experience cognitive dissonance vicariously, by witnessing the hypocritical behavior of an in-group member. Specifically, since an in-group member's hypocrisy threatens the in-group's integrity (similar to personal hypocrisy threatening self-integrity), witnessing an in-group member's transgression may trigger individual behavior change aimed to restore the in-group's integrity. Evidence shows that stronger identification with the in-group and higher prototypicality of the model (i.e., the person transgressing) increase the efficacy of vicarious hypocrisy in motivating individual action. Thus, Stone stresses the potential benefits of using the imperfect role model to promote sustainable behavior. Moreover, Stone suggests that hypocrisy-eliciting procedures may prove successful not only in triggering behavior initiation, but also in motivating learning and goal formation, as well as behavior maintenance.

Finally, in Chapter 16, Schwinghammer discusses the function and effectiveness of the contributions in this book in terms of the question, "What can practitioners learn from these insights and ideas?" Schwinghammer's analysis of the other chapters reveals some common themes and issues that need to be addressed in the future.

Together, these chapters provide a richness of theoretical perspectives which at the same time deepen our understanding of why people do not necessarily walk the talk in terms of sustainable consumption and clearly articulate how scientific theories and research findings can inform intervention strategies at the commercial and public policy level. Most probably, none of these theoretical perspectives will fully solve the problem of attitude–behavior gaps, let alone that of sustainable consumption. Complex and "wicked" problems like sustainable development require complex solutions that can only emerge at the interface— and through the interaction—of diverse theoretical perspectives and applied approaches. And yet, this book shows that these perspectives are largely comple- mentary, and also identifies a number of key themes that come back in different perspectives. We hope that the book stimulates further integration and cross- fertilization of these ideas and contributes to our understanding of sustainable consumer behavior.

Section 2

Enhancing Sustainable Behavior in Everyday Life

2

Marketing and Sustainable Development
A Social Marketing Perspective

JANNEKE DE JONGE, ARNOUT R.H. FISCHER, and HANS C.M. VAN TRIJP

INTRODUCTION

*T*he United Nations (UN, 2009) has projected that the world population will grow to over nine billion people in 2050. Importantly, most of this population growth will occur in developing countries and urban areas. Also, UN Millennium Development Goals have been agreed to for ensuring a fairer distribution of welfare across different parts of the globe through the eradication of extreme poverty and hunger worldwide. It is obvious that these demographic developments, the increased demand associated with it, the ecological restrictions, and the commitment to a fairer distribution of welfare will put a major burden on society and business, both in quantitative and qualitative terms of supply. As Dr. Jacques Diouf, Director General of the FAO, stated at the World Summit on Food Security 2009: "food production must expand by 70% in the world and double in developing countries, to meet the food needs of a world population expected to reach 9.1 billion in 2050" (FAO, 2009, p. 2). At the same time this will need to be realized at reduced social and ecological impact to prevent the depletion of non-renewable resources and to reduce the level of CO_2 emissions. It is unlikely that these "required" changes can be accommodated within existing production and marketing systems, simply because of the environmental and social constraints.

In order to meet these challenges, substantial changes at the systemic level (*doing better things*) are required, rather than incremental changes in existing business practices (*doing things better*). The need for system innovations not only

13

applies to business practices and production methods, but also includes the marketing of products and services. Commercial companies are increasingly being pressured to implement fundamental changes in their practices both by parastatal institutions (such as the United Nations and FAO), by national governments (legislation), and particularly also by nongovernmental organizations (NGOs) that call for fundamental changes in current production and marketing practices. Many companies have already incorporated corporate social responsibility (CSR) programs to take up their responsibility in the face of these global social and ecological challenges. For example, Unilever recently shifted toward a corporate sustainability strategy, with the ambitious aim of doubling its sales without increasing its environmental impact. Ben & Jerry's®, a Unilever ice cream brand, announced that all of its portfolio will be converted to Fair Trade Certified ingredients by the end of 2013. Another global Unilever brand (Lipton) has greened its total tea assortment and is now being marketed as Rainforest Alliance Certified™. Corporate social responsibility strategies have developed into a dominant business model for many companies, partly as a deliberate proactive choice and partly in response to environmental pressure. As a recent *Harvard Business Review* paper (Nidumolu, Prahalad, & Rangaswami, 2009, p. 56) stated: "There's no alternative to sustainable development."

Substantial improvements on sustainable development can be realized from a technical innovation perspective (e.g., environmental-friendly production on the basis of new technological breakthroughs) and changes in sourcing and primary production (e.g., with lower ecological impact and/or with fairer distribution of added value across all chain partners). Nevertheless, it is clear that greening the production in itself will not be sufficient for true sustainable development to become realized. Such efforts will need to be complemented by fundamental changes in consumers' lifestyles as well as purchase and consumption behavior.

This chapter takes the position that marketing can play a crucial role in helping to facilitate such behavioral changes of consumers toward more sustainable behavior. It needs to be acknowledged up front that central to the marketing approach is the concept of value exchange, based on the superior satisfaction of consumer needs in exchange for a profit gained by the party satisfying these consumer needs (Kotler, 1999). Marketing requires customer and/or end consumer demand, both in terms of willingness to buy and potentially in willingness to pay. This is where a major complication arises in the context of sustainability marketing. Although consumers express concerns with environmental and social issues and will express positive attitudes toward sustainable products and services, their actual demand and willingness to pay is typically very limited. In other words, there exists an attitude–behavior gap that needs to be closed for sustainable development to materialize. We argue that social marketing approaches provide a viable tool for sustainable development and point to directions in which this may occur.

MARKETING AND SUSTAINABILITY

Admittedly, commercial marketing does not hold a strong track record when it comes to sustainable development. More often, commercial marketing is seen as part of the problem, rather than as part of the solution. Within a marketing context, the achievement of organizational goals is dependent upon businesses delivering customer satisfaction in a more successful way than competitors do. In commercial marketing, there has been a strong tendency to define organizational goals largely in terms of monetary profit and continuity of the firm. As issues related to sustainable development have not been a strong emphasis in consumer demand, much of commercial marketing has focused on direct customer and consumer need satisfaction. To some extent, this has occurred at the disregard of negative externalities (i.e., costs) that business practices impose on society, such as unsustainable manufacturing processes (Biglan, 2009). However, this situation is now changing rapidly as production and marketing partners in the value chains are faced with increasing pressure from governments, NGOs, retailers, and consumers begin to take the consequences of direct need satisfaction into account in terms of its social and environmental impact. Furthermore, in the light of necessary value chain resources including human resources and availability of sufficient inputs, companies start to realize that their long-term continuity may be at stake. There is an increasing urge to consider externalities of product and marketing, beyond the focus on exchange of monetary profit for immediate consumer benefits only. This is implemented in the redefinition of the value concept beyond the one-dimensional economic profit focus to also include the social (people) and ecological (planet) impacts (Elkington, 1999). This so-called Triple P (people, planet, and profit) bottom-line concept is central to Transforum's (Veldkamp et al., 2009) approach to sustainable development and is increasingly being practiced by commercial organizations often in close integration with other relevant stakeholders in the value chain.

From a marketing point of view, the commitment to the Triple P bottom line is neither straightforward nor simple. For consumers, the social and ecological benefits of sustainable consumption manifest themselves often at larger social and temporal psychological distance than benefits derived from other goods, which provide instantaneous and personal need satisfaction. This poses a problem in (competitive) value exchange due to consumer biases toward need satisfaction *hic et nunc*. Sustainability marketing strategies involve the exchange of social and ecological values, in addition to direct need satisfaction from the physical product or service. Sustainability values should therefore be part of an organization's marketing efforts, and communicated to prospective consumers. Sustainability marketing has a dual role, first of all in "creating" increased demand for sustainable products and services across the whole sector ("enlarging the pie"), and second, effectively and efficiently delivering products that meet those social and environmental needs by the individual companies ("enlarging the piece of the pie"). The crucial question then becomes: How should companies achieve this?

Following Porter's (1985) strategies for competitive advantage in value chains, companies can embed sustainability proactively in their business strategy through differentiation, cost leadership, and focus on a specific segment of buyers. Increasingly, corporate social responsibility is also recognized as a strategy for competitive advantage (Ingenbleek & Frambach, 2012; Nidumolu et al., 2009). If a differentiation strategy is used, sustainable development should be central to the firm's core benefit proposition, supported by visible practices related to sourcing, production, and marketing. In other words, sustainability would be deeply embedded in the business process and would be actively communicated at the mass market level. A cost leadership approach would exploit the opportunity to lower production costs through more sustainable sourcing, increased energy efficiency, and/or waste reduction. In those instances, price advantage rather than sustainability would be the core benefit proposition. Finally, a focus strategy would aim to exploit the marketing potential of specific segments in the marketplace, from which a price premium could be extracted for sustainable products and services that specifically tailor the needs of this segment. Additionally, sustainability may be pursued to provide competitive advantage in the form of long-term continuity of the firm (ensuring availability of human and physical resources for the future), and as a positive corporate (social responsibility) image more generally. In the latter context, sustainable development can be incorporated without actively communicating it in the marketplace, or can be communicated as part of the corporate image of the company (e.g., through contributions to good causes as part of a CSR strategy). A final option is to ignore sustainable development altogether and to continue with business as usual. This reflects an inactive approach, where business practices are guided by external factors, such as the enforcement of new legislation, leading to incremental rather than the required discontinuous innovations in business performance.

One major complication with any sustainability strategy is that currently the size of the segment responsive to sustainability issues seems to be limited in size. The market share of, for example, organically produced food remains relatively constant at around 3 percent in Europe (Wier, O'Doherty Jensen, Andersen, & Millock, 2008), and total ethical consumption (including fair trade and animal welfare products) is estimated at only 5 percent of food sales (Young, Hwang, McDonald, & Oates, 2010). It is important to adequately serve this segment of front-runner consumers that express actual demand for sustainable options, but this is better achieved by niche players rather than mainstream players. The key challenge lies in enlarging consumer demand for sustainability, and specifically in appealing to the mass market segment in addition to the niche segment. However, the mass market segment seems to be caught between good intentions and poor behavior (Vermeir & Verbeke, 2006). This requires the mobilization of the "latent" demand for sustainable development among consumers. We argue that social marketing, which reflects the use of techniques from commercial marketing (Hastings, 2007) with the ultimate aim of "changing behavior to increase the well-being of individuals and/or society" (Peattie & Peattie (2009, p. 262) is an appropriate strategy to achieve this, and fitting well within the Triple P bottom-line optimization rather than just profit optimization. This will, however, require adjustment in the traditional operational tools of commercial marketing, the so-called marketing mix (Peattie & Peattie, 2009).

A SOCIAL MARKETING APPROACH TO SUSTAINABLE DEVELOPMENT

Social marketing is a subdiscipline of marketing, with the core objective to facilitate desirable social change (cf., Dann, 2010). The term was originally introduced by Kotler and Zaltman in the early 1970s (Kotler & Zaltman, 1971), but has been redefined since (see, for example, Dann, 2010). Kotler and Lee (2008, p. 7) define social marketing as a "process that applies marketing principles and techniques to create, communicate and deliver value in order to influence target audience behavior that benefit society (public health, safety, environment and communities) as well as the target audience." Social marketing has a wide application in different fields of social change, but is probably most advanced in the field of health (Grier & Bryant, 2005).

A useful perspective on social marketing is presented in a paper by Rothschild (1999) who distinguishes between three principal routes toward social change: law, education, and marketing. Law relies on involuntary changes in behavior, whereas both education and marketing take voluntary changes in behavior as their key route to intervention. Education largely relies on behavioral change at a cost to the individual, because it does not involve an exchange of valued goods. This is different in marketing approaches, which attempt to realize social change by providing something in direct return for behavioral change in the form of attractive alternatives with comparative advantage, which function as reinforcers (Rothschild, 1999). Social marketing is differentiated in that it focuses on voluntary exchange behavior, but induces change by (re-)positioning the desired behavior such that it becomes a personally desirable behavior (a reinforcer). Social change requires an integrated approach to inducing changes at the micro level (the individual consumer), as well as changes at the group and even overall community level (Brennan & Binney, 2008). In social marketing this is reflected in the distinction between upstream social marketing approaches aimed at influencing policy and government, and downstream social marketing approaches aimed at the level of individual consumers (Niblett, 2005).

In the context of marketing sustainable products, there are two key challenges. First, the assumption that behavior is largely driven by perceived self-interest on the part of the consumer provides a challenge, since sustainability primarily concerns *how a product is brought about* and less about *what the product is delivering*. In other words, products that are brought about in an environmentally friendly way or with more positive social impact do not impact the usage quality of the product. Such products relate to idealistic rather than pragmatic product qualities. A major complication is further that social and ecological impact is a credence quality (Nelson, 1970), which cannot be verified by the consumer from personal product experience. There is a considerable level of uncertainty in terms of which product is delivering what level of social and ecological impact, which is even more problematic from a communications point of view as experts do not necessarily agree on this complex matter. As a result, sustainability motivations are more likely to be a secondary rather than primary benefit of products and to many consumers not the *first reason* for product choice (Auger, Devinney, Louviere, & Burke, 2008). Sustainability motivations may guide product choice when the product's functional performance is not at stake.

A second complication with sustainable motivations is that the idealistic benefits manifest themselves at larger psychological distance in terms of social, temporal, physical, and hypothetical dimensions (Trope, Liberman, & Wakslak, 2007). This higher psychological distance will increase the weight of sustainability attributes in consumers' abstract evaluation (e.g., from survey research or political preferences), but is likely to reduce their impact in actual choice situations. The social and temporal dimensions also form the basis of social dilemma theory, which would argue that the choice for sustainable products is a trade-off between personal and societal benefit and between direct and delayed need satisfaction (Joireman, Van Lange, & Van Vugt, 2004). Social dilemma theory would predict that, without adequate governance, consumer behavior would be biased toward direct personal need satisfaction, which is in line with the limited market share of ecological and social products in the marketplace.

At the heart of the social marketing approach lies a careful analysis of the factors that stimulate and/or obstruct the expression of the desired behavior. Rothschild (1999) proposes that the motivation, opportunity, ability (MOA) framework provides a powerful tool to classify these factors. Essential to this framework is the assumption that desired behavior is more likely to be expressed if it is perceived to be in the self-interest of the consumer (motivation), if the environment provides the relevant information in a transparent way and the consumer has the skills and competencies to express the behavior (ability), and importantly the environment also provides the consumer with sufficient opportunity in terms of availability and accessibility of behavioral options (opportunity). The balance between motivation, ability, and opportunity factors also, to a large extent, determines the appropriateness of social marketing approaches compared to law and education approaches. Regulatory approaches are particularly appropriate if adequate motivation is lacking and primarily restrict the opportunity of the undesirable behavior. A key example would be the ban on smoking in the public domain. Education presumes basic motivation, but this motivation cannot be expressed properly due to lack of knowledge and/or lack of skills in expressing the behavior. However, the limited success of educational and informational campaigns in promoting more healthy and sustainable behavior among the mass public seems to suggest that sufficient motivation cannot be taken for granted. Marketing approaches similarly assume some level of basic motivation, but aim to make the requested behavior more desirable in relation to consumers' self-interest.

Social marketing theory would suggest three types of dominant influences for social change: opportunity, ability, and motivation (Rothschild, 1999).

Opportunity is an important determinant of behavior because a large part of consumer behavior is characterized by low involvement, where consumers devote limited time and effort to making consumption choices. As a result, by simply increasing the availability and accessibility of sustainable product options at the moment of choice, behavior may already be shifted in the desired direction without necessarily impacting sustainability motivation or the more deliberate information processing on the sustainability impact of the product. Providing ample opportunity for the consumer is an example of upstream social marketing and is receiving increasing attention in the context of nudging (Thaler & Sunstein, 2008). The idea behind nudging is that consumers are gently maneuvered into doing the right thing while still leaving consumers free to choose; an approach labeled *libertarian paternalism*. Nudging helps to preserve liberty in the sense that consumers are able to go their own way, but paternalistic in the sense that the choice context is deliberately designed to steer behavior to make people's lives better. The core of the responsibility for increasing choices for sustainable products in this approach lies with the people who decide how choice options are being offered to consumers (the *choice architects*), and not with the end consumer. One approach to nudging behavior in the desirable direction is by providing a default option; for example, a restaurant offering only fair trade coffee or a vending machine only offering healthy options. It is clear that such an availability route would not build on creating consumer demand, but rather requires policy and government intervention and/or self-regulation. However, nudging can also be exploited in more subtle ways, namely by affecting accessibility rather than availability. Accessibility of sustainable options can first of all be enhanced through assortment decisions (providing many sustainable options in mainstream outlets), through assortment layout (putting sustainable product in preferred shelf locations), and through the price mechanism (reducing price as a potential barrier to sustainable consumption). In either case, opportunity will be managed to increase the behavioral cost of *not* consuming the sustainable option, rather than the more common situation where the purchase of the sustainable option requires extra time and effort on the part of the consumer.

Ability can be a barrier to sustainable consumption in situations where consumers lack the necessary resources, for example, the relevant knowledge to purchase sustainable products. This can either relate to general (product class) knowledge on the issue of sustainability or to product-specific knowledge (the sustainability impact of any specific behavioral option). Educational campaigns would be the most appropriate instrument to enhance general product class knowledge on sustainability and to some degree product-specific knowledge as well. Given the credence nature of sustainability, product-specific knowledge would also require information transparency, best achieved through labeling on the product to allow identification at the point of purchase and consumption. However, such labels and on-product information are likely to be more influential if they are actively looked for from a sustainability motivation. Otherwise, much of the information front of pack may go unnoticed given the limited time and effort devoted to product choice behavior.

Although opportunity and ability are necessary requirements for increasing consumer demand of sustainable products, in light of consumers' focus on self-interest (Holmes, Miller, & Lerner, 2002), *motivation* is probably the most important underlying determinant of consumer behavior. Without motivation, consumers are unlikely to change their behavior, regardless of existing opportunity and ability

(Rothschild, 1999). Motivation is reflected in the decisional balance between the personal perceived costs and benefits of conducting the desired behavior. Thus to promote sustainable choices, the decisional balance has to swing toward the sustainable option at the moment of choice. Since consumer behavior is largely driven by self-interest (Holmes et al., 2002; Rothschild, 1999), sustainable products that have concrete consumer benefits that make them more attractive compared to nonsustainable alternatives may have the most potential to generate increased consumer demand for sustainable products. Additionally, perceived benefits may be the result of (mild) social pressure to conform to sustainable purchase and consumption behavior. The influence of social norms on consumer behavior is particularly high when an individual's behavior is public (White & Peloza, 2009). In the areas of health and traffic safety (the areas of public campaigning where social marketing was developed), remarkable successes, for example, in campaigns to prevent drunk driving, have been achieved in changing social norms (Hamilton, Biener, & Brennan, 2008; Stead, Gordon, Angus, & McDermott, 2007). Potentially, social marketing initiatives might stimulate the development of stronger social norms that put pressure on consumers to behave sustainably.

In summary, social marketing approaches would argue that factors related to opportunity, ability, and motivation together determine whether an individual is prone (all three factors positive), unable (no opportunity or ability), or resistant (lack of motivation) to behave sustainably (Rothschild, 1999). It suggests a combination of upstream and downstream social marketing techniques to bring about social change and to both enlarge the pie as well as to enlarge the piece from the pie. Creating opportunity is particularly supply driven, and therefore potential intervention strategies might focus on substantiating the availability and accessibility of sustainable products at purchase locations. Interventions to increase consumer ability to make sustainable product choices might consist of communication campaigns and consumer education combined with transparent product labeling. Increasing consumer motivation to consume in a more sustainable way may be achieved through product development, where innovative products have the potential to affect the decisional balance in favor of sustainable products. In addition to concrete product offerings in terms of attributes, a social route focusing on developing stronger social norms regarding sustainable consumption behavior might be followed to increase consumer motivation to consume sustainable products.

INTERVENTION STRATEGIES

The social marketing perspective on sustainability suggests a number of specific intervention routes toward sustainable development, structured around the key motivators of opportunity, ability, and motivation. These potential intervention routes will be illustrated from existing scientific publications and ongoing research from the Transforum research portfolio.

Opportunity. By analogy with the WHO (2006) slogan "make the healthy choice the easy choice," opportunity-related intervention strategies would focus on "make the sustainable choice the easy choice." This can be achieved through enlarging the availability and accessibility of sustainable options. Importantly, research conducted for Transforum (van Herpen, van Nierop, & Sloot, 2012) shows that the location of sustainable products on the shelf (i.e. accessibility) is more important for organic products, and that the amount of shelf space (i.e. availability) is more important for fair trade products. That is, the market share for organic products is higher when the unique aspects of different brands are emphasized by a shelf arrangement on brand (van Herpen et al., 2012). The availability and accessibility of sustainable options, furthermore, appear to have a larger influence on the market share of fair trade and organic products compared to the influence of price promotions. For both organic and fair trade products, van Herpen et al. (2012) find that the vertical position on the shelf is also important. Locating sustainable items at eye-level is a simple but highly effective choice-architectural heuristic to enlarge sustainable demand. The market share for sustainable products is not increased by price promotions. In general, consumers show very limited willingness to pay a price premium for products with a sustainability claim (Bhattacharya & Sen, 2004; van Doorn & Verhoef, 2011). In particular, larger price differences between fair trade products and a category's leading brand negatively influence the market share of fair trade products (van Herpen et al., 2012). In addition, van Doorn and Verhoef (2011) find that willingness to pay for organic products is limited because the positive effect through perceived prosocial product benefits is reduced through a negative relationship through perceived quality, particularly for vice products. This is a serious barrier in any (social) marketing program aimed at sustainable development and illustrates that company commitment towards sustainable development needs to be sincere and consistent to exert a viable marketing proposition (Becker-Olsen, Cudmore, & Hill, 2006; Yoon, Görhan-Canli, & Bozok, 2006).

Ability. To enhance ability, social marketing intervention strategies would point in the direction of increasing general awareness of sustainability issues, primarily through communication campaigns (e.g., The Netherlands goes for a better climate). Such campaigns would educate consumers about reducing their "household footprint," and providing them with the skills and competencies in making more deliberate choices regarding purchase and consumption of products, both on making category-level issues transparent (e.g., resources needed to produce meat products), and within category differentiation (e.g., fair trade chocolate). Such strategies would need to be complemented with transparent and clear labeling of sustainability attributes on products to facilitate informed choice. Research shows that such information needs to be actively communicated as consumers are not necessarily prone to actively search for it (Ehrich & Irwin, 2005), probably out of self-protection and in avoidance of negative emotions associated with the discrepancy between their *want* and *ought* motivations (Ehrich & Irwin, 2005).

Effective consumer use of labeling and certification issues depends to a large extent on trust and transparency. More is not necessarily better, as it may lead to confusion and information overload (Braun-LaTour, Puccinelli, & Mast, 2007; Verbeke, 2005), which may undermine the effective use of such information on the part of the consumer.

Motivation. The social marketing perspective would suggest two key routes to enhance motivation: (1) through shifting the decisional balance between perceived cost and benefit to the preference for the more sustainable option, and (2) impacting behavior through the activation of social norms and social identification.

As social attributes related to sustainability to most consumers constitute desirabilities rather than feasibilities, they tend to operate as secondary choice motivations at a disadvantage compared to primary benefits such as taste, convenience, and price, which deliver instant need gratification. Research shows that consumer willingness to pay a price premium for social attributes is very modest if present at all (Van Doorn & Verhoef, 2011), and that consumers show limited willingness to trade off primary benefits against product functionality more generally (Auger et al., 2008). However, in the absence of trade-off against (perceived) lowered product functionality, social attributes can direct choice behavior toward the more sustainable option (Auger et al., 2008). In terms of intervention strategies, this suggests at least three routes. First would be to ensure that sustainability values are activated at the point of sale in an attempt to make consumers' self-perceptions of being concerned about the environment salient (Cornelissen, Dewitte, Warlop, & Yzerbyt, 2007; Cornelissen, Pandelaere, Warlop, & Dewitte, 2008). This makes it more likely that sustainability motivations are being considered at all at the moment of choice. The second strategy would be to communicate sustainability benefits of products at a more concrete and tangible level for better fit with the lower construal level relevant to choice. As an example, consider the slogan of a campaign from a Dutch NGO promoting animal welfare: "This chicken has never had more room than it has in your oven tonight." Such lower-level construal of an abstract issue such as animal welfare would theoretically increase its impact on choice. A third strategy would be to link social attributes to support primary consumer benefits such as taste or price.

So rather than communicating that a product is tasty *and* organically produced, develop the proposition that the product is tasty *because* it is organically produced. This strategy can also be applied through technological and sourcing innovations that generate cost reductions from sustainable sourcing and production (Nidumolu et al., 2009). A key example here is a more concentrated detergent in a smaller package size, which would be communicated on better (more active) performance, as well as more convenience (easier to carry) and with considerable sustainability advantages in terms of transportation and storage costs.

A second approach toward enhancing motivation for sustainable consumption would come from the activation of social norms and social identification. Rather than reducing the temporal dimensions of psychological distance (as in the previous examples), this strategy would reduce social distance primarily. Such a strategy would focus on providing information about the approval or compliance behavior of others and build on social identification (e.g., Goldstein, Cialdini, & Griskevicius, 2008). A recent meta-analysis (Melnyk, van Herpen, & van Trijp, 2012) suggests that descriptive norms (making salient what relevant other people do) are more effective in stimulating (sustainable) behavior than injunctive norms (social influence expressed as "they should"), while the reverse is true for attitudes. Descriptive social norms may be communicated in quite subtle ways as was illustrated in research by Van Herpen et al. (2009), which shows that consumers (implicitly) follow the example of people who went before them, by choosing products that were relatively scarce. A possible intervention to increase purchase of sustainable products might be to communicate a descriptive norm stating that other people in the same context chose the particular product, potentially accompanied by partly empty shelf space, implicitly indicating that other people have also chosen the product.

CONCLUSION

This chapter has argued that for marketing, the key challenge in enhancing sustainable demand is twofold. Given current limited demand for sustainability, a first challenge is to *create* demand for sustainability (enlarging the pie). Social marketing approaches are particularly appropriate to help achieve this and suggest a number of intervention routes. Such social marketing approaches would fit nicely with corporate social responsibility and can be implemented together with other key stakeholders (e.g., governments and NGOs), which share the objective of enhancing sustainable development. It will involve both upstream social marketing efforts, aimed at informing policy and strategic development, and downstream social marketing efforts, aimed at achieving immediate (behavioral) goals, and sometimes require legislation and education as partners in the process.

Understanding the key consumer and business drivers of sustainable demand provides a strong competitive basis on which commercial marketing strategies can be built. In that respect, the objectives of enlarging the pie and enlarging the pieces of the pie would easily go hand in hand as they build on the same set of core competitive resources within the firm (Nidumolu et al., 2009). Such strategic resources involve an understanding of sustainability motivations of business and end consumers, sourcing strategies for cost effectiveness on the basis of sustainable development, and creative product development and positioning strategies.

Understanding the key drivers of consumer choice for sustainable products and services is a key requisite for their management and particularly to bridge the existing gap between good intentions and poor behavior on the part of the consumer. This is where the other chapters in this volume can provide input to the design and execution of effective marketing strategies and programs that would ultimately help to transform the marketing discipline from a perceived enemy to an inevitable partner in sustainable development.

REFERENCES

Auger, P., Devinney, T. M., Louviere, J. J., & Burke, P. F. (2008). Do social product features have value to consumers? *International Journal of Research in Marketing, 25*(3), 183–191.

Becker-Olsen, K. L., Cudmore, B. A., & Hill, R. P. (2006). The impact of perceived corporate social responsibility on consumer behavior. *Journal of Business Research, 59*(1), 46–53.

Bhattacharya, C. B., & Sen, S. (2004). Doing better at dong good: When, why, and how consumers respond to corporate social initiatives. *California Management Review, 47*(1), 9–24.

Biglan, A. (2009). The role of advocacy organizations in reducing negative externalities. *Journal of Organizational Behavior Management, 29*(3–4), 215–230.

Braun-LaTour, K. A., Puccinelli, N. M., & Mast, F. W. (2007). Mood, information congruency, and overload. *Journal of Business Research, 60*(11), 1109–1116.

Brennan, L., & Binney, W. (2008). Concepts in conflict: Social marketing and sustainability. *Journal of Nonprofit & Public Sector Marketing, 20*(2), 261–281.

Cornelissen, G., Dewitte, S., Warlop, L., & Yzerbyt, V. (2007). Whatever people say I am, that's what I am: Social labeling as a social marketing tool. *International Journal of Research in Marketing, 24*(4), 278–288.

Cornelissen, G., Pandelaere, M., Warlop, L., & Dewitte, S. (2008). Positive cueing: Promoting sustainable consumer behavior by cueing common environmental behaviors as environmental. *International Journal of Research in Marketing, 25*(1), 46–55.

Dann, S. (2010). Redefining social marketing with contemporary commercial marketing definitions. *Journal of Business Research, 63*(2), 147–153.

Ehrich, K. R., & Irwin, J. R. (2005). Willful ignorance in the request for product attribute information. *Journal of Marketing Research, 42*(3), 266–277.

Elkington, J. (1999). *Cannibals with forks: The triple bottom line of 21st century business.* Stony Creek, CT: New Society Publishers.

Food and Agriculture Organization. (2009). Opening Statement of FAO Director-General, Dr Jacques Diouf. World Summit on Food Security. Rome, November 16–18, 2009. Retrieved 30 May , 2012, from ftp://ftp.fao.org/docrep/fao/meeting/018/k6628e.pdf.

Goldstein, N. J., Cialdini, R. B., & Griskevicius, V. (2008). A room with a viewpoint: Using social norms to motivate environmental conservation in hotels. *Journal of Consumer Research, 35*(3), 472–482.

Grier, S., & Bryant, C. A. (2005). Social marketing in public health. *Annual Review of Public Health, 26,* 319–339.

Hamilton, W. L., Biener, L., & Brennan, R. T. (2008). Do local tobacco regulations influence perceived smoking norms? Evidence from adult and youth surveys in Massachusetts. *Health Education Research, 23*(4), 709–722.

Hastings, G. (2007). *Social marketing: Why should the Devil have all the best tunes?* Oxford, UK: Butterworth Heinemann.

Holmes, J. G., Miller, D. T., & Lerner, M. J. (2002). Committing altruism under the cloak of self-interest: The exchange fiction. *Journal of Experimental Social Psychology, 38*(2), 144–151.

Ingenbleek, P. T. M., & Frambach, R. T. (2012). *Value creation from corporate social responsibility.* Working paper.

Joireman, J. A., Van Lange, P. M., & Van Vugt, M. (2004). Who cares about the environmental impact of cars?: Those with an eye toward the future. *Environment and Behavior, 36*(2), 187–206.

Kotler, P. (1999). *Principles of marketing.* London: Prentice Hall Europe.

Kotler, P., & Lee, N. R. (2008). *Social marketing: Influencing behaviors for good* (3rd ed). Thousand Oaks, CA: Sage Publications.

Kotler, P., & Zaltman, G. (1971). Social marketing: An approach to planned social change. *Journal of Marketing, 35*(3), 3–12.

Melnyk, V., van Herpen, E., & van Trijp, H. (2012). The influence of social norms on consumer decision making: A meta-analysis. *Working paper.*

Nelson, P. (1970). Information and consumer behavior. *Journal of Political Economy, 78*(2), 311–329.

Niblett, G. R. (2005). Stretching the limits of social marketing partnerships, upstream and downstream: Setting the context for the 10th Innovations in Social Marketing Conference. *Social Marketing Quarterly, 11*(3), 9–15.

Nidumolu, R., Prahalad, C. K., & Rangaswami, M. R. (2009, September). Why sustainability is now the key driver of innovation. *Harvard Business Review, 87*(9), 55–64.

Pan American Health Organization (PAHO). (2009). PAHO/WHO launches private–public partnership to promote healthy lifestyles, reduce chronic diseases. Retrieved 30 May, 2012 from http://new.paho.org/hq/index.php?option=com_content&task=view&id=2 075&Itemid=1.

Peattie, K., & Peattie, S. (2009). Social marketing: A pathway to consumption reduction? *Journal of Business Research, 62*(2), 260–268.

Porter, M. E. (1985). *Competitive advantage.* New York: Free Press.

Rothschild, M. L. (1999). Carrots, sticks, and promises: A conceptual framework for the management of public health and social issue behaviors. *Journal of Marketing, 63*(4), 24–37.

Stead, M., Gordon, R., Angus, K., & McDermott, L. (2007). A systematic review of social marketing effectiveness. *Health Education, 107*(2), 126–191.

Thaler, R. H., & Sunstein, C. R. (2008). *Nudge: Improving decisions about health, wealth, and happiness.* New Haven, CT: Yale University Press.

Trope, Y., Liberman, N., & Wakslak, C. (2007). Construal levels and psychological distance: Effects on representation, prediction, evaluation, and behavior. *Journal of Consumer Psychology, 17*(2), 83–95.

United Nations. (2009). *World population prospects: The 2008 revision* (No. ST/ESA/ SER.A/287/ES). New York: Department of Economic and Social Affairs, United Nations.

Van Doorn, J., & Verhoef, P. C. (2011). Willingness to pay for organic products. Differences between Virtue and Vice products. *International Journal of Research in Marketing, 28*(3), 167–180

van Herpen, E., Pieters, R., & Zeelenberg, M. (2009). When demand accelerates demand: Trailing the bandwagon. *Journal of Consumer Psychology, 19*(3), 302–312.

Van Herpen, E., van Nierop, E., & Sloot, L. (2012). The relationship between in-store marketing and observed sales for organic versus fair trade products. *Marketing Letters, 23,* 293–308.

Veldkamp, A., Van Altvorst, A. C., Eweg, R., Jacobsen, E., Van Kleef, A., Van Latesteijn, H., et al. (2009). Triggering transitions towards sustainable development of the Dutch agricultural sector: TransForum's approach. *Agronomy for Sustainable Development, 29*(1), 87–96.

Verbeke, W. (2005). Agriculture and the food industry in the information age. *European Review of Agricultural Economics, 32*(3), 347–368.

Vermeir, I., & Verbeke, W. (2006). Sustainable food consumption: Exploring the consumer "attitude–behavioral intention" gap. *Journal of Agricultural and Environmental Ethics, 19*(2), 169–194.

White, K., & Peloza, J. (2009). Self-benefit versus other-benefit marketing appeals: Their effectiveness in generating charitable support. *Journal of Marketing, 73*(4), 109–124.

World Health Organization (WHO). (2011). WHO reforms for a healthy future. Report by the Director-General. Retrieved 30 May, 2012 from http://apps.who.int/gb/ ebwha/pdf_files/EBSS/EBSS2_2-en.pdf.

Wier, M., O'Doherty Jensen, K., Andersen, L. M., & Millock, K. (2008). The character of demand in mature organic food markets: Great Britain and Denmark compared. *Food Policy, 33*(5), 406–421.

Yoon, Y., Görhan-Canli, Z., & Bozok, B. (2006). Drawing inferences about others on the basis of corporate associations. *Journal of the Academy of Marketing Science, 34*(2), 167–173.

Young, W., Hwang, K., McDonald, S., & Oates, C. J. (2010). Sustainable consumption: Green consumer behaviour when purchasing products. *Sustainable Development, 18*(1), 20–31.

3

Twenty-Seven Thoughts About Multiple Selves, Sustainable Consumption, and Human Evolution

GEOFFREY MILLER

*M*y ideas about multiple selves and green consumerism are fragmentary, premature, and speculative. So there's little point in pretending that I can craft a smooth scientific narrative that deploys a consilient theory and compelling evidence to yield crisp policy recommendations. It's too early for that. Instead I'll simply list some thoughts that bubbled up from my interest, as an evolutionary psychologist, in how people display their traits to others. If I'm lucky, some of these thoughts might prove irritating or intriguing enough to provoke others to explore the suggested readings at chapter's end, and to test a few of these thoughts empirically.

1. There's nothing mysterious about growing, displaying, and switching among multiple selves. We all do it all the time. It's perfectly natural. It's the basic texture and tempo of social life for a species of big-brained narcissists like us, in all of our status-seeking, sexual strategizing, self-deceptive glory.

2. Our capacities for displaying different selves in different social contexts have a deep evolutionary history: 85 million years as primates, 35 million years as social apes, 4 million years as hypersocial hominids. That's plenty of time for our ancestors to get good at crafting different masks for different audiences, even before language. Then, about 10,000 years ago, some human populations started to develop agriculture, cities, trade, money, divisions of labor, social classes, subcultures, professions, named roles, and specialized mating markets. The demand for multiple selves boomed, and the supply of selves followed. We learned to apply our evolved capacities

for self-display to these more complex and intricate conditions. The number and diversity of selves multiplied, both per society and per individual.

3. As species genetically adapt to specific ecosystems and mating systems, our selves developmentally adapt to specific economic, social, and sexual roles.

4. Prehistoric hominids played just a few roles calling for a few different selves in their small-scale societies—roles such as hunter, gatherer, lover, parent, friend, ally, enemy, leader, follower, mentor, and student. Such roles recurred millions of times over human evolutionary history, so we evolved genetic propensities to form certain types of selves with certain features well adapted to those roles. We are neurogenetically well adapted to inhabit such ancient selves, so they feel comfortable and natural, like Jungian archetypes.

5. By contrast, after civilization, we were forced to grow a wider variety of selves for more diverse roles. Economic divisions of labor called for roles such as warrior, priest, scribe, craftsman, trader, customer, investor, and, eventually, marketer. More intricate mating markets, family structures, inheritance norms, and political systems called for differentiations between dads and cads, wives and whores, firstborns and later-borns, extroverts and introverts, conservatives and liberals, police and criminals, zealots and apostates, optimists and pessimists. For such evolutionarily novel social roles, we acquire useful selves as best we can, given the role models and social norms available in our cultures. These novel selves may feel alienated, awkward, and mutually contradictory. Evolution has not had time to optimize, ritualize, and compartmentalize them. In each such modern role we may feel cognitive dissonance, ambivalence, uncertainty, and alienation. They don't fit as comfortably as those old Jungian archetypes.

6. Some of our selves interact with markets for goods and services, as buyers, sellers, consumers, workers, investors, observers, critics, and gossips—but most of our selves do not. Among the selves that interact with markets, there are diverse and often contradictory goals in the acquisition, use, and display of products, so these selves feel internally fragmented. Further, even our economic selves are never just economically oriented (much less economically rational); all are alloyed with social, sexual, familial, and status concerns.

7. A game theorist might observe that the markets for different goods and services are different sorts of positive-sum, mixed-motive games, with different players, rules, principles, payoffs, discourses, equilibrium selection heuristics, coordination focal points, information asymmetries, commitment mechanisms, and signaling strategies. But we need not explore such technical details here. It's sufficient to say that these different games demand different strategic attitudes, which are ritualized over our lives into different selves called forth by different economic and social contexts.

8. From a psychologist's viewpoint, each *self* includes and comprises:

- A set of habits and compromises to play a social role
- A performance, both well practiced and creatively improvised
- A narrator for a certain genre of life story
- A mode of operation for the human brain, like a smartphone app
- A profile of hormones, neurotransmitters, and other physiological parameters
- A set of perceptual and attentional filters
- A system of beliefs and desires
- A set of activation thresholds for various emotions, moods, and cognitive styles
- An altered state of consciousness, sparked by a role rather than a drug
- A style of adaptive self-deception, with a self-justifying ideology
- A way of being-in-the-world (in Heidegger's sense)
- A certain style of bad faith (in Sartre's sense)
- A specialized defense against the existential dread of death and cosmic meaninglessness (if terror management theory is right)
- A set of costly signals displayed, unconsciously, for a particular audience
- A way of manipulating other people's theory of mind (mind reading, perspective taking, person perception), so they draw certain inferences about our traits and propensities.

9. Different selves are different modes of judgment and decision making that unconsciously seek different *fitness affordances*—different objects, situations, experiences, and relationships that tend to promote survival and reproductive success. But each self is also a specialized mode of display, a different *fitness indicator*, a form of costly, reliable, hard-to-fake signaling that displays certain traits through certain signals to certain audiences.

10. Here are my *selves* at the time of writing, each semiconscious and semi-salient, ready for specific modes of perception and action as needed:
    - A psychology professor drafting a book chapter on multiple selves in relation to sustainable consumerism
    - A machine for turning coffee into science
    - A father worrying about his daughter's well-being during her school trip to Bhutan
    - A homeowner waiting for a plumber to arrive, to fix a root-damaged pipe
    - A daydreamer covetous of a BMW 550i, but grudgingly content with a 13-year-old Toyota.

11. These selves show different degrees and styles of green consumerism in different circumstances. The coffee drinker may favor fair-trade, shade-grown, organic coffee when grocery shopping, but may not care about the beans' provenance when grabbing a cappuccino before a faculty meeting. The worried father may favor other tourists using small, efficient hybrid vehicles when exploring developing countries, but may wish his own daughter to be cocooned in an armored, five-ton truck with 26 air bags and the acceleration to outrun would-be kidnappers. The homeowner may attend to the sustainability of retail PVC pipe when shopping at Home

Depot, but may not question the plumber's own choice of wholesale piping. As for the BMW, no comment.

12. For some goods and services, I may be aware of green branding, sustainability issues, socially responsible companies, ethnical investment opportunities, and local social norms concerning morally acceptable consumerism. These green-salient markets, at this moment in Euro-American capitalism, include food, clothing, cars, houses, tourism, charities, and equities. In other markets, green issues remain invisible, inactionable, undiscussed with friends or family, and unshaped by social norms so far. These nongreen (or pregreen) markets, at the moment, concern goods and services such as knives, smartphones, paintings, televisions, furniture, pets, recreational drugs, live music, spectator sports, movies, casinos, treasury bonds, educational credentials, research grants, parties, holidays, and feasts. Many will disagree with this list, which illustrates the culture-specific, subculture-modulated, ever-expanding nature of green consumerism.

13. Each self is a different brand aimed at a different market segment (lovers, friends, family members) through different advertising content and channels. Selves as brands undergo updates, makeovers, brand extensions, differentiations, mergers, and co-branding relationships, in response to shifting market conditions.

14. For example, if one's lover is relaxed at home, she/he may value one's displaying cues of kindness and sensitivity (high agreeableness), as manifest in soft-hearted green consumerism. Yet if one's lover is threatened in public by a mugger or rapist, she/he may value one's displaying cues of aggressiveness and formidability (low agreeableness), as manifest in hard-hearted pugilism.

15. The couple in love, early in courtship, may value consumerist decisions that display high openness, impulsivity, status seeking, and romantic sentimentalism. Later, once the woman is pregnant, she may value consumerist attitudes that signal conservatism, cautiousness, humility, and practical rationality. Standards of green consumerism may shift as relationships develop. They may slip as constraints of time and money loom larger for families. As mates, friends, and relatives become enthused or burned out about various green issues, our moral accountabilities to them shift.

16. For example, my daughter watches the documentaries *Food, Inc.* and *Our Daily Bread* about the food industry, and learns that eating battery-farmed chickens and nonorganic beef is immoral, disgusting, and harmful. She decides never to eat chicken or beef again. In response, my behavior as her grocery-shopping father changes so our family dinners include more fish and tofu. But I still eat chicken or beef for lunch sometimes in restaurants. This is an inconsistency, but is it maladaptive? Perhaps only if my daughter finds out about it.

17. Alternatively, my wife learns how cheap it is to prevent iodine deficiency in India, which causes serious mental retardation in millions of children, and wants to support charities that promote salt iodization in India. So we may buy fewer organic vegetables and more conventionally grown vegetables, so we can donate the difference to the Network on Sustained Elimination of Iodine Deficiency Disorders. Our food choices now look less sustainable, but our spending overall may be more virtuous according to the triple bottom line: financial, social, and environmental good. Asked about our eating or charity habits, we may downplay the iodine-over-organic decision in the company of organic food zealots, but we may highlight it when visiting Bangalore or Mumbai. Another case of adaptive inconsistency.

18. This last example highlights the complexity of trade-offs in green consumer decision making. Economists expect consumers to maximize subjective expected utility across all possible product choices. This is hard enough even given perfect rationality, including stable, transitive preferences. It is exponentially harder if one is trying to maximize welfare across all living and future generations of all people, animals, plants, and environments. The problem of achieving rational consistency across consumer choices then becomes impossible, given uncertainties about the total welfare impacts of each product choice.

19. In particular, the media present consumers with an ever-changing set of research results concerning the welfare side effects (negative externalities) of each consumer decision. One week, new hybrid cars seem obviously superior to old SUVs; the next week, concerns about the toxic side effects of manufacturing hybrid car batteries makes the old SUVs seem worth keeping. Information about product externalities is a dynamic kaleidoscope of consumer confusion. Almost no consumer externalities are reliably measured, widely reported, or rationally comparable to qualitatively different externalities (e.g., how should we compare carcinogens vs. child labor vs. global warming?).

20. Ralph Waldo Emerson: "A foolish consistency is the hobgoblin of little minds." Consistency may be laudable integrity, or rigid inflexibility. Where a philosopher may see logical inconsistency, a biologist may see adaptive flexibility. So what is the optimal degree of inconsistency among our distinct selves, for us imperfect humans in an imperfect world with conflicting demands?

21. Some see multiple selves as broken fragments of some original, integral, and hypothetical soul. I see multiple selves as the biological norm for any social species in a complex, dynamic environment.

22. Some of our consumer selves become self-consciously green, and strive for rational consistency of green principles across different products, markets, and social relationships. Most do not bother. If our selves are multiple, domain specific, relationship specific, shaped by different habits

and social norms, influenced by different sets of genes, environments, and random developmental nudges, we should not expect a principled consistency across selves. Further, if our propensity to develop, use, and display multiple selves is adaptive, then forcing consistency among those multiple selves is likely to be maladaptive, even if theoretically possible.

23. Consistency among selves may be maladaptively reduced in those with schizophrenia, bipolar disorder, borderline personality disorder, high neuroticism, high impulsivity, or addiction. Consistency may be adaptively reduced among spies, psychopaths, con men, politicians, philanderers, and marketers.

24. Consistency among selves may become a conspicuous, costly display of "integrity" in its own right, pursued by those with unusually strong conscientiousness, obsessive-compulsive disorder, self-critical depression, or religious zealotry. For them, consistency of principles and values—and hence consumer preferences—is a personal achievement driven by metacognition, critical self-reflection, a vivid autobiographical memory, and a misguided existential yearning for unity of personhood across time and context. Consistency arises only if demanded by some sort of internalized Immanuel Kant, Peter Singer, or Dalai Lama. Seeking moral consistency across selves and across consumer domains would become just another costly signal of one's moral virtues, intelligence, or personality traits such as conscientiousness, agreeableness, or openness. The superconsistent seek a stable identity through a backbone of articulated principles, not through the stable genotype that suffices for all other organisms.

25. We shouldn't expect moral or ideological consistency across multiple selves any more than we should expect different software applications to operate according to the same principles. The computer's multiple selves—Word, Excel, Powerpoint, Outlook, Explorer—are all consistent with the hardware of the CPU, RAM, and hard drive, as our multiple selves are all consistent with our brains. But they have different personalities, and so they should.

26. Policy implications? Don't try to force consistency among people's existing consumer selves, which are already brittle and rusty with age, and mutually repellent like neodymium magnets. Instead, encourage the growth of fresh new consumer selves who owe nothing to old habits or identities. Inject each person with a new green consumer conscience, rather than trying to engineer an awkward compromise among existing selves. This will work best when there are intense new social norms that demand a rebranding of each human identity.

27. Change the soul's social environment, and the soul will adapt. A new green costume ball will demand new green masks, and that's OK. Old selves die, new selves arise. We are free to play whatever tricks upon our minds that we can, to save our civilization, species, and planet.

FURTHER READING

General Background

Miller, G. F. (2009). *Spent: Sex, evolution, and consumer behaviour*. New York: Viking.

Evolutionary Psychology, Evolutionary Biology, Animal Behavior

Alcock, J. (2005). *Animal behavior*. (8th Ed.). Sunderland, MA: Sinauer.
Buss, D. M. (Ed.). (2005). *The handbook of evolutionary psychology*. Hoboken, NJ: John Wiley.
Pinker, S. (2002). *The blank slate*. New York: Viking.
Schaller, M., Kenrick, D. T., & Simpson, J. A. (Eds.). (2006). *Evolution and social psychology*. New York: Psychology Press.
Wilson, D. S. (2007). *Evolution for everyone*. New York: Delacorte Press.

Costly Signaling, Sexual Selection, Mate Choice

Andersson, M., & Simmons, L. W. (2006). Sexual selection and mate choice. *Trends in Ecology and Evolution, 21*(6), 296–302.
Bird, R. B., & Smith, E. A. (2005). Signaling theory, strategic interaction, and symbolic capital. *Current Anthropology, 46*(2), 221–248.
Donath, J. (in press). *Signals, truth, and design*. Cambridge, MA: MIT Press.
Geher, G., & Miller, G. F. (Eds.). (2007). *Mating intelligence*. Mahwah, NJ: Erlbaum.
Maynard Smith, J., & Harper. D. (2004). *Animal signals*. New York: Oxford University Press.
Miller, G. F. (2000). *The mating mind*. New York: Doubleday.
Miller, G. F. (2007). Sexual selection for moral virtues. *Quarterly Review of Biology, 82*(2), 97–125.
Neiva, E. (2007). *Communication games*. New York: Mouton de Gruyter.
Searcy, W. A., & Nowicki, S. (2005). *The evolution of animal communication*. Princeton, NJ: Princeton University Press.

Status, Positional Goods, Conspicuous Consumption

De Botton, A. (2004). *Status anxiety*. New York: Penguin.
English, J. F. (2005). *The economy of prestige*. Cambridge, MA: Harvard University Press.
Frank, R. H. (2000). *Luxury fever*. Princeton, NJ: Princeton University Press.
Heffetz, O., & Frank, R. H. (2011). Preferences for status: Evidence and economic implications. In J. Benhabib, M. O. Jackson, & A. Bisin (Eds.), *Handbook of social economics*, Volume 1A (pp. 69–91). Amsterdam: Elsevier
Mason, R. S. (2000). Conspicuous consumption and the positional economy: Policy and prescription since 1970. *Managerial and Decision Economics, 21*(3–4), 123–132.
Solnick, S. J., & Hemenway, D. (2005). Are positional concerns stronger in some domains than in others? *American Economic Review, 95*(2), 147–151.
Spence, M. (2002). Signaling in retrospect and the informational structure of markets. *American Economic Review, 92*(3), 424–459.
Trigg, A. B. (2001). Veblen, Bourdieu, and conspicuous consumption. *Journal of Economic Issues, 35*(1), 99–115.

Veblen, T. (1899). *The theory of the leisure class: An economic study in the evolution of institutions*. New York: Macmillan.

Evolutionary Consumer Psychology

Conniff, R. (2002). *The natural history of the rich: A field guide*. New York: W. W. Norton.

Cronk, L., & Dunham, B. (2007). Amounts spent on engagement rings reflect aspects of male and female mate quality. *Human Nature, 18*(4), 329–333.

Godoy, R. et al. (2007). Signaling by consumption in a native Amazonian society. *Evolution and Human Behavior, 28*(2), 124–134.

Griskevicius, V., et al. (2007). Blatant benevolence and conspicuous consumption: When romantic motives elicit costly displays. *Journal of Personality and Social Psychology, 93*(1), 85–102.

Haselton, M. G., Mortezaie, M., Pillsworth, E. G., Bleske-Rechek, A., & Frederick, D.A. (2007). Ovulation and human female ornamentation: Near ovulation, women dress to impress. *Hormones and Behavior, 51*, 40–45.

Iredale, W., Van Vugt, M., & Dunbar, R. (2008). Showing off in humans: Male generosity as a mating signal. *Evolutionary Psychology, 6*(3), 386–392.

Kruger, D. J. (2008). Young adults attempt exchanges in reproductively relevant currencies. *Evolutionary Psychology, 6*(1), 204–212.

McMillan, J. (2003). *Reinventing the bazaar: A natural history of markets*. New York: W. W. Norton.

Miller, G. F. (2007). Runaway consumerism explains the Fermi paradox. In J. Brockman (Ed.), *What is your dangerous idea?* (pp. 240–243). New York: Harper Perennial.

Plourde, A. M. (2009). The origins of prestige goods as honest signals of skill and knowledge. *Human Nature, 19*(4), 374–388.

Saad, G. (2007). *The evolutionary bases of consumption*. Mahwah, NJ: Lawrence Erlbaum.

Seabright, P. (2005). *The company of strangers*. Princeton, NJ: Princeton University Press.

Shermer, Michael (2007). *The mind of the market*. New York: Times Books.

Sozou, P. D., & Seymour, R. M. (2005). Costly but worthless gifts facilitate courtship. *Proceedings of the Royal Society of London B, 272*(1575), 1877–1884.

Van Kempen, L. (2003). Fooling the eye of the beholder: Deceptive status signaling among the poor in developing countries. *Journal of International Development, 15*(2), 157–177.

Individual Differences, Person Perception, Multiple Selves, Consumer Identities

Akerlof, G. A., & Kranton, R. E. (2000). Economics and identity. *Quarterly Journal of Economics, 115*(3), 715–753.

Ambady, N., & Skowronski, J. J. (Eds.). (2008). *First impressions*. New York: Guilford Press.

Berger, J., & Heath, C. (2007). When consumers diverge from others: Identity signaling and product domains. *Journal of Consumer Research, 34*(2), 121–134.

Funder, D. C. (2006). *The personality puzzle* (4th ed.). New York: W. W. Norton.

Gosling, S. D. (2008). *Snoop: What your stuff says about you*. New York: Basic Books.

Matthews, G., Deary, I., & Whiteman, M. (2004). *Personality traits* (2nd ed.). Cambridge University Press.

Plomin, R., et al. (2008). *Behavioral genetics* (5th ed.). New York: Worth Publishers.

Sustainable Consumption, Human Nature, Public Policy

Borgerhoff Mulder, Monique, & Coppolillo, P. (2005). *Conservation: Linking ecology, economics, and culture*. Princeton, NJ: Princeton University Press.

Crawford, Charles, & Salmon, C. (Eds.). (2004). *Evolutionary psychology, public policy, and personal decisions*. Mahwah, NJ: Lawrence Erlbaum.

Farley, Joshua, & Daly, H. E. (2003). *Ecological economics: Principles and applications*. Washington, DC: Island Press.

Myers, Norman, & Kent, Jennifer. (2004). *The new consumers: The influence of affluence on the environment*. Washington, DC: Island Press.

Penn, Dustin J. (2003). The evolutionary roots of our environmental problems: Toward a Darwinian ecology. *Quarterly Review of Biology, 78*(3), 275–301.

Sachs, Jeffrey. (2008). *Common wealth: Economics for a crowded planet*. New York: Penguin.

Singer, Peter. (2004). *One world: The ethics of globalization* (2nd ed.). New Haven, CT: Yale University Press.

Somit, Albert, & Peterson, S. A. (Eds.). (2003). *Human nature and public policy: An evolutionary approach*. New York: Palgrave Macmillan.

4

Goal-Framing Theory and Norm-Guided Environmental Behavior

SIEGWART LINDENBERG and LINDA STEG

INTRODUCTION

P ro-environmental behavior must be guided by values and norms. New developments in cognitive sociology and psychology and related fields have produced a number of insights about values and norms in relation to behavior
that allow us to generate quite concrete policy implications for promoting behavior
that aids pro-environmental behavior and thereby sustainable development. In the
following, we will first describe these insights in some detail, after which we will
apply them to pro-environmental behavior.

THE STATE OF THE ART WITH REGARD
TO NORM-GUIDED BEHAVIOR

There are many definitions of social norms, but one of them can be taken to be
dominant in sociology: Social norms are informally enforced rules about which
there is at least some consensus (see Horne, 2001, p. 5). Norms may also be for-
mally enforced (say, by the police), but it belongs to the defining characteristic of
social norms that they are in any case informally enforced. Thus, if people are in
a position to do so, they also negatively react to norm transgressions in which they
are not directly involved. This is what makes social norms so important for social
life and so special for sociologists. There are cases in which people experience
group pressure to enforce norms they do not believe in (see Willer, Kuwabara, &
Macy, 2009), but by and large, informal enforcement presupposes that norms are
activated and that people experience a degree of *oughtness* with regard to these
norms (see Hechter & Opp, 2001; Falk, Fehr, & Fischbacher, 2005).

A feeling of oughtness of a social norm has at least three components. The first component is a sense of importance, meaning that the particular norm is not to be taken lightly in comparison to other considerations (such as mood, preference gain). Second, oughtness implies that one disapproves of others' transgressing the norm (i.e., the core motivation for informal enforcement derives from the oughtness of the norm itself). Third, oughtness implies that one feels obliged to follow the norm oneself (i.e., the core motivation for informal enforcement is also directed toward oneself). The stronger the sense of oughtness, the more directly relevant a social norm will be for action (Sripada & Stich, 2006). The degree of activation of a norm is tantamount to the strength of the sense of oughtness with regard to this norm at a given moment.

If one would have to summarize the main message of what we will discuss, it is the fact that norm-guided behavior is precarious. It needs chronic broad social support to be sustained. Neither internalization nor sanctions are enough to maintain the level of norm conformity that is socially desirable. In the following, we will present in some detail why norm-guided behavior is so precarious, after which we will turn to the consequences for environmental behavior and for social policy.

THE PRECARIOUSNESS OF NORM-GUIDED BEHAVIOR

There are at least four processes that make norm-guided behavior itself or its positive collective effects precarious. First, with norms, small numbers often matter. The positive result of norm-guided behavior is a collective good. In many cases this good is highly vulnerable. It can be tainted or even ruined by a relatively small percentage of people who deviate. For example, in a neighborhood, a few people who persistently throw garbage on the sidewalk, or scream during the night, or get drunk sitting on your doorstep, can lower the quality of life for almost everybody else in the neighborhood. In buses and trains, even one person who abuses the conductor or who treats the other passengers to his music or loud cell phone conversation is able to turn the trip into a very unpleasant experience. This also holds for the workplace, for car traffic, and behavior in public places. Deviant behavior of seemingly "nice" people in high positions can have grave consequences for others, as is well known from cases like Enron. Corruption of a few civil servants in state bureaucracies can create havoc for people who need licenses or seek help or justice. This small-number vulnerability also holds for many forms of environmental behavior of individuals and organizations.

Second, the deviance of a few tends to spread to others; that is, deviance is contagious (Keizer, Lindenberg, & Steg, 2008; Gino, Ayal, & Ariely, 2009). This holds for simple things like littering (Cialdini, Reno, & Kallgren, 1990), but also big things like corruption (see Goel & Nelson, 2007; Sah, 2007).

Third, norm-conforming behavior depends on the accessibility of the goal to behave in a norm-guided way, yet this goal-frame has a tendency to decay unless it is strongly supported by social forces (Andreoni, 1988; Fehr & Gächter, 2002). As we will see in more detail later on, without considerable extra support, the normative goal is weaker than the competing self-interest goals in the sense that its accessibility is easily reduced by the accessibility of competing self-interest goals.

This makes people's norm-conforming behavior highly vulnerable to cues that reduce the support for a normative goal. It implies that the violation of one rule will weaken the normative goal and will thereby lead to the violation of other rules. For example, graffiti is a cue that somebody violated the norm against disfiguring other people's property, and it has been shown that it can induce littering and even stealing in those who see it (Keizer, Lindenberg, & Steg, 2008). By this *cross-norm* inhibition effect, deviance in one area can spread to very different areas of life. Small cues can have large consequences.

Fourth, there is a secular trend that norms become more abstract (Lindenberg, 2005). This means that more and more norms become *smart norms* that need to be translated to a given situation (Lindenberg, 2009). For example, the norm not to hurt others needs to be translated by an individual into very different concrete actions, depending on the situation. In one case, it could mean that one tells the truth; in another, it could mean that one hides the truth from somebody. People have to use their wits to behave normatively. This has the advantage that it allows normative behavior to flexibly adapt to changing situations. Yet, there is also a large disadvantage: smart norms open the door wide for moral hypocrisy, allowing individuals to twist and stretch the translation of the abstract norm in such a way that they feel morally good about themselves while they do not pay the price attached to conformity (cf. Batson et al., 1999; Dana, Weber, & Kuang, 2007; Lindenberg & Steg, 2007).

GOAL-FRAMING THEORY

The power of goals. Goal-framing theory (Lindenberg 2001, 2006, 2008; Lindenberg & Steg, 2007) is based on the evidence that human perception, thinking, and deciding are organized in a modular way. However, as we will see later on, this modularity is porous or "semi." The adaptive advantages of modularity are evident. The possible interpretations of sensory input are legion and the organism cannot react fast enough without being *selective* with regard to inputs and *prepared* with regard to the processing of inputs. There are hardwired modules, such as face recognition, and learned modules, such as word recognition and habits, each characterized by functional specificity (Barret & Kurzban, 2006).

Modularity is thus tantamount to functional specialization. But social life is rife with uncertainty and sudden changes and requires flexible forms of modularity. It is thus more than likely that evolutionary pressure will have selected for a form of modularity that allows for flexibility. Flexible modularity is achieved by the power of goals to organize cognitive and emotional processes. Goals are the most flexible form of functionality in the sense that they can change according to situational cues and affordances *and* make the organism both selective with regard to inputs and prepared with regard to processing them. Take as an example the effect of being hungry. If somebody is very hungry he is likely to have a strong focal goal to eat something. What this goal does is to make him particularly sensitive to cues that something is edible, make it easy to imagine what something would taste like, increase liking for objects that are edible and tasty, suppress attention to goal-irrelevant or possibly distracting aspects (such as monetary costs, possible negative long-term effects of what you eat, etc.). Goals can become focal as an automatic reaction to cues, without deliberation (see Bargh et al., 2001). When they are focal, they create modularity by affecting what we attend to, what information we are sensitive to, what information we neglect, what chunks of knowledge and what concepts are being activated at a given moment, what we like and dislike, what we expect others to do, what criteria for goal achievement are being applied, and so on (see Gollwitzer & Bargh, 1996; Kruglanski & Köpetz, 2009; Marsh, Hicks, & Bink, 1998; Förster, Liberman, & Higgins, 2005). This can be compared to different selves. However, these selves are connected by the background goals and thus not really independent, as explained in the next paragraph.

Three overarching goals. If we are looking for the most inclusive flexible modules, we thus must look at overarching goals, each of which comprises a great number of subgoals and representations of means and causal relations among them. When such an overarching goal is focal, it organizes cognitions and evaluations in a modular way and it selectively activates hardwired and learned modules. A focal high-level goal can thus be seen as a composite module (a *goal-frame*), comprising a particular selection of modules and hardwired and learned submodules. These overarching goals thus create domain specificity and selective sensitivity to specific inputs. In that sense, they create different selves. For example, the high-level goal "to act appropriately" is likely to make situationally relevant norms cognitively more accessible, make people particularly sensitive to information about what is expected, activate the modules to process information on gaze and on certain facial expressions of approval and disapproval, and activate response tendencies and habitual behavioral sequences concerning conformity to norms (such as facial expression, shaking hands, keeping a certain distance from the other person, helping someone in need, etc.) and activating positive evaluations of the means to reach the goal (Ferguson & Bargh, 2004). This is the basis for goal-framing theory. The modularity is only *semi* because the workings of the goal-frame are affected by background goals, which can shift the goal criteria in their direction. For example, even if the normative goal to act appropriately is focal, a gain goal in the background can affect what one considers appropriate when the costs of norm conformity go up (Straub & Murnighan, 1995).

Human beings seem to be predisposed to strive for improving their condition. However, due to modularity, nobody is able to improve his or her total condition. Behavior is chronically one-sided. Improvement will be selective, depending on the overarching goal that is focal at a given moment. Which are the most important overarching goals? Here, it helps to look at evolutionary developments. Three overarching goals seem to have evolved for human beings: A goal "to improve the way one feels right now" (a hedonic goal); a goal to "act appropriately" for the group, and a goal "to guard and improve one's resources" (a gain goal).

The most basic overarching goal is related to how one feels right now and how one can improve the way one feels at this moment. This is called a hedonic goal. When this goal is focal (i.e., when it is a goal-frame), it will sharpen the sensitivity toward opportunities for need satisfaction (such as a piece of cake left on their kitchen counter) and toward events that affect the way one feels (mood swings, pain, the friendliness or unfriendliness of people at this moment, mishaps, losses, etc.). The evolving brain added two important overarching goals to the hedonic one. With the evolution of deriving adaptive advantages from living in groups, brain power that allows individuals in groups to jointly create more complex collective goods (such as hunting parties, defense of water holes) grew as well (what Dunbar [2003] calls the social brain). One of the main features of this added brain power is an improved ability to put oneself into the shoes of others, most notably of the group. Groups cannot create adaptive advantages for individuals unless they create collective goods, and for that, individuals must be able to temporarily identify with group goals rather than their individual goals. Thus evolutionary selection on the group level has very likely occurred as well (Wilson, 2006). Doing what is right for the group at a given moment implies that one's modularity is focused on what is appropriate for the group (Tomasello et al., 2005). This overarching goal is called the normative goal, because in many cases, groups work out what needs to be done for the realization of group goals in terms of social norms.

The increased ability to put oneself into the shoes of another added yet another overarching goal. When people are able to put themselves into the shoes of themselves in the future, they can make plans, invest, and generally be focused on the goal to increase their resources. This is called the gain goal. The added brain power thus also greatly advanced the possibility for prospective behavior. It created additional abilities to increase the individual adaptive advantages within the group by acting strategically, by making plans, by being able to identify with and invest in one's own future self. For example, one could invest in improving one's status position within the group by strategically entering coalitions, by deceiving, and by manipulating others. This resource and future orientation requires a very different selectivity and preparedness than focusing on improving the way one feels right now (say, by eating, or having fun, or venting one's anger) or for acting appropriately.

SHIFTING WEIGHTS BETWEEN THE OVERARCHING GOALS: INCREASING THE RELATIVE WEIGHT OF THE NORMATIVE GOAL-FRAME

All three overarching goals are chronically influential, but which of the three goals is focal (i.e., which is the goal-frame) and thus has the greatest influence on cognitive and motivational processes depends on internal and external cues that trigger the goal and give it temporarily a weight that is stronger than that of the other two (Lindenberg, 2012). The term *triggered* is used to indicate that goal-frames are not chosen but are subject to automatic priming effects. Semantic primes (concepts) and primes that label situations are likely to be at the same time also goal primes, just as primes that refer directly to goals. For example, Liberman, Samuels, and Ross (2004) used the cue "this is a community game," which triggered in most subjects a normative goal-frame (with actual norm-guided behavior), whereas the cue "this is a Wall Street game" triggered in most subjects a gain goal-frame (with actual behavior guided by gain). Activating normative precepts will also make the normative goal-frame more salient. For example, just trying to recall the Ten Commandments made people less likely to cheat (Mazar, Amir, & Ariely, 2008). There is no deliberate decision involved. Similarly, people are quite easily influenced by instructions from (and even by the sheer psychological presence of) significant others and by the goals of others without any deliberate choice involved (*goal-frame resonance* [see Lindenberg, 2000], and *goal contagion* [see Aarts, Gollwitzer, & Hassin, 2004]).

Other people. Cues can also shift the relative weight of the goal-frame in relation to the background goals without changing the goal-frame itself. Importantly, the normative goal-frame can thereby be strengthened by cues. For example, eyes looking at you will have this effect. In a field experiment, Bateson, Nettle, and Roberts (2006) found that, when payment for tea and coffee was based on people's own honesty, a poster with eyes looking at you as you help yourself to coffee or tea almost tripled the amount of money people paid compared to a poster with flowers. Thus, socially *empty* environments, such as parking garages, office buildings at night, empty streets, corridors in hotels, and so on, will activate social norms less than socially *full* environments and will thus have a higher chance of deviant behavior and of making people feel unsafe. In a similar vein, it has been shown that darkness decreases norm-guided behavior in favor of dishonesty and self-interest (Zhong, Bohns, & Gino, 2010).

Environments in which others support the norms will activate norms even more than simply peopled environments (Cialdini et al., 1990). This effect is even stronger if these others are especially important, such as parents, teachers, and religious leaders. Organizational leaders can also have this effect. For example, in a vignette study, Lauer, Rockenbach, and Walgenbach (2008) found that information that the leadership of an organization of which one is a member puts a high premium on cooperation, commitment, and fairness in team work will make people significantly cooperate more and free-ride less. Another powerful cue that will strengthen the normative goal-frame is that one is involved in *joint production*, that a common goal is jointly achieved (cf. Lindenberg & Foss, 2012; Sebanz, Bekkering, & Knoblich, 2006; Tomasello, Carpenter, Call, Behne, & Moll, 2005).

Social values. Social values people hold are likely to activate a normative goal-frame if there is no strong competition from hedonic and/or gain goals (Lindenberg, 2009). In analogy to social norms, social values can be defined as shared evaluations and priorities that are at least informally enforced by sanctions. In turn, social values themselves can be said to protect a way of life (including the identities that go with the way of life) (see Lindenberg, 2009). For example, for many circles in Western countries, democracy is an important part of a way of life and is seen as worthy of protection. To give the defense of democracy high priority is then a value in these circles, and public expressions that denigrate the value of democracy will be met with social disapproval and possibly worse.

Next to activating a normative goal-frame directly, social values also make it more likely that significant others and other factors supporting the normative goal-frame will be successful in this support. For example, if cleanliness is a value for people, then a reminder by significant others not to litter will make the anti-litter norm more accessible than if cleanliness is not a value they hold.

In turn, social value can be boosted by public campaigns that moralize certain evaluations and priorities. Moralization (Lindenberg, 1983; Rozin, Lowery, Imada, & Haidt, 1999) links certain evaluations and priorities to the common good, to the protection against threats to a valued way of life. Going against such evaluation is then a sign of lacking moral integrity, of being a bad person, which in turn is likely to clash with people's goal to maintain a moral identity (Aquino, Freeman, Reed, Lim, & Felps, 2009). Governments, media, and widely dispersed expert opinions are strong vehicles for creating consensus on threats to our way of life and on promoting values to protect it. The bigger the perceived threat and the more this threat remains on the public agenda, the more likely that social values are moralized and that joint production in realizing this value is called for.

Decreasing the Relative Weight of the Normative Goal-Frame

Other people. Even though the normative goal-frame can be boosted, goal-framing theory predicts that it is very vulnerable to the a priori stronger forces of hedonic and gain goals and can be weakened by situational factors priming hedonic or gain goals. For example, people in a normative goal-frame can experience a hedonic shift in the sense that the hedonic goal in the background, even though it remains in the background, becomes stronger than it was. This can happen by lowering the relative strength of the normative goal-frame or by strengthening the relative weight of the hedonic background goal. Being a priori the weakest of the three overarching goals, it does not take much to weaken the normative goal-frame, unless there is little competition from the other two goals in the particular situation or unless it is strongly supported by social priming (say, by significant others). For example, moving about in public space generally favors the normative goal-frame if there are no competing claims by the other two goals in the background. However, that goal-frame can easily be weakened by cues that favor one of the other goals in the background. This was recently demonstrated in a field experiment by Keizer, Lindenberg, and Steg (2008) on littering. Responsibly disposing of a flyer under the windshield in a parking garage takes effort. A weakening of the normative goal-frame increases the relative weight of the hedonic goal and thereby also the likelihood of experiencing effort as a cost. The experiment showed that people who are exposed to the sight of others not conforming to a norm (unreturned shopping carts in conjunction with a sign asking people to return these carts) litter flyers significantly more than people who have not been exposed to this sight. Conversely, ambient odors can be enough to weaken the normative goal-frame by strengthening the hedonic goal in the background. For example, Lindenberg and Steg (2012) could show that people exposed to pleasant or unpleasant ambient odors were significantly less willing to put in the effort needed to help, compared to people who were not exposed to these odors. As mentioned above, the cue that others don't conform to a norm can also increase the relative weight of the gain goal and make people more likely to steal. In sum, the normative goal-frame is very easily pushed aside by hedonic or gain goals unless it is chronically supported by social forces, such as significant others, prominent examples, sanctions, and values.

Self-Regulation

In goal-framing theory, self-regulatory capacity becomes a central concept because goal-frames make behavior chronically one-sided, and people can and will try to influence the strong effect of cues in the environment on goal-frames. Even though people differ in this capacity, they are all equipped with the ability to self-regulate (Vohs & Baumeister, 2004). In this context, this means especially two things: (1) people can actively try to influence the sensitivity to situational cues that shift the relative weight of their goals, and (2) people can actively choose environments with an eye to exposing themselves to or avoiding certain cues. For example, people who want to lose weight can resolve not to have enticing food lying on the kitchen counter (Schachter, 1968). People who want to avoid getting drunk can decide not to go to a party, knowing that once they are there they will drink too much. Interventions can be directed at increasing self-regulatory capacity and/or at reducing the need for self-regulation (for example, offering defaults that make it relatively more effortful to choose unwanted hedonic products). As we will see, there are also forms of self-regulation that make moral hypocrisy quite likely under favorable circumstances. In such cases, hedonic and/or gain goals in the background will shift the normative goal-frame toward self-serving outcomes if it is not sufficiently supported, a process that is compatible with the findings of Gino and Pierce (2009). This process is aided by abstract norms ("smart norms") that need intelligent effort to be applied to a given situation (Lindenberg, 2005). Abstract norms are more flexible and situational peculiarities can be better accommodated. However, they also allow more normative wiggle room, more opportunity to let hedonic or gain goals prevail while one believes one acted normatively. Because the normative goal-frame is a priori weaker than the hedonic or gain goals, abstract norms will easily lead to moral "stretching," to let self-interest dictate what is normative (Dana, Weber, & Kuang, 2007). In this way, self-regulation with moral hypocrisy will make norm-guided behavior even more precarious when norms allow for ambiguity or when the costs in terms of gain or hedonic goals rise. However, self-regulatory capacity can be influenced by intervention and authorities can make it more or less necessary for various important areas of life (Lindenberg, 2013).

NORMS, VALUES, AND BOOSTING ENVIRONMENTAL BEHAVIOR

What we have said about norms and values in general also holds for norms and values with regard to environmental behavior. In terms of boosting pro-environmental behavior, the goal-framing theory of norm-guided behavior (as just described) points to three large blocks of instruments: (1) pro-environmental values, (2) demonstrated support of pro-environmental norms, and (3) support of self-regulation. In the remainder of this chapter, we will discuss all three in order.

Pro-Environmental (Biospheric) Values

With increasing interdependence, the way of life of different groups also becomes more similar and dependent on similar core elements (such as various forms of freedom, without which a social market system could not operate). As a consequence, what values to protect also becomes more inclusive, with a secular trend toward universalism (Schultz et al., 2005; Schwartz, 2007). In turn, this increasing inclusiveness of social values increases the likelihood that the moral universe is extended beyond the realm of human beings. *Human* rights and nature rights thus become part of our way of life, which social values are supposed to protect. Recent studies revealed that in Western societies, social values have indeed become more inclusive and that environmental concerns have even become part of many people's morality (De Groot & Steg, 2007, 2008; Steg, Dreijerink, & Abrahamse, 2005; Stern, 2000; Stern, Dietz, & Kalof, 1993 ; Steg, De Groot, Dreijerink, Abrahamse, & Siero, 2011; see also Steg & De Groot (2012) for a review). Many pro-environmental behaviors, such as limiting car use, energy conservation, and the purchase of organic food, require individuals to go against egoistic values in order to benefit the environment. Yet, as can be expected on the basis of goal-framing theory, these studies showed that environmental behaviors are not only influenced by egoistic values (concerning evaluation of individual outcomes), but also by social values (reflecting concern for the welfare of other human beings) and especially by biospheric (or ecocentric) values, which have developed as a separate realm of values.

Together with these biospheric values, many new norms developed, about dealing with nonrenewable resources, with trash, with poisons, with spray cans, and so on. These values and norms are special, yet what was said previously about values and norm conformity in general also holds for them. Conformity to pro-environmental norms is just as precarious as conformity to other social norms, and the danger of moral hypocrisy applies to the environmental sphere as to other valued spheres. In other words, for conformity to these norms, it is just as important that the normative goal-frame be socially supported as it is for other kinds of norms. In the following, we will discuss how knowledge of the roots of precariousness helps us to specify ways to encourage environmental behavior.

Research revealed that values indeed matter for environmental behavior. The more strongly individuals subscribe to values beyond their immediate own interests, that is, to self-transcendent, prosocial, altruistic, but particularly biospheric values, the more likely they are to have pro-environmental beliefs and to engage in pro-environmental behavior, while those who strongly endorse egoistic values are less likely to have pro-environmental beliefs and to act pro-environmentally (De Groot & Steg, 2007, 2008, 2009a; Nordlund & Garvill, 2002; Steg et al., 2005; Stern & Dietz, 1994; Stern, Dietz, & Kalof, 1993; Stern, Dietz, Kalof, & Guagnano, 1995; Schultz & Zelezny, 1999). This influence can be direct (Schultz & Zelezny, 1998; Steg et al., 2005; Stern, 2000; Thøgersen & Ölander, 2002), but mostly it is indirect, via activating a feeling of joint production (with individual responsibilities) and thus a normative goal-frame, and within it behavior-specific beliefs (especially on adverse consequences of their behavior for others or for the environment) and norms (see also Stern, 2000; Stern, Dietz, Abel, Guagnano, & Kalof, 1999). In turn, this creates a heightened feeling of moral obligation (oughtness), which makes people more likely to choose what they consider the appropriate course of action (De Groot & Steg, 2009b; Steg & De Groot, 2010; Steg et al., 2005). By the same token, given biospheric values, increasing occasions of joint pro-environmental activity will boost activation of the normative goal-frame with regard to environmental obligations. For example, a joint spring cleaning in a neighborhood activates people's sense of belonging and their willingness to sacrifice time and effort for the common goal (Frieling, Lindenberg, & Stokman, 2012).

This ability of biospheric values to activate norms that are relevant to pro-environmental behavior also points to possible ways of intervention. Whatever increases the salience of biospheric values will also increase the salience of the normative goal-frame in situations that call for pro-environmental behavior (Maio & Olson 1998; Verplanken & Holland, 2002; cf. Aquino et al., 2009). As it is with social values, the salience of biospheric values can be increased by moralization, a process during which values are linked to supporting emotions ranging from "you are a bad person if you act against biospheric values and norms" all the way to expressions of disgust as reaction to deviance, say, to somebody who uses a gas-guzzler car just for fun (Lindenberg & Steg, 2007). Through moralization, the expression of value-deviant evaluations and beliefs (either through words or actions) is subject to informal sanctions. This increases the likelihood that biospheric values are chronically accessible.

Other People

Presence of people. As we mentioned previously, observing the sheer presence of people in a given environment can activate norms that are relevant in this environment, given that people have already internalized these norms. Thus, empty environments (such as deserted streets, parking garages, etc.) will not be conducive to the activation of norms, and also not of pro-environmental norms. In such environments, people will be more prone to littler, throw away toxic waste, and let lights burn needlessly, although they are less likely to do so if they have strong values and internalized norms against such actions.

There is an important additional aspect to this power of people's presence to activate norms: a cross-norm reinforcing effect, in which cues that others respect a particular norm will increase the likelihood that the observer will conform to pro-environmental norms. For example, Keizer, Lindenberg, and Steg (in press) showed that people who see a resident sweep the sidewalk in front of his house will be subsequently more willing to act prosocially. They observed somebody caring for the cleanliness norm which, in turn, increased the relative weight of their normative goal-frame, thus spreading the effect to the observance of other norms.

Behavior of others. The presence of others is even more of a powerful influence on norm conformity when the others clearly show that they care for norms. This creates a cross-norm reinforcement effect. For example, Keizer, Lindenberg, and Steg (in press) showed that people who see a resident sweep the sidewalk in front of his house will be subsequently more willing to act prosocially. They observed somebody caring for the cleanliness norm which, in turn, increased the relative weight of their normative goal-frame, thus spreading the reinforcement effect across different norms. Conversely, if others do not conform to or show disrespect for the norm, it will weaken one's goal to act appropriately. This point was clearly illustrated by a study of Schultz, Nolan, Cialdini, Goldstein, and Griskevicius (2007). They showed that when people learned that their neighbors used comparatively less energy, they decreased their energy use as a reaction. That this is not a pure case of imitation but rather related to the activation of norms can be seen from the fact that if they received information about their neighbors' energy consumption with a clear signal it is the lower and not the higher energy consumption that conforms to the norm, they did not increase their own consumption when the neighbors ostensibly used more energy than they did. This effect has proven to have real-life applications on energy savings (see Allcott, 2010). Above, it was already mentioned that Keizer et al. (2008) showed the generality of such cross-norm inhibition effects on norm-guided behavior.

For example, if people observe graffiti as a sign of disrespect for the antigraffiti norm, they are more likely to litter. In other words, any clear sign of disrespect for one particular norm is likely to make people also disrespect environmental norms. In order to boost norm-guided behavior in this area, city governments should clean up and also remove graffiti as quickly as possible. In addition, they should do so when people see it, when the clean-up itself will be a signal that the city government cares for cleanliness and environmental norms.

An even stronger effect on the (de)activation of environmental norms can be expected from the demonstrated support (or lack thereof) for these norms from significant others. For example, in a field experiment, Keizer, Lindenberg, and Steg (2010) showed that students littered a flyer significantly more when the flyer included the (false) text that professors plagiarized on a large scale (as opposed to fellow students doing so). This implies that people who wield authority in the public eye can have a considerable positive or negative influence on the activation of environmental norms.

Self-Regulation

Because a stable normative goal-frame largely depends on people's self-regulatory capacity, an important set of possible interventions to boost pro-environmental behavior is to improve this capacity. There are several ways to do this. First and foremost are ways to reduce the likelihood that self-regulation leads to moral hypocrisy in the area of environmental behavior. As explained previously, the abstractness of social norms and the inclusiveness of ego-transcendent values create moral wiggle room space within which the individual can rationalize hedonic and gain-oriented behavior as moral behavior. For example, the norm to act pro-environmentally is too abstract to tell us what to do. Information that it is bad to throw batteries into one's trash bin because they contain toxic substances is much more concrete. But then, additional information that rechargeable batteries are especially toxic makes it easier to throw regular batteries into the trash with a good conscience. Given abstract norms, concrete information is often not enough to prevent stretching the norm in favor of economizing on effort or expense. What is needed is concrete low-level norms that are clearly instrumentally linked to the abstract norm, so that they can be flexibly replaced when the technology changes. For example, in some communities, garbage has to be separated into various containers; in other communities, this is not necessary. Sometimes the norm changes from separating to no-separating or vice versa. People may use this confusing situation to be excused from making any effort with regard to garbage. Unless the instrumental link of low-level norms to high-level norms (and biospheric values) is made clear, people will use ambiguities in norms for morally hypocritical behavior (Babcock & Loewenstein, 1997). Authorities and environmental organizations should come up with concrete norms about what people should do to behave pro-environmentally and provide enough information for each norm, so that the link to the higher abstract norm and the biospheric values is made both explicit and flexible as technology changes (see also Abrahamse, Steg, Vlek, & Rothengatter, 2005). Low-level concrete norms work like implementation intentions (if–then sequences) with focused *if* cue detection (Parks-Stamm & Gollwitzer, 2007), which in turn lowers attention to cues that lower the strength of the normative goal-frame. This mechanism is also able to help break the power of hedonically supported, environmentally "bad" habits (for example, with regard to car use; see Steg, 2005).

Second, another important means for aiding a form of self-regulation that does not lead to moral hypocrisy is concrete and frequent feedback, especially on energy use. As mentioned previously, this feedback may also concern information on averages of relevant others (such as neighbors). Concrete and frequent feedback helps self-regulation in the sense that with this information, it is more difficult to believe that one is saving energy (say, by turning off some lamps) while in fact this is not so. It also helps prevent compensatory strategies that are bad for norm-oriented self-regulation (Mazar & Zhong, 2010; Sachdeva, Iliev, & Medin, 2009). Acting pro-environmentally in one way (say, buying green products) may make it easier to feel entitled to be easy on some other kind of behavior (such as turning off standby appliances). Concrete and frequent feedback on energy use makes such forms of hypocrisy much more difficult.

A third way to aid self-regulation is to reduce the impact of hedonic and/or gain goals that are contrary to pro-environmental behavior (see Lindenberg & Steg, 2007). This can be done by making them compatible. For example, given biospheric values, pro-environmental behavior may yield status. Griskevicius, Tybur, and Van den Bergh (2010) showed that people primed with status motives were more likely to choose green products, in particular in public situations, and when green products were more rather than less expensive than a luxurious alternative, which suggests that in this case, gain goals (i.e., status motives) were compatible with normative goals, easing the burden of pro-environmental self-regulation. Another such way is to reduce costs in terms of hedonic or gain goals. For example, recycling facilities can be provided to make recycling easier and more convenient (Vining & Ebreo, 1992). Similarly, subway use can be promoted by offering reduced fares or free tickets (Hunecke, Blöbaum, Matthies, & Höger, 2001). Environmentally harmful behavior can also be made less attractive, for example, by increasing the costs of car use (Eliasson, Hultkrantz, Nerhagen, & Rosqvist, 2009; Santos, 2008; Schuitema,

Steg, & Vlek, 2007). However, from our goal-framing analyses about what it takes to boost pro-environmental behavior, it should be clear that cost interventions will only work in concert within the other interventions that boost the activation of a normative goal-frame in a more direct way.

Finally, it is also possible to make self-regulation itself less necessary. This kind of intervention has recently been pushed by Thaler and Sunstein (2008) and consists of default options and perceptual nudges offered by governments and organizations. For example, default options could be offered in terms of consumer goods and foods with green labels, default green energy contract options, default green construction options for houses, default green car rental contract options, and so on. In restaurants, a green menu could be the default option, and in supermarkets, green products could be displayed at eye level, which creates a default effect (Drèze, Hoch, & Purk, 1994).

CONCLUSION

Goal-framing theory deals with the power of goals to govern cognitive and motivational processes, and focuses on three overarching goals: hedonic, gain, and normative goals. One of these is in the cognitive foreground with the strongest influence on selective attention, selective accessibility of knowledge chunks, evaluations, emotion regulation, and so on. It is called the goal-frame. The other two overarching goals are in the background, with a weaker influence on these processes. Stable norm-guided behavior depends on the stability of the normative goal-frame. The most important message for the purpose of this chapter is that the normative goal needs the most support to withstand being pushed into the background by hedonic or gain goals. This makes norm-guided behavior chronically precarious and chronically in need of external (social) support. Goal-framing theory also specifies the factors that are most important for supporting the normative goal-frame: social values, the presence of other people, the behavior of other people (especially of significant others), and self-regulatory capacity.

Stable pro-environmental behavior depends on a stable normative goal-frame in situations that call for this kind of behavior. Boosting pro-environmental behavior is then tantamount to boosting the stability of the normative goal-frame in such situations. The most important message here is that for the purpose of stable pro-environmental behavior, a broad spectrum of support for the normative goal-frame is needed. Biospheric values need to be pushed by governments and environmental organizations, positive information on norm conformity by others needs to be widely disseminated, signs of disrespect for environmental norms (such as litter) should be quickly removed, and pro-environmental self-regulation should be aided by supplying concrete pro-environmental norms and standards, easy feedback on one's own energy use, cheap ways to dispose of toxic materials, and finally a wide range of default options. This wide spectrum is not the sum of measures that are substitutes. Rather, it should be seen as a list of complements. Lastly, it is clear from this chapter that pro-environmental behavior will decay and keep decaying even after it has been widely adopted unless the full spectrum of measures is chronically dedicated to the stability of the normative goal-frame in this realm of behavior.

REFERENCES

Aarts, H., Gollwitzer, P. M., & Hassin, R. R. (2004). Goal contagion: Perceiving is for pursuing. *Journal of Personality and Social Psychology, 87*(1), 23–37.

Abrahamse, W., Steg, L., Vlek, Ch., & Rothengatter, J. A. (2005). A review of interventions aimed at household energy conservation. *Journal of Environmental Psychology, 25*(3), 273–291.

Allcott, H. (2010). Social Norms and Energy Conservation. MIT Center for Energy and Environmental Policy Working Paper, 09–14, 2010.

Andreoni, J. (1988). Why free ride? Strategies and learning in public goods experiments. *Journal of Public Economics, 37*, 291–304.

Aquino, K., Freeman, D., Reed II, A. Lim, V. K. G., and Felps, W. (2009). Testing a social-cognitive model of moral behavior: The interactive influence of situations and moral identity centrality. *Journal of Personality and Social Psychology, 97*(1), 123–141.

Babcock, L., & Loewenstein, G. (1997). Explaining bargaining impasse: The role of self-serving biases. *Journal of Economic Perspectives 11*(1), 1099–1126.

Bargh, J. A., Gollwitzer, P. M., Lee-Chai, A., Barndollar, K., & Trötschel, R. (2001). Automated will: Nonconscious activation and pursuit of behavioral goals. *Journal of Personality and Social Psychology, 81*(6), 1014–1027.

Barret, H. C., & Kurzban, R. (2006). Modularity in cognition: Framing the debate. *Psychological Review, 113*(3), 628–647.

Bateson, M., Nettle, D., & Roberts, G. (2006). Cues of being watched enhance cooperation in a real-world setting. *Biology Letters, 2* (June), 412–414.

Batson, C. D., Thompson, E. R., Seuferling, G., Whitney, H., & Strongman, J. (1999). Moral hypocrisy: Appearing moral to oneself without being so. *Journal of Personality and Social Psychology, 77*(3), 525–537.

Cialdini, R. B., Reno, R. R., & Kallgren, C. R. (1990). A focus theory of normative conduct: Recycling the concept of norms to reduce littering in public places. *Journal of Personality and Social Psychology, 58*(6), 1015–1026.

Dana, J., Weber, R. A., & Kuang, Xi, J. (2007). Exploiting moral wiggle room: Experiments demonstrating an illusory preference for fairness. *Economic Theory, 33*(1), 67–80.

De Groot, J., & Steg, L. (2007). Value orientations and environmental beliefs in five countries: Validity of an instrument to measure egoistic, altruistic and biospheric value orientations. *Journal of Cross-Cultural Psychology, 38*(3), 318–332.

De Groot, J., & Steg, L. (2008). Value orientations to explain beliefs related to environmental significant behavior: How to measure egoistic, altruistic, and biospheric value orientations. *Environment and Behavior, 40*(3), 330–354.

De Groot, J. I. M., & Steg, L. (2009a). Mean or green: Which values can promote stable pro-environmental behavior? *Conservation Letters, 2*(2), 61–66.

De Groot, J. I. M., & Steg, L. (2009b). Morality and prosocial behavior: The role of awareness, responsibility and norms in the norm activation model. *Journal of Social Psychology, 149*(4), 425–449.

Drèze, X., Hoch, S. J., & Purk, M. E. (1994). Shelf-management and space elasticity. *Journal of Retailing, 70*(4), 301–326.

Dunbar, R. I. M. (2003). The social brain: Mind, language, and society in evolutionary perspective. *Annual Review of Psychology, 32*, 163–181.

Eliasson, J., Hultkrantz, L., Nerhagen, L., & Rosqvist, L. S. (2009). The Stockholm conges-
tion–charging trial 2006: Overview of effects. *Transportation Research Part A: Policy
and Practice*, 43(3), 240–250.

Falk, A., Fehr, E., & Fischbacher, U. (2005). Driving forces behind informal sanctions.
Econometrica, 73(6), 2017–2030.

Fehr, E., & Gächter, S. (2002). Altruistic punishment in humans. *Nature*, 415, 137–140.

Ferguson, M. J., & Bargh, J. A. (2004). Liking is for doing: The effects of goal pursuit on
automatic evaluation. *Journal of Personality and Social Psychology*, 87(5), 557–572.

Förster, J., Liberman, N., & Higgins, E. T. (2005). Accessibility from active and fulfilled
goals. *Journal of Experimental Social Psychology*, 41(3), 220–239.

Frieling, M., Lindenberg, S., & Stokman, F. N. (2012). Collaborative communities through
co-production: Two case studies. *American Review of Public Administration Online*.
DOI: 10.1177/0275074012456897.

Gino, F., Ayal, S., & Ariely, D. (2009). Contagion and differentiation in unethical behavior.
The effect of one bad apple on the barrel. *Psychological Science*, 20(3), 393–398.

Gino, F., & Pierce, L. (2009). Dishonesty in the name of equity. *Psychological Science*,
20(3), 1153–1160.

Goel, Rajeev K., & Nelson, Michael A. (2007). Are corrupt acts contagious? Evidence from
the United States. *Journal of Policy Modeling*, 29(6), 839–850.

Gollwitzer, P. M., & Bargh, J. (Eds.). (1996). *The psychology of action. Linking cognition
and motivation to behavior*. New York: Guilford Press.

Griskevicius, V., Tybur, J. M., & Van den Bergh, B. (2010). Going green to be seen:
Status, reputation, and conspicuous conservation. *Journal of Personality and Social
Psychology*, 98(3), 392–404.

Hechter, Michael, & Opp, Karl-Dieter. (2001). What have we learned about the emergence
of social norms?" In Michael Hechter and Karl-Dieter Opp (Eds.), *Social norms* (pp.
394–415). New York: Russell Sage.

Horne, C. (2001). Sociological perspectives on the emergence of norms. In Michael Hechter
and Karl-Dieter Opp (Eds.), *Social norms* (pp. 3–34). New York: Russell Sage.

Hunecke, M., Blöbaum, A., Matthies, E., & Höger, R. (2001). Responsibility and environment: Ecological norm orientation and external factors in the domain of travel mode
choice behavior. *Environment and Behavior*, 33(6), 830–852.

Keizer, K., Lindenberg, S., & Steg, L. (2008). The spreading of disorder. *Science*, 322(5908),
1681–1685.

Keizer, K., Lindenberg, S., & Steg, L. (2010). Higher-ups make especially influential norm
violators. Working paper. University of Groningen.

Keizer, K., Lindenberg, S., and Steg, L. (in press). The importance of demonstratively
restoring order. *PLOS ONE*

Kruglanski, A. W., & Kopetz, C. (2009). *What is so special (and non-special) about goals?
A view from the cognitive perspective*. In G. B. Moskowitz and H. Grant (Eds.), *The
psychology of goals* (pp. 27–55). New York: Guilford Press.

Lauer, T., Rockenbach , B., & Walgenbach, P. (2008). Not just hot air: Normative codes of
conduct induce cooperative behaviour. *Review of Management Science*, 2(3), 183–197.

Liberman, V., Samuels, S. M., & Ross, L. (2004). The name of game: Predictive power of
reputations versus situational labels in determining prisoner's dilemma game moves.
Personality and Social Psychology Bulletin, 30(9), 1175–1185.

Lindenberg, S. (1983). Utility and morality. *Kyklos*, 36(3), 450–468.

Lindenberg, S. (2000). The extension of rationality: Framing versus cognitive rationality. In J.
Baechler, F. Chazel, and R. Kamrane (Eds.), *L'Acteur et ses raisons: Mélanges en l'honneur
de Raymond Boudon* (pp. 168–204). Paris: Presses Universitaires de France (PUF).

Lindenberg, S. (2001). Social rationality versus rational egoism. In J. Turner (Ed.), *Handbook
of sociological theory* (pp. 635–668). New York: Kluwer Academic/Plenum.

Lindenberg, S. (2005). Smart norms: How do they work and does the school have an important function for making them work? In W. Veugelers & M. H. Bosman (Eds.), *De strijd om het curriculum* (pp. 85–107). Leuven-Apeldoorn: Garant.

Lindenberg, S. (2006). Prosocial behavior, solidarity and goal-framing processes. In D. Fetchenhauer, A. Flache, B. Buunk, & S. Lindenberg (Eds.), *Solidarity and prosocial behavior. An integration of sociological and psychological perspectives* (pp.23–44). Amsterdam: Kluwer.

Lindenberg, S. (2008). Social rationality, semi-modularity and goal-framing: What is it all about? *Analyse & Kritik*, *30*(2), 669–687.

Lindenberg, S. (2009). Values: What do they do for behavior? In Mohamed Cherkaoui and Peter Hamilton (Eds.), *Boudon: A life in sociology, Vol III* (pp. 59–89). Oxford: Bardwell Press.

Lindenberg, S. (2012). How cues in the environment affect normative behavior. In L. Steg, A. E. van den Berg, & J. I. M. de Groot (Eds.), *Environmental psychology: An introduction* (pp.119–128). New York: Wiley.

Lindenberg, S. (2013). Social rationality, self-regulation and well-being: The regulatory significance of needs, goals, and the self. In R. Wittek, T.A.B. Snijders, & V. Nee (Eds.), *Handbook of rational choice social research* (pp.72–112). Stanford: Stanford University Press.

Lindenberg, S., & Foss, N. (2011). Managing joint production motivation: The role of goal-framing and governance mechanisms. *Academy of Management Review*, *36*(3), 500–525.

Lindenberg, S., and Steg, L. (2007). Normative, gain and hedonic goal-frames guiding environmental behavior. *Journal of Social Issues*, *65*(1), 117–137.

Lindenberg, S., & Steg, L. (2012). The hedonic shift. How odors can reduce prosocial behavior and increase moral hypocrisy. Working paper. University of Groningen.

Maio, G. R., & Olson, J. M. (1998). Values as truisms: Evidence and implications. *Journal of Personality and Social Psychology*, *74*(2), 294–311.

Marsh, R. L., Hicks, J. L., & Bink, M. L. (1998). Activation of completed, uncompleted, and partially completed intentions. *Journal of Experimental Psychology: Learning, Memory, and Cognition*, *24*(2), 350–361.

Mazar, N., Amir, O., & Ariely, D. (2008). The dishonesty of honest people: A theory of self-concept maintenance. *Journal of Marketing Research*, *45*(6), 633–644.

Mazar, N., & Zhong, Chen-Bo. (2010). Do green products make us better people? *Psychological Science*, *21*(4), 494–498.

Nordlund, A. M., & Garvill, J. (2003). Effects of values, problem awareness, and personal norm on willingness to reduce personal car use. *Journal of Environmental Psychology*, *23*(4), 339–347.

Parks-Stamm, E. J., & Gollwitzer, P. M. (2007). Action control by implementation intentions: Effective cue detection and efficient response initiation. *Social Cognition*, *25*(2), 248–266.

Rozin, P., Lowery, L., Imada, S., & Haidt, J. (1999). The CAD triad hypothesis: A mapping between three moral emotions (contempt, anger, disgust) and three moral codes (community, autonomy, divinity). *Journal of Personality and Social Psychology*, *76*(4), 574–586.

Sachdeva, S., Iliev, R., & Medin, D. L. (2009). Sinning saints and saintly sinners. The paradox of moral self-regulation. *Psychological Science*, *20*(4), 523–528.

Sah, Raaj K. (2007). Corruption across countries and regions: Some consequences of local osmosis. *Journal of Economic Dynamics and Control*, *31*(8), 2573–2598.

Santos, G. (2008). The London experience. In E. Verhoef, B. Van Wee, L. Steg, & M. Bliemer (Eds.), *Pricing in road transport: A multi-disciplinary perspective* (pp. 273–292). Cheltenham: Edgar Elgar.

Schachter, S. (1968). Obesity and eating. *Science*, *161*(3843), 751–756.

Schuitema, G., Steg, L., & Vlek, C. (2007). Are pricing policies effective to change car use? *IATSS Research*, 31(1), 21–31.

Schultz, P. W., Gouveia, V. V., Cameron, L. D., Tankha, G., Schmuck, P., & Franek, M. (2005). Values and their relationship to environmental concern and conservation behavior. *Journal of Cross-Cultural Psychology*, 36(4), 457–475.

Schultz, P. W., Nolan, J. M., Cialdini, R. B., Goldstein, N., & Griskevicius, V. (2007). The constructive, destructive, and reconstructive power of social norms. *Psychological Science*, 18(5), 429–434.

Schultz, P. W., & Zelezny, L. C. (1998). Values and pro-environmental behaviour. A five-country study. *Journal of Cross-Cultural Psychology*, 29(4), 540–558.

Schultz, P. W., & Zelezny, L. C. (1999). Values as predictors of environmental attitudes: Evidence for consistency across 14 countries. *Journal of Environmental Psychology*, 19(3), 255–265.

Schwartz, S. H. (2007). Universalism values and the inclusiveness of our moral universe. *Journal of Cross-Cultural Psychology*, 38(6), 711–728.

Sebanz, N., Bekkering, H., & Knoblich, G. (2006). Joint action: Bodies and minds moving together. *TRENDS in Cognitive Science*, 10(2), 70–76.

Sripada, C. S., & Stich, S. (2006). A framework for the psychology of norms. In P. Carruthers, S. Laurence, and S. Stich (Eds.), *The innate mind, Vol. 2* (pp. 280–301). Oxford: Oxford University Press.

Steg, L. (2005). Car use: Lust and must. Instrumental, symbolic and affective motives for car use. *Transportation Research A*, 39(2), 147–162.

Steg, L., & De Groot, J. I. M. (2010). Explaining prosocial intentions: Testing causal relationships in the Norm Activation Model. *British Journal of Social Psychology*, 49(4), 725–743.

Steg, L., & De Groot, J.I.M. (2012). Environmental values. In S. Clayton (ed.), *The Oxford handbook of environmental and conservation psychology* (pp. 81–92). New York: Oxford University Press.

Steg, L., De Groot, J. I. M., Dreijerink, L., Abrahamse, W., & Siero, F. (2011). General antecedents of personal norms, policy acceptability, and intentions: The role of values, worldviews, and environmental concern. *Society and Natural Resources*, 24(4), 349–367.

Steg, L., Dreijerink, L., & Abrahamse, W. (2005). Factors influencing the acceptability of energy policies: A test of VBN theory. *Journal of Environmental Psychology*, 25(4), 415–425.

Stern, P. C. (2000). Toward a coherent theory of environmentally significant behavior. *Journal of Social Issues*, 56(3), 407–424.

Stern, P. C., & Dietz, T. (1994). The value basis of environmental concern. *Journal of Social Issues*, 50(3), 65–84.

Stern, P. C., Dietz, T., & Kalof, L. (1993). Value orientations, gender, and environmental concern. *Environment and Behavior*, 25(3), 322–348.

Stern, P. C., Dietz, T., Kalof, L., & Guagnano, G. A. (1995). Values, beliefs, and pro-environmental action: Attitude formation toward emergent attitude objects. *Journal of Applied Social Psychology*, 25(18), 1611–1636.

Stern, P. C., Dietz, T., Abel, T., Guagnano, G. A., & Kalof, L. (1999). A value-belief-norm theory of support for social movements: The case of environmentalism. *Human Ecology Review*, 6(2), 81–97.

Straub, P. G., & Murnighan, J. K. (1995). An experimental investigation of ultimatum games: Information, fairness, expectations, and lowest acceptable offers. *Journal of Economic Behavior and Organization*, 27(3), 345–364.

Thaler, R. H., & Sunstein, C. R. (2008). *Nudge: Improving decisions about health, wealth, and happiness.* New Haven, CT: Yale University Press.

Thøgersen, J., & Ólander, F. (2002). Human values and the emergence of a sustainable consumption pattern: A panel study. *Journal of Economic Psychology*, 23(5), 605–630.

Tomasello, M., Carpenter, M., Call, J., Behne, T., & Moll, H. (2005). Understanding and sharing intentions: The origin of cultural cognition. *Behavioral and Brain Sciences*, 28(5), 675–735.

Verplanken, B., & Holland, R. W. (2002). Motivated decision making: Effects of activation and self-centrality of values on choices and behaviour. *Journal of Personality and Social Psychology*, 82(3), 434–447.

Vining, J., & Ebreo, A. (1992). Predicting recycling behavior from global and specific environmental attitudes and changes in recycling opportunities. *Journal of Applied Social Psychology*, 22(20), 1580–1607.

Vohs, K. D., & Baumeister, R. F. (2004). Understanding self-regulation: An introduction. In R. F. Baumeister and K. D. Vohs (Eds.), *Handbook of self-regulation. Research, theory, and applications* (pp. 1–9). New York: The Guilford Press.

Willer, R., Kuwabara, K., & Macy, M.W. (2009). The false enforcement of unpopular norms. *American Journal of Sociology*, 115(2), 451–490.

Wilson, D.S. (2006). Human groups as adaptive units: Towards a permanent consensus. In P. Carruthers, S. Laurence, and S. Stich, *The Innate Mind* (Vol. 2, pp. 78–90). Oxford: Oxford University Press.

Zhong, C., Bohns, V. K., & Gino, F. (2010). Good lamps are the best police: Darkness increases dishonesty and self-interested behavior. *Psychological Science*, 21(3), 311–314.

5

A Fairly Mechanical Method for Policy Innovation

DANIEL G. GOLDSTEIN and ISAAC M. DINNER

INTRODUCTION

Defaults exert a strong and predictable influence over behavior (Goldstein et al., 2008; Johnson, Belman, & Lohse, 2002). In European countries with opt-in organ donor pools, it is rare for greater than 20% of the population to opt in, while in opt-out countries it is not unusual to find that over 99% of the population are organ donors (Johnson and Goldstein, 2003). This example is a situation where a *no-action default* drastically affects outcome. More generally, as argued by Thaler and Sunstein (2008), defaults can be used to encourage individual behavior to increase societal welfare in a way that a law, which removes all personal responsibility for the decision, cannot.

The effect of defaults can be measured in millions or even billions of dollars. For example, two US states, Pennsylvania and New Jersey, underwent a legal change in the early 1990s such that all motorists had to pick between a high-cost insurance policy that provided the right to sue or a low-cost insurance policy that lacked this right. The two states chose opposite defaults, setting up an interesting natural experiment. New Jersey chose the limited policy as the default and Pennsylvania chose the more comprehensive one. In New Jersey, 21% of residents purchased the right to sue, while 70% of Pennsylvania residents purchased that same right (Johnson et al., 1993). That is, 70% to 79% of people on both sides of the river went with the default, leading to large financial consequences for the insurance sales industry. More recently, Beshears et al. (2009) find that when employees are defaulted to participate in a pension program through their employer, nearly all do, while less than two-thirds follow suit when the default is to not participate.

TABLE 5.1   Matrix of Objectives and Tools

	Tool 1	Tool 2	...	Tool n
Objective 1	Idea (1,1)	Idea (1,2)	...	Idea (1,n)
Objective 2	Idea (2,1)	Idea (2,2)	...	Idea (2,n)
...	...	...	...	...
Objective m	Idea (m,1)	Idea (m,2)	...	Idea (m,n)

Defaults can have strong implications in nearly all societal policy, and in particular, ones pertaining to mobilizing consumers to execute actions that are more sustainable. In this chapter we examine ways that default situations can be used to induce actions that boost sustainable development. Specifically, we employ a fairly mechanical and simple method to generate ways in which default configurations can be used to reduce carbon emissions. We choose carbon emissions as the objective focus because, as recently shown by Attari et al. (2010), this is an area where individuals have difficulty quantifying energy savings and defaults can lead the decision process and also have a serious impact. We begin by outlining an idea-generation method before discussing ways in which default options can reduce carbon emissions, and then close with a discussion of policy.

IDEA GENERATION: A FAIRLY MECHANICAL AND SIMPLE METHOD

Here we outline an easy method for generating ideas that can impact policy using a set of *tools* and *objectives*. In the following example, the objectives will be a set of carbon-decreasing activities, although any social objective could be used. The tools will be different types of default frames that can impact social policy, but could also include other methods of information sharing and policy. The simplicity of this method should not necessarily undermine the quality of the ideas it generates, as even important scientific discoveries are thought to have arisen from the application of heuristics for discovery (Langley et al., 1987; Gigerenzer & Goldstein, 1996). To apply this method, a policy maker begins with a list of objectives to be achieved. This list is then crossed with a list of policy tools to generate a matrix populated with strategic ideas as shown in Table 5.1.

For each possible combination of objective and tool, the policy designer asks how each tool could be applied to each objective. The creative process was helped along by flattening the matrix so that each combination of tool and objective is given unique inspiration as a *tool*-based approach to an *objective*. The spreadsheet to model this arrangement might be structured as shown in Table 5.2.

The method is described as fairly mechanical because the steps listed do only some of the work. The rest is left to the creativity of the policy maker. As a caveat, this has not been tested against other methods of generating ideas, structured or unstructured. However, since the process is quick, pleasant, and may at least generate a few good ideas, there is little risk in its implementation.

For this volume, we applied the method using sustainable actions as objectives and defaults as the tools. We will now step through both in detail.

TABLE 5.2   Spreadsheet Model of a Tool-Based Approach to an Objective

Objective	Tool	Imaginary Article Title	Idea
Objective 1	Tool 1	A tool 1-based approach to objective 1	Idea (1,1)
Objective 1	Tool 2	A tool 2-based approach to objective 1	Idea (1,2)
...	...	...	
Objective 1	Tool n	A tool n-based approach to objective 1	Idea (1,n)
Objective 2	Tool 1	A tool 1-based approach to objective 2	Idea (2,1)
Objective 2	Tool 2	A tool 2-based approach to objective 2	Idea (2,2)
...	...	...	
Objective 2	Tool n	A tool n-based approach to objective 2	Idea (2,n)
...	...	...	
Objective m	Tool n	A tool n-based approach to objective m	Idea (m,n)

OBJECTIVES: ACTIONS THAT REDUCE CARBON EMISSIONS

To best suit a general audience, we searched for a list of sustainable actions that could plausibly be achieved by typical households, as opposed to specialized corporations. Thomas Dietz and colleagues' paper "Household Actions Can Provide a Behavioral Wedge to Rapidly Reduce US Carbon Emissions" in the *Proceedings of the National Academy of Sciences* (2008) lists a series of actions, which, if undertaken in the United States, would reduce carbon emissions by an amount roughly equal to the carbon emissions of France (p. 18452). We took said actions and re-expressed them in the form of measurable objectives, as follows:

1. Increase the proportion of windows without drafts
2. Better align heating and air-conditioning settings to time of day, season, and presence of people home
3. Decrease the average amount of standby electricity used by appliances
4. Decrease the average temperature settings of clothes washers
5. Decrease the average temperature settings of water heaters
6. Decrease the weight carried in automobile trunks
7. Increase air-conditioner tune-up rates
8. Increase automobile oil change rates
9. Increase heating, ventilation, and air-conditioning filter change rates
10. Increase the proportion of insulated attics
11. Increase the proportion of drivers who minimize acceleration and deceleration rates
12. Increase the proportion of highway drivers who maintain a speed of 55 mph
13. Increase the proportion of drivers who use cruise control
14. Increase the proportions of Energy Star furnaces, air-conditioners, water heaters, refrigerators, and clothes washers and dryers in use
15. Increase the proportion of fuel-efficient vehicles in use

16. Increase the proportion of LED televisions in use (relative to plasma screens)
17. Increase the proportion of low-flow showerheads in use
18. Increase the proportion of low-rolling-resistance tires in use
19. Increase the proportion of triple-pane windows in use
20. Increase the proportion of wash loads dried on the line
21. Increase tire inflation rates
22. Increase vehicle tune-up rates
23. Reduce the number of motor vehicle trips made per day
24. Reduce the proportion of single-passenger motor vehicle trips
25. Reduce the time vehicles spend idling.

Dietz et al. categorize the actions as: a onetime investment in building shells, purchases made to increase the energy efficiency of household appliances, infrequent actions that can be maintained by habit, infrequent actions that are maintained automatically, and frequently repeated actions maintained by habit or conscious choice (p. 18454). Since these particular categorizations contain ideas about how to achieve the objectives, they were not included in the spreadsheet to avoid interfering with generation of different solutions. With an ambitious set of concrete and measurable objectives before us, we turn to the tools of policy: defaults.

TOOLS: A VARIETY OF DEFAULTS

While the effects of defaults are great, they have garnered limited academic attention and literature. A few years back, Goldstein et al. (2008, pp. 102–103) proposed a taxonomy of default types and ideas about choosing the most appropriate default for specific situations. This list is a starting point for policy idea generation, and will ultimately be revised as a result of this exercise.

To understand these examples, consider a product that is available in various configurations. For instance, a new car might come with a passenger-side airbag enabled (but can be switched off) or disabled (but can be switched on) by default. The enabled default would be ideal if the passenger is a large adult, but potentially fatal if the passenger is a small child. Nonetheless, the manufacturer ultimately must choose one of these two settings as a default. In addition to product defaults, services can have default settings as well. For example, by default, employees might participate or not participate in their company's pension plan. Note: For something to be a default, the customer must have the ability to switch states. If the customer was not able to switch, defaults would not preserve freedom of choice. Here is the list of tools of policy that will be applied:

Benign Defaults. When policy makers set a benign default, they take their best guess about which configuration would be most acceptable and present the least risk to most people. These are *mass defaults*, meaning that they are applied to all people uniformly, and not on a case-by-case basis.

Random Defaults. To enact random defaults, policy makers randomly assign customers to one of several default configurations and track change rates. They are often used to learn about preferences or the consequences of alternatives. They are only recommended when there is little foreseeable harm in someone receiving either default.

Hidden Options. When a single default configuration is presented as the only choice when alternatives do exist, the policy maker is using hidden defaults. For instance, the availability of special meals on airlines is not widely publicized, though customers who are knowledgeable enough to know of the hidden option are able to switch. Hidden options violate the spirit of choice-preserving defaults in that they limit the ability of the consumer to switch states.

Forced Choice. In forced choice, the default is to deny providing the product or service unless a configuration is actively chosen. In some cases, defaults exist even when forced choice is used. For instance, if people must answer a question about whether they consent to be organ donors when applying for a driver's license, those who do not apply for licenses dodge the question and would be classified according to the prevailing regional law (e.g., they would not be considered donors in the United States). In other cases, forced choice implies no default at all. For instance, imagine an installer for a web browser that will not proceed unless a default search engine is chosen. Those who do not answer the question will not be able to install the browser and their default search engine for that browser will be undefined.

Persistent Defaults. A persistent defaults policy assumes that a customer's last choice should be used as the default for the next choice. For example, if a customer requests an aisle seat on one flight, they might be assigned one by default on the next flight. This last choice could be a result of an application of a default, an active departure from the default, or a forced choice question.

Reverting Defaults. A reverting defaults policy ignores a customer's last active choice that departed from the default, treating it as an exception, and reverts back to the long-term default.

Smart Defaults. This is a kind of personalized default that can sense and react; smart defaults use information about an individual or a situation to generate tailored configurations. An example would be assigning employees in a pension program to one of several target retirement funds based on their age.

Adaptive Defaults. Another kind of personalized default, adaptive defaults dynamically update based on current, often real-time, decisions that a person has made and attempt to guess remaining defaults. Examples include product configurators that use a small set of questions to guess a user's needs (e.g., home or business) and recommend finished products.

Applying the Process

A spreadsheet was constructed like that in Table 5.2, nesting tools within objectives (though the alternative nesting, or a random order, might have its merits). This sheet was filled in 200 rows (8 tools by 25 objectives) where possible. While completing the task, certain cells failed to create ideas or raised unappealing ones. These cells were left blank and we moved on to the next row to avoid hindering the flow of ideas. It was also decided that the spreadsheet would not be made public, for the thought of doing so may have caused internal censorship. Instead, we took the chance of possibly generating many bad ideas in the hopes of ending up with a few good ones. A creative writing teacher of Dan's once referred to this as "letting the faucet run to clear out the rusty water."

Revising the Classification of Defaults

An unexpected benefit of the exercise was that it caused us to rethink the classification of defaults cited previously. Here is a revised classification:

1. Policies for establishing initial configurations
   a. *Forced choice*: Ask user one or more questions to determine the configuration.
   b. *Simple defaults*: Use a default configuration set by the policy maker.
   c. *Sensory defaults*: Choose among multiple sets of configuration based on any available data other than individual usage data (which does not exist at initial use).
   d. *Random defaults*: Choose a configuration randomly from several alternatives.
2. Policies for establishing configurations for reuse
   a. *Predictive defaults*: Apply learning algorithms to the past configuration and user data to adjust the configuration automatically.
   b. *Persistent defaults*: Reuse the configuration from the last session.
   c. *Reverting defaults*: Establish the configuration anew according to the initial default policy; that is, treat each use as the first use.
3. Techniques for adjusting configurations
   a. *Manual adjustment*: Ask the user to review each setting, thus providing the user with the opportunity to change. The choice default for each choice must be determined by another method.
   b. *Predictive adjustment*: Review each setting, thus providing the user with the opportunity to change. Each change causes the subsequent choice option defaults to update dynamically so that they are likely to be acceptable.

What's new? One realization is the distinction between the default and the configuration. The *configuration* is the collection of settings. *Default policies* determine the default configuration, which can be adjusted. When adjusting a configuration, *choice option defaults* are preselected options that a person can simply approve or make an active choice to change. The policy designer may choose to have the system prompt the user to adjust the configuration, or simply respond to users' requests to adjust. With *predictive adjustment* the process can be streamlined by a kind of autocompletion, taking educated guesses about the levels of the remaining choice-option defaults on the basis of past choices.

Policies for determining a configuration differ between the initial use of a product or service and its subsequent reuses. At the first use, there is no previous use data about the user to exploit for determining the configuration. However, in *sensory defaults* the system may be able to detect some things about the user (demographics, a case-history file, directly observable information) that it may use to make an educated guess when setting the configuration. At reuse, this sensory data is still available, but now the system also has data on how the user interacts with the product or service and can start to extrapolate, updating the configuration through *predictive defaults*. For instance, a thermostat, after noticing that the user increases it two degrees each morning and decreases it three degrees each night, might adjust the daytime and nighttime settings in the configuration accordingly. The distinction between *sensory* and *predictive* defaults is that the former do not have past usage data and take the form of if–then rules, while the latter have past usage data and take the form of learning algorithms.

REFLECTIONS COMING OUT OF THE PROCESS

In applying this process, we found that one idea might apply to a range of objectives that group together thematically. To begin, we flesh out some of these higher-level ideas.

Defaults and Shopping

Many of the actions suggested by Dietz et al. involve purchasing new products. An unappealing and narrow application of defaults to shopping involves placing a product in a customer's cart by default, a process actually tried by some airlines trying to sell trip insurance alongside airline tickets. One does not see this attempted much these days, perhaps due to laws concerning unintentional purchases as well as a general distaste for the practice by consumers. Seeing this as unviable, we thought that defaults might apply not to the product itself, but to the presentation of the product. In online settings, what appears first is favored. In auctions by Google and Yahoo!, for instance, advertisers bid to be placed above the others on the page knowing that, all else equal, this top position will yield more clicks. Online retailers could set defaults such that Energy Star products (those meeting a certain standard of efficiency in the United States) could be presented to customers first on vendors' web pages that display products within a category. For it to truly be a default, consumers would need the ability to change the ordering of products, so an Energy Star First checkbox would be visible in the filtering options of the page. Setting product displays to list energy-efficient appliances first is a *simple defaults* solution. Vendors could be incented to present and precheck such a box through tax breaks or by selective membership to a responsible business organization. With the sale of many products moving online, the domain of Internet commerce could be the ideal territory to test defaults.

Previous research on a customer's self-proclaimed consideration set predicts that an item will be chosen over an item not in the set (Hauser, 1978), and a hypothesis worth testing is whether items placed into an artificial consideration set have a similar favored status. Today, virtual consideration sets are routinely created in the form of online product comparison engines and recommender systems. It would be instructive to place energy-efficient products in virtual consideration sets by default. Doing so would not lead to unintentional purchases, but it could increase the probability of an efficient device being chosen. Smart consideration sets are an instance of *predictive defaults* because the users' virtual consideration set is originally set to be empty and is endowed with an appropriate energy-efficient product only after the user has specified what they are shopping for.

A *forced-choice* mechanism for online purchases might allow shoppers to proceed as usual, but then, before checkout, ask them to decide between the product they have chosen and a comparable energy-efficient model, presented alongside cost-of-ownership information.

Predictive defaults and *persistent defaults* could also be employed online when customers shop for multiple products from the same retailer on one or multiple visits. For instance, imagine someone in the market for a refrigerator, clothes washer, dryer, and television. After they choose one energy-efficient good, the website could learn to display energy-efficient models at the top of their list of search results for the other products. That is, predictive defaults would be responsible for changing the sort order of products to Energy Star First on the basis of the first product placed in the cart. Persistent defaults would be responsible for retaining this configuration for future visits by this customer.

Defaults and Services

Many energy-inefficient goods are, unfortunately, already in use. Replacing or improving them will cause a great decrease in carbon emissions according to Dietz et al. (2008), but old products cannot replace or improve themselves by default. A service provider is thus desirable to do jobs such as servicing air-conditioners, replacing an automobile's oil or tires, inflating tires, insulating an attic, or replacing thin, drafty windows.

Consumers are accustomed to some services, such as sanitation, taking place by default, but in the case of some paid services, provision by default is unthinkable. At the same time, many people wish that certain maintenance activities would simply happen by themselves, even if they are just a phone call away.

One solution would be to create appointments by default, or more specifically *options for appointments* by default. An option for an appointment means that one has the right to convert the option into an appointment, but if one does not, nothing will happen. Consider the servicing of an air-conditioner. Imagine that every five years you received an e-mail from the local government stating that an appointment has been made for you to have your air-conditioner serviced at a certain date and time. If you don't want that appointment, you do nothing and nothing happens. If you do want the service at that time, you click through on the e-mail to accept, and a service person shows up at your house at the specified time. If you want the appointment at a different time, you can click to reschedule. This example employs two configuration settings. The first is to receive options for appointments via e-mail. The *simple default* for this is to be "yes", and can be set to "no" to preserve choice. The second is to have the appointment take place. The *choice-option default* for this setting is "no" (the appointment will not take place unless confirmed), but the consumer has the opportunity to change this through prompted *manual adjustment* (the prompt being the e-mail). One might think that this is nothing more than getting reminders by default, but it is. A unilateral offer to commit to a particular time does have value, just as options in financial markets do. They save the consumer some deliberation and effort because it is easier to confirm than it is to generate a proposed time and reach out to the other party. (Consider how often you get e-mails asking you to propose a meeting time from a person who could have done the same.)

Beyond visits that take place at home, appointment options could be used to schedule services at the vendor's place of business (such as changing oil or inflating or replacing tires). The result could be better maintained equipment and shelter that consumes less energy. Vendors should appreciate the business as well, though coordination by a trusted authority (e.g., a local government) would be necessary.

Defaults and Devices

Defaults built into technology have strong effects. When installing software, many of us click Next in response to most every question the installer asks. When installing web browsers, many people do not reset the default home page, and it has been argued that AOL's $4 billion purchase of Netscape was motivated less by its software and more by its default home page, which was not changed by some 40% of users (Kesan and Shah, 2006). Technology defaults are so powerful that companies like Google and Microsoft face legal regulations regarding the degree to which they can make a search engine a default (Johnson and Goldstein, 2006).

Changing human behavior is hard, but changing the behavior of devices usually boils down to trivial engineering. We live in an age in which the size and cost of computers is approaching zero and the cost of powerful software (such as the Linux operating system) is free, both in the sense of *gratis* and *libre*. We suspect that many of the ideas that follow have already been implemented, or could be implemented at very low cost.

Consider the case of standby electricity, the small amounts of power consumed by appliances (such as television sets) in a sleeping state that allows them to be powered on by remote control (as opposed to manually flipping a switch). Standby electricity is estimated conservatively by Dietz et al. (2009, Appendix, p. 6) at 440 kilowatt hours per household annually. That is roughly 4% of household electricity consumption in the United States, and by appliances that no one is using. Since widespread adoption of Energy Star appliances would reduce standby power consumption by 80%, some improvement could be made with the above ideas for influencing energy-efficient online purchasing decisions.

The remaining 20% could be attacked as well. The default configuration of many appliances is to enter standby mode when turned off by remote control. The alternate setting of shutting appliances all the way down is unattractive as it would essentially undo the convenience of standby power. A *predictive default* solution would be to move an appliance from standby to off when no one is around to use it, and to move it from off to standby when someone might. What is needed is a *people presence detector* that monitors when people are at home and awake (via sensors at the doors and light switches, or by motion and sound detectors) incorporated into a meta-appliance that controls the standby power consumption of televisions, stereo systems, computer monitors, or anything the requires a human being present to be used. No magic is necessary to move an appliance between standby and off—all one needs is to plug it into an outlet that can be turned on or off remotely. Ironically, the meta-appliance would itself consume standby electricity, but the net savings are obvious because of the one-to-many effects.

Predictive defaults could reduce the energy needed for heating water and regulating the temperature of homes. Going beyond people presence detectors, *people presence predictors* could record people's comings, goings, and behaviors (again by monitoring light switches, doors, and manual adjustments to thermostats) and use simple learning algorithms to predict when they would likely want the heat or air-conditioning on, or hot water available. On a daily basis, it could switch appliances from low- to regular-power modes when they are likely to be used. Similarly, it could detect when the occupant is out of town and reduce power consumption accordingly.

As a result of engaging in this exercise, the previous classification of defaults (Goldstein et al., 2008) is refined to introduce some new concepts, clean out some old ones, and to clarify some terminology. In addition, some general purpose policy ideas like options for appointments and smart consideration sets have arisen. Before concluding, we offer some suggestions as to how these concepts and ideas might apply to the 25 objectives that aided in their creation.

25 Objectives and at Least 25 Ideas

1. Increase the proportion of windows without drafts.
    a. Options for appointments (simple defaults and prompted manual adjustment)
    b. Smart consideration sets for new purchases (predictive defaults)
    c. "Energy Star First" display options for new purchases (simple defaults).
2. Better align heating and air-conditioning settings to time of day, season, and presence of people in the home.
    a. People presence detectors (sensory default)
    b. People presence predictors (predictive default).
3. Decrease the average amount of standby electricity used by appliances.
    a. Smart consideration sets for new purchases (predictive defaults)
    b. "Energy Star First" display options for new purchases (simple defaults)
    c. People presence detectors (sensory default)
    d. People presence predictors (predictive default).
4. Decrease the average temperature settings of clothes washers.
    a. Clothes washers that detect the color of clothing and set temperatures accordingly (sensory default)
    b. Clothes washers that ask color and set temperature accordingly (forced choice then adaptive auto completion).
5. Decrease the average temperature settings of water heaters.
    a. For new purchases, manufacturers set heaters to recommended levels, which user can readjust (simple default)
    b. Smart consideration sets for new purchases (predictive defaults)
    c. "Energy Star First" display options for new purchases (simple defaults)

    d.   People presence detectors (sensory default)

    e.   People presence predictors (predictive default).

6. Decrease the weight carried in automobile trunks.

    a.   No good ideas arose.

7. Increase air-conditioner tune-up rates.

    a.   Options for appointments (simple defaults and prompted manual adjustment).

8. Increase automobile oil change rates.

    a.   Options for appointments (simple defaults and prompted manual adjustment).

9. Increase heating, ventilation, and air-conditioning filter change rates.

    a.   Options for appointments (simple defaults and prompted manual adjustment).

10. Increase the proportion of attics insulated.

    a.   Options for appointments (simple defaults and prompted manual adjustment).

11. Increase the proportion of drivers who lessen acceleration and deceleration rates.

    a.   No good ideas arose.

12. Increase the proportion of drivers who maintain 55 mph speed.

    a.   Have cruise control turn on by default when 55 mph speed or greater is maintained for more than 10 minutes (predictive default).

13. Increase the proportion of drivers who use cruise control.

    a.   Have cruise control turn on by default when 55 mph speed or greater is maintained for more than 10 minutes (predictive default).

14. Increase the proportion of Energy Star furnaces, air-conditioners, water heaters, refrigerators, and clothes washers in use.

    a.   Smart consideration sets (predictive defaults)

    b.   "Energy Star First" display options for new purchases (simple defaults).

15. Increase the proportion of fuel-efficient vehicles in use.

    a.   Smart consideration sets (predictive defaults)

    b.   "Energy Star First" display options for new purchases (simple defaults).

16. Increase the proportion of LED televisions in use (relative to plasma screens)

    a.   Smart consideration sets (predictive defaults)

    b.   "Energy Star First" display options for new purchases (simple defaults).

17. Increase the proportion of low-flow showerheads in use.

    a.   Smart consideration sets (predictive defaults)

    b.   "Energy Star First" display options for new purchases (simple defaults)

    c.   Options for appointments for replacement (simple defaults and prompted manual adjustment).

18. Increase the proportion of low-rolling-resistance (LRR) tires in use.

    a.   Smart consideration sets (predictive defaults)

    b.   "LRR First" display options for new purchases (simple defaults)

    c. Options for appointments for tire replacement (simple defaults and prompted manual adjustment).

19. Increase the proportion of triple-pane windows in use.
    a. Smart consideration sets (predictive defaults)
    b. "Energy Star First" display options for new purchases (simple defaults)
    c. Options for appointments for window replacements (simple defaults and prompted manual adjustment).

20. Increase the proportion of wash loads dried on the line.
    a. If the outdoor temperature is warm, clothes washer asks if it should tumble dry (sensory default)
    b. Options for deliveries. Like options for appointments, but recipient would receive an option to have a free clothes-line delivered to their home (simple defaults and prompted manual adjustment).

21. Increase tire inflation rates.
    a. Options for appointments, combined with other auto maintenance objectives (simple defaults and prompted manual adjustment).

22. Increase vehicle tune-up rates.
    a. Options for appointments (simple defaults and prompted manual adjustment).

23. Reduce the number of motor vehicle trips made per day.
    a. Online mapping software could list public transportation alternatives before providing driving directions (simple defaults).

24. Reduce the proportion of single-passenger motor vehicle trips.
    a. Online mapping software could list public transportation alternatives before providing driving directions (simple defaults).

25. Reduce the time vehicles spend idling.
    a. After 5 minutes of idling, automobile asks driver if it should shut down (sensory default)
    b. For buses, a GPS tracks places where a bus idles for more than 5 minutes on its route. When the bus next stops at such a place for 1 minute, it automatically shuts off after a warning period (predictive defaults).

CONCLUSION: PRESERVING CHOICE

Since defaults are so powerful, one might expect that the changes proposed would have substantive effects. Are defaults acceptable in societies that put a high value on freedom of choice? In the strict sense, defaults preserve free choice, and advocates of libertarian paternalism emphasize this (e.g., Sunstein and Thaler, 2003). At the same time, defaults are manipulative: the evidence is great that they change behavior.

In practice, decisions need defaults. Attempts to make all choice into forced choices would result in citizens spending all their time deciding, and still would not address those who choose not (or who are unable) to choose. Free choice and defaults may seem at odds, but even the most choice-loving societies require them. Furthermore, while a given default configuration may be seen as manipulative, so are its alternatives. One configuration must be chosen and ultimately there is no short cut to weighing the costs and benefits of making courageous policy decisions.

The acceptability of defaults has much to do with the reasons why defaults are effective in a particular situation. People follow defaults for various reasons. They may interpret them as recommendations (McKenzie, Liersch, and Finkelstein, 2006), or they may see them as indications of what other people might do (Samuelson and Zeckhauser, 1988). People are capable of reasoning about defaults, as consumers make shrewd assumptions about a vendor's motives when they see its choice-option defaults (Brown and Krishna, 2004).

However, apart from situations in which people think and reason about defaults, some default effects may be due to transaction costs or ignorance. If people find it too difficult to choose against the default, or if they do not know how to, we depart from the practice of setting defaults and enter the territory of creating obstacles to choice. Defaults whose effects depend on such barriers are not ideal instruments of policy. Policy makers should design defaults that are nearly as easy to change as to follow, and they may be surprised at how many people prefer intelligent defaults to bans and appeals.

REFERENCES

Attari, Shahzeen, DeKay, Michael L., Davidson, Dliff, I., & Bruine de Bruin, Wandi. (2010). *Public perceptions of energy consumption and savings.* 107(37), 16054–16059.

Beshears, John, Choi, James J., Laibson, David, & Madrian, Brigitte C. (2009). *The importance of default options for retirement saving objectives: Evidence from the United States.* In Jeffrey Brown, Jeffrey Liebman, and David A. Wise (Eds.), *Social security policy in a changing environment,* (pp. 167–200). Chicago: University of Chicago Press.

Brown, Christina L., & Krishna, Aradhna. (2004). The skeptical shopper: A metacognitive account for the effects of default options on choice. *Journal of Consumer Research,* 31(3), 529–539.

Dietz, Thomas, Gardner, Gerald T., Gillgian, Jonathan, Stern, Paul C., & Vandenbergh, Michael P. (2009). Household actions can provide a behavioral wedge to rapidly reduce US carbon emissions. *Proceedings of the National Academy of Sciences,* 106(44), 18452–18456.

Gigerenzer, G., & Goldstein, D. G. (1996). Mind as computer: The birth of a metaphor. *Creativity Research Journal,* 9(2–3), 131–144.

Goldstein, Daniel G., Johnson, Eric J., Herrmann, Andreas, & Heitmann, Mark. (2008). Nudge your customers toward better choices. *Harvard Business Review,* 86(12), 99–105.

Hauser, John R. (1978). Testing the accuracy, usefulness, and significance of probabilistic models: An information-theoretic approach. *Operations Research,* 26 (May/June), 406–421.

Johnson, Eric J., Belman, Steven, & Lohse, Gerald L. (2002). Defaults, framing, and privacy: Why opting in is not equal to opting out. *Marketing Letters,* 13(1), 5–15.

Johnson, Eric J., & Goldstein, Daniel G. (2003). Do defaults save lives? *Science,* 302(5649), 1338–1339.

Johnson, E. J., & Goldstein, D. G. (2006, August 29). The daily defaults that change lives. *Financial Times.*

Johnson, Eric J., Hershey, John, Meszaros, Jacqueline, & Kunreuther, Howard. (1993). Framing, probability distortions, and insurance decisions. *Journal of Risk and Uncertainty*, 7(1), 35–53.

Kesan, Jay P., & Shah, Rajiv C. (2006). Setting software defaults: Perspectives from law, computer science and behavioral economics. *Notre Dame Law Review*, 82(2), 583–634.

Langley, P., Simon, H. A., Bradshaw, G. L., & Zytkow, J. M. (1987). *Scientific discovery: Computational explorations of the creative processes.* Cambridge, MA: MIT Press.

McKenzie, Craig R. M., Liersch, Michael J., & Finkelstein, Stacey R. (2006). Recommendations implicit in policy defaults. *Psychological Science*, 17(5), 414–420.

Samuelson, William, & Zeckhauser, Richard. (1988). Status quo bias in decision making. *Journal of Risk and Uncertainty*, 1(1), 7–59.

Sunstein, Cass R., & Thaler, Richard H. (2003). Libertarian paternalism is not an oxymoron. *The University of Chicago Law Review*, 70(4), 1159–1202.

Thaler, Richard H., & Sunstein, Cass R. (2008). *Nudge: Improving decisions about health, wealth, and happiness.* New Haven, CT: Yale University Press.

Section 3

Strengthening the Sustainability Goal

6

I Just Recycled. Can I Use the Car Now?

When People Continue or Discontinue Behaving Sustainably after an Initial Sustainable Act

MARIJN H.C. MEIJERS, MARRET K. NOORDEWIER, and YANA R. AVRAMOVA

*I*magine that John had a party last night. The next morning he looks around at the mess that is left behind: empty plastic and glass bottles lying around, wrapping paper and confetti on the floor, beer cans in the kitchen. Instead of throwing all the waste in one big garbage bag, John decides to separate his waste. He starts collecting the empty glass bottles and puts them in a crate. Then he moves on to the plastic packaging and bottles that are lying around. Next, he decides to collect the cans in the kitchen. Finally, he gathers all the paper lying on the tables and puts it in a big paper bag. When he is done, he walks all the way to the waste-disposal bins and disposes of his separated waste. His arms are tired from the heavy bags, but he is done. Finally! He walks back home and remembers that he needs to get some groceries for dinner. Normally, he would bike to the supermarket as it is quite close by. Today, however, John decides to go by car. After all, did he not already behave sustainably enough today? This thought probably sounds familiar to many people; sometimes you just feel you've done enough.

In this chapter, we present a framework on what happens *after* people behave sustainably. On the one hand, one might expect that people will continue to behave sustainably after a sustainable act (i.e. a carry-over effect). Since they behaved sustainably once, they are likely to continue doing so because that is how they apparently behave. On the other hand, the opposite could also happen, such that people stop behaving sustainably after an initial sustainable act (i.e., a balance effect). Like John, people might feel that they are "done" with behaving sustainably after a sustainable act. They did what they needed to do and thus feel exempt from having to behave sustainably again. As our example showed, this may ultimately lead to performing unsustainable behaviors.

We will first review research on when balance effects, rather than carry-over effects, are likely to occur. Then we will discuss the role of self-view in balance versus carry-over effects. In the last section, we will propose ways in which our framework can be implemented in sustainability campaigns so as to enhance the chance of carry-over effects after an initial sustainable behavior. In doing so, we will provide recommendations on how to encourage continued sustainable behavior by using the social labeling technique (e.g., Allen, 1982).

TO CONTINUE OR NOT TO CONTINUE?

What do people do once they have behaved sustainably? It seems logical to assume that people continue behaving sustainably after an initial sustainable act (i.e., a carry-over effect). Indeed, research suggests that people are likely to perform continued sustainable behavior. For example, research on self-perception and cognitive consistency shows that people often prefer to behave consistently over time to maintain a particular self-view (Bem, 1967; Festinger, 1957; Swann & Gilbert, 1990). Furthermore, research on habits shows that people who are in the habit of behaving environmentally sustainably are more likely to show repetitive sustainable behavior (Aarts, Verplanken, & Van Knippenberg, 1998; Ouellette & Wood, 1998). Finally, research on priming suggests that constructs that are accessible in people's minds may guide subsequent behavior (Bargh, Chen, & Burrows, 1996). Based on this, one would expect that sustainable behavior can activate sustainable constructs, motivating continued sustainable behavior.

In contrast to these findings supporting carry-over effects, recent research suggests that people do not always show continued sustainable behavior. In fact, after performing an environmentally sustainable act people may stop behaving sustainably or even start behaving environmentally unsustainably (i.e., a balance effect). From this perspective, people who make sustainable choices are actually less likely to make environmentally sustainable choices later. Below, we will review research on licensing effects and goal pursuit, suggesting that balance effects (rather than carry-over effects) are likely to occur.

BALANCE EFFECTS

Licensing

Recent research on *moral licensing* suggests that performing a sustainable act may actually lead to performing an unsustainable act. Moral licensing entails that after performing a virtuous deed people feel that they are allowed to refrain from further virtuous behavior (Monin & Miller, 2001). The explanation for this finding is that a moral act temporarily satisfies people's sense of being a moral person, permitting them to behave in a morally questionable way. Since sustainable behavior is often perceived as moral behavior (Schmuck & Schultz, 2002), this research suggests that committing a moral act, such as behaving sustainably, may license people to subsequently behave unsustainably. Research on licensing thus suggests that people balance their sustainable and unsustainable behaviors, making an unsustainable act after an initial sustainable act more likely.

In a series of experiments, Monin and Miller (2001) provided compelling evidence for this balance effect. For example, they demonstrated that opposing sexist views initially resulted in more sexist choices later on. Specifically, male participants who first disagreed with sexist statements like "Most women should stay at home" were in a second task more likely to indicate that men were more suitable than women for a stereotypically male job. Presumably, these male participants had built up moral credentials on their "non-sexist person account" by indicating that most women should not stay at home. Having established their non-sexist selves, they later felt licensed to make a more sexist choice. In contrast, participants who agreed with sexist statements in the first task were more likely to indicate that women would be equally suitable for the job as men in the second task. These male participants did not build up non-sexist credentials, so they were not licensed to make a more sexist choice in the second task. In line with this, research shows that recalling general moral behaviors performed in the past leads to immoral behaviors in the present. For example, it has been demonstrated that recalling general moral behaviors leads to more cheating behavior on a math task (Jordan, Mullen, & Murnighan, 2011) and to donating less money to charity (Sachdeva, Iliev, & Medin, 2009).[1]

When applying these balance effects findings to sustainability, it seems likely that after performing a sustainable behavior people may actually perform *less* sustainable behaviors since they feel they are granted to. In fact, there is some recent evidence that balance effects also occur in the domain of sustainable behavior. Research by Sachdeva and colleagues (2009) shows, for example, that people are less likely to make environmentally sustainable choices after being prompted to think of themselves as a moral person rather than as an immoral person. A study by Mazar and Zhong (2010) provides additional evidence for the possibility of balance effects in the domain of sustainability. They showed that people are more likely to behave selfishly after shopping at an environmentally sustainable store than after shopping at a conventional store. Together, these studies on moral licensing thus suggest that carry-over effects are not always to be expected after an initial sustainable act. In fact, sometimes balance effects may be more likely to occur. Next, we will review research in the domain of goal pursuit that points to a similar conclusion.

---

[1] The balance effect also works the other way around, such that after doing something immoral, people are more likely to display moral behavior (e.g., Sachdeva et al., 2009). This effect has been referred to as *moral cleansing* and has been shown to hold for a wide range of behaviors. For example, after considering selling and buying human body parts for transplantations (i.e., immoral behavior), people were more likely to subsequently volunteer (i.e., moral behavior; Tetlock, Kristel, Elson, Green, & Lerner, 2000). An interesting question for future research might be whether this type of balance effect (i.e. moral cleansing effects) could also trigger sustainable behaviors.

Goal Pursuit

Research shows that setting a goal (a desired end state that people want to attain) initially has a positive effect on the behavior aimed for (Locke & Latham, 1990). So, recycling is more likely when a recycling goal is set and saving energy is more likely when an energy-saving goal is set (Abrahamse, Steg, Vlek, & Rothengatter, 2007; Becker, 1978; McCalley, Kaiser, Midden, Keser, & Teunissen, 2006; McCalley & Midden, 2002). Consistent with classic goal pursuit findings, this type of research thus suggests that when people set the goal to behave sustainably, they will be more likely to actually behave sustainably than when this goal is not set (e.g., Bargh, Gollwitzer, Lee-Chai, Barndollar, & Trotschel, 2001; Förster, Liberman, & Friedman, 2007; Lewin, 1935; Zeigarnik, 1927).

Crucial to the present framework, however, research has also shown that setting goals may have a negative side effect. As long as the goal is unfulfilled, the motivation to attain the goal is strong and goal-related constructs are accessible (Atkinson & Birch, 1970; Bargh et al., 2001; Förster et al., 2007; Förster, Liberman, & Higgins, 2005; Lewin, 1935; Zeigarnik, 1927). But, as soon as a goal is fulfilled, motivation and accessibility *decrease* (Förster et al., 2007; Förster et al., 2005; Zeigarnik, 1927). From a cognitive perspective, this is functional, as the immediate deactivation of goal-related motivations and constructs prevents interference of these constructs with other tasks (Carver & Scheier, 1999; Förster et al., 2007; Lindenberg & Steg, 2007). From the perspective of encouraging sustainable behavior, however, this is detrimental since deactivated goals make goal-congruent behavior less likely. If people have the goal to behave sustainably and they replace high energy bulbs with low energy bulbs, they may subsequently leave the lights on because their goal to behave sustainably is fulfilled and is thus pushed into the background.

A nice illustration of the balance effect upon goal fulfillment can be found in research on helping behavior by Bargh, Green, and Fitzsimons (2008). Participants were assigned to help a fellow student decipher visual ambiguous images, thereby activating a helping goal. Then another student dropped by with a questionnaire and asked participants whether they would be willing to help her with a research project she was going to conduct in the future. Participants were more likely to comply with the second student's request when they were asked for help while still working on the helping task with their fellow student than when they had already finished the helping task. In other words, when the participants were still pursuing the helping goal they were more likely to help out the student who was dropping by for help than when the helping goal was fulfilled. Activating a goal may thus initially motivate goal-congruent behavior, but once the goal is fulfilled goal-congruent behavior (i.e., a carry-over effect) is unlikely and balance effects might occur. This ironically suggests that trying to act sustainably by setting goals will initially work but in the end may in fact decrease rather than increase continued sustainable behavior.

In sum, both the goal-fulfillment and the licensing literature support the perspective that balance effects are more likely after an initial sustainable act than carry-over effects. In other words, this literature suggests that continued sustainable behavior is unlikely after an initial environmentally sustainable act. Based on this, John will probably take his car instead of his bike to the supermarket after recycling waste which is detrimental for initiatives encouraging repetitive sustainable behavior. At the same time, however, the picture might not be so bleak: As we previously mentioned, there is also evidence for carry-over effects, suggesting that performing environmentally sustainable behavior is more likely after an initial sustainable act. Integrating these two perspectives might offer valuable insights into what drives balance versus carry-over effects, enabling us to offer concrete recommendations for how to encourage continued sustainable behavior and avoid balance effects.

INTEGRATING BALANCE AND CARRY-OVER EFFECTS

In this section, we will particularly look at the role of one factor that may determine whether carry-over effects or balance effects occur after an initial sustainable act, namely self-view.

Self-Perception and Self-View

There are various sources that suggest that people continue to behave in a certain way when this behavior is part of their self-view (Bem, 1967; see also Eagly & Chaiken, 1993; Taylor, 1975). People infer from their past behavior what is important to them and what kind of person they are, and this self-view subsequently guides their behavior (Bem, 1967). Thus, after voluntarily performing a behavior people seem to reason that this behavior is desirable, making engagement in similar behaviors more likely (Albarracín & Wyer, 2000; Bem, 1967).

In a classic study, Freedman and Fraser (1966) found evidence for this self-perception phenomenon. First, under the guise of belonging to the "Community Committee for Traffic Safety Group," the researchers asked a number of households to place a small sign in their window that advocated safe driving. Some time later, the same households were contacted again with the request to place a large, unattractive billboard promoting safe driving on the front lawn for a couple of weeks. However, this time the researchers contacted them under the pretext of being from another group—the "Citizens for Safe Driving Group." In addition, another group of households who did not receive the initial request was also contacted by the "Citizens for Safe Driving Group" with the request to place the large, unattractive billboard promoting safe driving on their front lawn for a couple of weeks.

It turned out that people who agreed to place a small sign in the window were more likely to also place a large billboard on their front lawn than people who were not asked to place a small sign in the window in the first place. In other words, complying with an initial small request made people more prone to comply with a second, larger request (Freedman & Fraser, 1966). Placing a small sign for safe driving in their window apparently signaled to people that they are the kind of people who care about this, making subsequent placement of a larger sign more probable (see also Bem, 1967; Eagly & Chaiken, 1993; Snyder & Cunningham, 1975). With regard to sustainability, this suggests that if one infers from one's initial sustainable behavior that one is an environmentally sustainable person (i.e., a sustainable self-view), subsequent sustainable behavior will be more likely.

Indirect support for this notion can be found in a recent study by Effron, Cameron, and Monin (2009). Their study concerned the 2008 US presidential elections when Barack Obama was the first Black candidate from a major party running for president. They showed that endorsing Barack Obama produced either balance or carry-over effects, depending on whether people were relatively racist or not. That is, people who scored relatively low on the Modern Racism Scale (i.e., who viewed themselves as non-racists) were more likely to favor Blacks over Whites after indicating they would vote for Obama, and thus showed carry-over effects. In contrast, people who scored relatively high on the Modern Racism Scale (i.e., who viewed themselves as racist) were more likely to favor Whites over Blacks after indicating they would vote for Obama and thus showed balance effects. In line with this, research by Fishbach and Dhar (2005) suggests that carry-over effects are more likely when people are strongly committed to a goal and they see it as a defining characteristic of their self-concept. These findings suggest that people who view themselves as sustainable are more likely to show carry-over effects than balance effects.

In sum, these studies suggest that a crucial determinant of whether one continues to behave sustainably after engaging in a sustainable act is one's self-view. Viewing oneself as a sustainable person makes carry-over, rather than balance effects, more likely. Thus, in order to prevent balance effects and encourage carry-over effects it is important to make people perceive themselves as being environmentally sustainable. In the next section, we will provide some guidelines on how to accomplish this.

I JUST RECYCLED. NOW WHAT? HOW TO STIMULATE CARRY-OVER EFFECTS

In this section, we will use theoretical insights on social labeling to offer concrete recommendations on how to increase the likelihood of carry-over effects such that continued sustainable behavior becomes more likely. As reviewed above, self-view plays a vital role in producing carry-over effects. When people see themselves as sustainable, they are more likely to show continued sustainable behavior. Therefore, the question is: How can such a self-view be elicited? We propose that one particularly useful technique is the social labeling technique.

Social Labeling

When using social labeling, people are provided with a cue that they can use to form beliefs about themselves (Allen, 1982; Bem, 1967). By providing people with, for example, the social label "you are a sustainable person" they are more likely to come to see themselves as a sustainable person and also to behave accordingly. Through social labeling, a certain self-view is thus established which then influences subsequent choices (Allen, 1982). As such, social labeling seems a relatively simple, and therefore promising, method to alter people's self-views and motivate continued sustainable behavior.

One of the first studies showing this social labeling effect is a classic study by Miller, Brickman, and Bolen (1975). They demonstrated that children who were repeatedly told that they are tidy littered less than children who were told that they should be tidy. Similarly, a study by Allen (1982) showed that when people were labeled as environmentally friendly, they subsequently made more environmentally sustainable choices. Based on these findings, it seems likely that by labeling people as "environmentally sustainable consumers" they actually come to see themselves in this way and, as a result, also behave more environmentally sustainably. Given that these effects are driven by the relative salience of one's self-view, social labeling seems to be a promising technique for enhancing carry-over effects.

Indeed, there is some recent evidence in line with this view. In a set of clever studies, Cornelissen and colleagues (2007) first provoked participants to make an environmentally sustainable choice (i.e., to choose a TV set which was superior in comparison with the other televisions on various attributes, including sustainability). Then, participants received information on their choice that allowed them to attribute their (sustainable) choice to their personal values (i.e., people who choose this TV set are sustainable people). Being provided with the social label, participants actually came to see themselves as sustainable. As a result, they were subsequently more likely to also make sustainable choices (e.g., choose a more expensive but more energy-efficient light bulb).

Another way in which the social labeling technique may be employed is by stressing the environmental friendliness of common behaviors such as "not littering" (Cornelissen, Pandelaere, Warlop, & Dewitte, 2008). Most people do not litter and can recall many instances of not littering. At the same time, most people also fail to see "not littering" as a sustainable act. Cornelissen and colleagues (2008) showed that reminding people that their past behaviors, such as not littering, are actually environmentally sustainable activates a more sustainable self-view. As a result, people were more likely to later behave sustainably, for example, picking more environmentally friendly products and using less scrap paper (Cornelissen et al., 2008).

A study by Conway and Peetz (2012) further emphasizes the role of social labeling, by making a distinction between interpreting a behavior in terms of something a person did, or in terms of who the person is. When participants in their experiments visualized having certain moral traits (e.g., I am a generous person), they were more likely to donate to charity as compared to when they visualized behaving in a certain moral way (e.g., act caringly toward a person who is sad), (Conway & Peetz, 2012). This research suggests that the chance of performing continued sustainable behavior increases when a behavior is framed in terms of "being a sustainable person" rather than "performing a sustainable act." In sum, these studies suggest that the social labeling technique may prove effective in making people view themselves as sustainable, thereby increasing the chance of carry-over effects—rather than balance effects—after an initial sustainable behavior.

Besides increasing the chance of continued sustainable behavior on the individual level, the social labeling technique is also easily applicable in mass communication. The study by Allen (1982) showed that the social labeling technique may even work when being communicated over a mass medium such as television. In his study, he appealed to people living in the USA by labeling American consumers as willing to help solve the energy problem. In this way, a big group of people can be targeted. A way the social labeling technique could be used in practice is, for instance, by stating on packages of sustainable products (e.g., low energy light bulb, ecological detergent) that one is a sustainable person given that one bought the product. Similarly, on bottle banks there could be slogans stating that the people disposing of their bottles must be sustainable people since they recycled their waste.

Another factor contributing to the efficiency and applicability of social labeling is that this technique works especially well in conditions where people are not processing information very deeply and instead rely on automatic processes and heuristics (Cornelissen et al., 2007). Specifically, research has shown that when people's cognitive resources are partially occupied, people are more likely to rely on social labels than when they process or retrieve these social labels with full cognitive resources (Cornelissen et al., 2007). This is advantageous, as in everyday life people often make automatic, unconscious decisions (e.g., Bargh et al., 1996; Dijksterhuis, Smith, Van Baaren, & Wigboldus, 2005). While shopping for (sustainable) products in the supermarket, for example, people may also be deliberating on what to cook for dinner, thinking about their work appointments for the next morning, and recalling a nice dinner they had in the weekend. Under such circumstances, people's cognitive resources are thus often directed elsewhere, increasing the efficiency of the social labeling technique.

In sum, the social labeling technique seems to be a promising strategy for eliciting sustainable self-views, thereby triggering continued sustainable behavior. It can be efficiently incorporated in mass communication, package labels, and slogans, and it might be extra effective in conditions where people have limited processing resources which is a common situation in people's everyday busy lives.

CONCLUSION

In this chapter, we discussed the consequences of performing an environmentally sustainable act. We showed that although people may sometimes continue to behave sustainably after performing an initial sustainable act (e.g., carry-over effects) there is evidence that this is not always the case. In some cases, engaging in sustainable behavior may actually lead to *less* sustainable behavior later on (e.g., balance effects). We suggested that an important determinant of whether carry-over or balance effects ensue is people's self-view. When people have a sustainable self-view (or such a view is made temporarily salient), they are more likely to exhibit carry-over effects. Finally, we discussed how social labeling can be used as an efficient technique to induce a sustainable self-view and thus elicits continued sustainable behavior.

REFERENCES

Aarts, H., Verplanken, B., & Van Knippenberg, A. (1998). Predicting behavior from actions in the past: Repeated decision-making or a matter of habit? *Journal of Applied Social Psychology, 28*(15), 1355–74.

Abrahamse, W., Steg, L., Vlek, C., & Rothengatter, T. (2007). The effect of tailored information, goal setting, and tailored feedback on household energy use, energy-related behaviors, and behavioral antecedents. *Journal of Environmental Psychology, 27*(4), 265–76.

Albarracín, D., & Wyer, R. S. (2000). The cognitive impact of past behavior: Influences on beliefs, attitudes, and future behavioral decisions. *Journal of Personality and Social Psychology, 79*(1), 5–22.

Allen, C. T. (1982). Self-perception based strategies for stimulating energy conservation. *Journal of Consumer Research, 8*(4), 381–90.

Atkinson, J. W., & Birch, D. (1970). *A dynamic theory of action*. New York: Wiley.

Bargh, J. A., Chen, M., & Burrows, L. (1996). Automaticity of social behavior: Direct effects of trait construct and stereotype activation on action. *Journal of Personality and Social Psychology, 71*(2), 230–44.

Bargh, J. A., Gollwitzer, P. M., Lee-Chai, A., Barndollar, K., & Trotschel, R. (2001). The automated will: Nonconscious activation and pursuit of behavioral goals. *Journal of Personality and Social Psychology, 81*(6), 1014–27.

Bargh, J. A., Green, M., & Fitzsimons, G. (2008). The selfish goal: Unintended consequences of intended goal pursuits. *Social Cognition, 26*(5), 534–54.

Becker, L. J. (1978). Joint effect of feedback and goal setting on performance: A field study of residential energy conservation. *Journal of Applied Psychology, 63*(4), 428–33.

Bem, D. J. (1967). Self-perception: An alternative interpretation of cognitive dissonance phenomena. *Psychological Review, 74*(3), 183–200.

Carver, C. S., & Scheier, M. F. (1999). Themes and issues in the self-regulation of behavior. In R. S. Wyer Jr (Ed.), *Perspectives on behavioral self-regulation: Advances in social cognition* (Vol. 12). Mahwah, NJ: Erlbaum.

Conway, P., & Peetz, J. (2012). When does feeling moral actually make you a better person? Conceptual abstraction moderates whether past moral deeds motivate consistency or compensatory behavior. *Personality and Social Psychology Bulletin, 38*(7), 907–19.

Cornelissen, G., Dewitte, S., Warlop, L., & Yzerbyt, V. (2007). Whatever people say I am, that's what I am: Social labeling as a social marketing tool. *International Journal of Research in Marketing, 24*(4), 278–88.

Cornelissen, G., Pandelaere, M., Warlop, L., & Dewitte, S. (2008). Positive cueing: Promoting sustainable consumer behavior by cueing common environmental behaviors as environmental. *International Journal of Research in Marketing, 25*(1), 48–55.

Dijksterhuis, A., Smith, P. K., Van Baaren, R. B., & Wigboldus, D. H. J. (2005). The unconscious consumer: Effects of environment on consumer choice. *Journal of Consumer Psychology, 15*(3), 193–202.

Eagly, A. H., & Chaiken, S. (1993). *The psychology of attitudes*. Fort Worth, TX: Harcourt, Brace, Jovanovich.

Effron, D. A., Cameron, J. S., & Monin, B. (2009). Endorsing Obama licenses favoring Whites. *Journal of Experimental Social Psychology, 45*(3), 590–93.

Festinger, L. A. (1957). *Theory of cognitive dissonance*. Evanston, IL: Row & Peterson.

Fishbach, A., & Dhar, R. (2005). Goals as excuses or guides: The liberating effect of perceived goal progress on choice. *Journal of Consumer Research, 32*(3), 370–77.

Förster, J., Liberman, N., & Friedman, R. S. (2007). Seven principles of goal activation: A systematic approach to distinguishing goal priming from priming of non-goal constructs. *Personality and Social Psychology Review*, *11*(3), 211–33.

Förster, J., Liberman, N., & Higgins, E. T. (2005). Accessibility from active and fulfilled goals. *Journal of Experimental Social Psychology*, *41*(3), 220–39.

Freedman, J. L., & Fraser, S. C. (1966). Compliance without pressure: The foot-in-the-door technique. *Journal of Personality and Social Psychology*, *4*(2), 195–202.

Jordan, J. M., Mullen, E., & Murnighan, J. K. (2011). Striving for the moral self: The effects of recalling past moral actions on future moral behavior. *Personality and Social Psychology Bulletin*, *37*(5), 701–13.

Lewin, K. (1935). The conflict between Aristotelian and Galilean modes of thought in contemporary psychology. In *A dynamic theory of personality: Selected papers* (pp. 1–42). New York: McGraw-Hill.

Lindenberg, S., & Steg, L. (2007). Normative, gain and hedonic goal frames guiding environmental behavior. *Journal of Social Issues*, *63*(1), 117–37.

Locke, E. A., & Latham, G. P. (1990). *A theory of goal-setting and task performance.* Englewood Cliffs, NJ: Prentice Hall.

Mazar, N., & Zhong, C. B. (2010). Do green products make us better people? *Psychological Science*, *21*(4), 494–98.

McCalley, L. T., Kaiser, F. G., Midden, C. J. H., Keser, M., & Teunissen, M. (2006). Persuasive appliances: Goal priming and behavioral response to product-integrated energy feedback. In W. A. IJsselsteijn, Y. A. W. de Kort, C. J. H. Midden, J. H. Eggen, & E. A. W. H. van den Hoven (Eds.), *Persuasive Technology* (Vol. 3962, pp. 45–49). Berlin: Springer-Verlag.

McCalley, L. T., & Midden, C. J. H. (2002). Energy conservation through product-integrated feedback: The roles of goal-setting and social orientation. *Journal of Economic Psychology*, *23*(5), 589–603.

Miller, R. L., Brickman, P., & Bolen, D. (1975). Attribution versus persuasion as a means for modifying behavior. *Journal of Personality and Social Psychology*, *31*(3), 430–41.

Monin, B., & Miller, D. T. (2001). Moral credentials and the expression of prejudice. *Journal of Personality and Social Psychology*, *81*(1), 33–43.

Ouellette, J. A., & Wood, W. (1998). Habit and intention in everyday life: The multiple processes by which past behavior predicts future behavior. *Psychological Bulletin*, *124*(1), 54–74.

Sachdeva, S., Iliev, R., & Medin, D. L. (2009). Sinning saints and saintly sinners: The paradox of moral self-regulation. *Psychological Science*, *20*(4), 523–28.

Schmuck, P., & Schultz, P. W. (Eds.). (2002). *The psychology of sustainable development.* Norwell, MA: Kluwer.

Snyder, M., & Cunningham, M. R. (1975). To comply or not comply: A testing of the self-perception explanation of the foot-in-the-door technique. *Journal of Personality and Social Psychology*, *31*(1), 64–67.

Swann, W. B., & Gilbert, D. T. (1990). The fleeting gleam of praise: Cognitive processes underlying behavioral reactions to self-relevant feedback. *Journal of Personality and Social Psychology*, *59*(1), 17–26.

Taylor, S. E. (1975). On inferring one's attitudes from one's behavior: Some delimiting conditions. *Journal of Personality and Social Psychology*, *31*(1), 126–31.

Tetlock, P. E., Kristel, O. V., Elson, S. B., Green, M. C., & Lerner, J. S. (2000). The psychology of the unthinkable: Taboo trade-offs, forbidden base rates, and heretical counterfactuals. *Journal of Personality and Social Psychology*, *78*(5), 853–70.

Zeigarnik, B. (1927). Das Behalten erledigter und unerledigter Handlungen [The memory of completed and uncompleted actions]. *Psychologisch Forschung*, *9*(1), 1–85.

7

Think Globally, Act Locally
Construal Levels and Environmentally Relevant Decision Making

KENTARO FUJITA, SHERI L. CLARK,
and ANTONIO L. FREITAS

A s measured by the rates of depletion of its vital resources, such as water suitable for drinking or irrigation, the Earth's environment is widely recognized to require active stewardship such that it may continue to sustain human life. Because this stewardship needs to be realized not only through large-scale (e.g., governmental) policy but also through the culmination of the many decisions individuals make each day, targeting individuals' environmentally relevant decision making is an increasingly intense focus of psychological theory and research. Understanding principles by which individuals might be persuaded to consistently curtail their water and energy usage, for example, can be expected to yield large overall benefits to the Earth's environment.

In this chapter, we propose that the adage frequently used by environmentalists—think globally, act locally—illuminates in part what some psychological research suggests is critical to understanding environment-relevant decision making and behavior. Specifically, we suggest that many decision-making contexts present a situation in which the rewards of deciding in favor of environment-sustaining options usually are relatively abstract, whereas the rewards of alternate less environmentally friendly decisions are relatively concrete. Although taking a very brief, lukewarm shower, for example, may benefit overall water and energy supplies in the abstract, the concrete cold of a winter morning may tempt one to take a longer, hotter shower. It is the immediate salience of the local features in our social environment that so frequently prompts us to make decisions and to behave in ways that maximize concrete rewards (e.g., a luxuriously warm shower) rather than abstract rewards (e.g., protecting the environment). Moreover, because environmental resources are communal, there often may be a diffusion of responsibility with respect to their stewardship. Individual decision makers may not clearly link communitywide environmental goals to their own particular actions and decisions, and thus make decisions that benefit their own situation at the expense of the community's. Powerful alternative rationales also often compete with environment-sustaining options, as when a land owner considers clearing a small patch of forest in pursuit of an agricultural or commerce goal. When confronted with such decision-making contexts, we argue that how globally or abstractly people think about or understand a situation plays a critical role in whether people heed their environmental goals and values. In what follows, we elaborate on what we mean by *thinking globally* and describe research that indicates its relevance for decision making and behavior.

THINKING GLOBALLY: LEVELS OF ABSTRACTION IN SUBJECTIVE CONSTRUAL

Research in psychology reveals that key to understanding judgment, decision, and behavior is recognizing that they represent responses not to the objective features of events, but rather people's subjective interpretation or *construal* of those features (e.g., Bruner, 1957; Griffin & Ross, 1991; Hastorf & Cantril, 1954; Kunda, 1990; Trope & Liberman, 2003). Whereas throwing a plastic bottle in the trash might represent *preventing litter* to one person and be viewed as meritorious, the same act might equally represent *failing to recycle* to another and be viewed as blameworthy. The same event can thus prompt very different responses depending on one's subjective construal of that event.

One important way in which people's subjective construals differ is in their level of abstraction (e.g., Liberman & Trope, 2008; Trope & Liberman, 2003, 2010; Vallacher & Wegner, 1987). People can construe the same event both abstractly and concretely. For example, bicycling to work can be construed abstractly as reducing one's carbon footprint or concretely as pushing pedals. Both abstract and concrete construals accurately describe bicycling to work, but underscore different features. More abstract (high-level) construals highlight the essential, invariant properties that are common to a more general class of events. The process of abstraction renders these subjective representations more schematic and organized. Information is structured around one's global goals and values. More concrete (low-level) construals, in contrast, highlight the more incidental, concrete features of events that render them unique from others. These mental representations are more disparate and disorganized, focused more on calling attention to those contextual specifics that distinguish the particular focal event. Thus, whereas the higher-level construal of *reducing one's carbon footprint* highlights the goals and values exemplified by actions that include bicycling to work, the lower-level construal of *pushing pedals* highlights the unique challenges and opportunities afforded by biking rather than riding the public bus.

We propose that taking account of the level of abstraction at which decision makers construe events may prove useful in promoting environmentally responsible decisions and behavior. Using this idea to promote environmentally responsible decisions requires understanding both those factors that promote higher- versus lower-level construals and what impact these subjective construals have on various decision-making and behavioral processes.

WHAT MAKES PEOPLE "THINK GLOBALLY"?

Research suggests that one central factor that determines the level of abstraction of people's subjective construals is the psychological distance of an event (e.g., Liberman & Trope, 2008; Trope & Liberman, 2003, 2010). An event is psychologically distant to the degree that it is removed from a person's direct and immediate experience. Events can be distant on a number of dimensions, including time, space, social distance, and hypotheticality. For example, an event that occurs a year from today is more psychologically distant on the basis of time relative to one that occurs a week from today. Research suggests that psychologically distant events tend to be construed more abstractly than psychologically proximal events. That is, events that are more distant versus proximal in time (e.g., Liberman, Sagristano, & Trope, 2002; Semin & Smith, 1999), space (e.g., Fujita, Henderson, Eng, Trope, & Liberman, 2006; Henderson, Fujita, Trope, & Liberman, 2006), social distance (Smith & Trope, 2006; Liviatan, Trope, & Liberman, 2008), and hypotheticality (e.g., Todorov, Goren, & Trope, 2007; Wakslak, Trope, Liberman, & Alony, 2006) all are construed in higher-level rather than lower-level terms. Research also shows that distance-related cues facilitate the processing of abstract concepts (e.g., Bar-Anan, Liberman, & Trope, 2006) and that this association between distance and construal can operate in a bidirectional manner, such that abstract concepts promote perceptions of greater distance (e.g., Liberman, Trope, McCrea, & Sherman, 2007).

Other research has revealed that the difficulty people have in performing particular actions influences the abstractness of their construals. Behavior is cognitively represented in means–ends hierarchies (Carver & Scheier, 1982, 1990; Kruglanski, Shah, Fishbach, Friedman, Chun, & Sleeth-Keppler, 2002; Vallacher & Wegner, 1987). Whereas the most concrete levels of these hierarchies detail those specific behaviors necessary for performing an action (means), more abstract levels increasingly reference the goals and values for which these actions are performed (ends). The level of abstraction at which people construe their actions represents an informational trade-off between understanding the more abstract implications of their behavior and successfully accomplishing the desired action. In essence, higher-level construals of behavior specify *why* someone might engage in an action, whereas lower-level construals specify *how* one executes that action. Although people prefer to construe behavior more abstractly, when more abstract construals fail to provide sufficient informational guidance for performing a behavior (particularly when the behavior is difficult, complex, or novel), they increasingly prefer more concrete construals. Trying to drink coffee out of a cumbersome mug, for example, promotes construing coffee drinking concretely as *swallowing* rather than abstractly as *becoming alert* (Wegner, Vallacher, Macomber, Wood,

& Arps, 1984). Beyond performance difficulty, research also suggests individual differences in the chronic tendency to construe action in high- or low-level terms (Vallacher & Wegner, 1989).

Other situational factors that tend to promote more abstract construals include positive versus negative moods (e.g., Beukeboom & Semin, 2005, 2006; Gasper & Clore, 2002; Isen & Daubman, 1984; Mikulincer, Kedem, & Paz, 1990; Mikulincer, Paz, & Kedem, 1990), states of self-affirmation (Schmeichel & Vohs, 2009; Wakslak & Trope, 2009), and adoption of third-person versus first-person visual perspectives (Libby, Shaeffer, & Eibach, 2009; Libby Shaeffer, Eibach, & Slemmer, 2007; see also Kross, Ayduk, & Mischel, 2005). The abstractness of people's construals of one event also tends to "carry over" and affect construals of subsequent events. Imagining one's life in the distant future versus near future, for example, not only promotes more abstract construals of the imagined event, but also of subsequent unrelated performance tasks (Förster, Friedman, & Liberman, 2004). Considering the abstract ends achieved by a target behavior (*why* one engages in a behavior) rather than the concrete means by which to perform that behavior (*how* one engages in a behavior) promotes higher-level construals of events that are semantically unrelated (Freitas, Gollwitzer, & Trope, 2004). Similarly, categorizing objects into broader superordinate versus narrower subordinate categories in one task can also promote more abstract construals of unrelated objects and events in subsequent tasks (Fujita, Trope, Liberman, & Levin-Sagi, 2006).

THE IMPACT OF THINKING GLOBALLY VERSUS LOCALLY ON DECISION MAKING AND BEHAVIOR

As noted earlier, understanding people's subjective construals is important because they systematically impact judgment, decisions, and actions (e.g., Liberman & Trope, 2008; Trope & Liberman, 2003, 2010; Vallacher & Wegner, 1987). Higher-level construals highlight and promote more abstract, global considerations of events, structuring information processing around one's general goals and values. Lower-level construals, by contrast, highlight and promote more concrete, local considerations, directing attention to those specific details that render an event unique. Consider, for example, the previously discussed example of bicycling to work. An environmentalist who wakes up one morning feeling particularly tired might make very different decisions about how to get to work, depending on level of construal. A higher-level construal is likely to reference his or her concern for the environment (e.g., reducing one's carbon footprint), and thus promote positive evaluations and increase the likelihood of biking to work. A lower-level construal of the same act, however, is likely to reference those concrete features that individuate this act from other acts; that is, how unusually tired the environmentalist is feeling this particular morning. In this latter example, a lower-level construal (e.g., pushing pedals) is likely to promote more negative evaluations and decrease the likelihood of biking to work.

In what follows, we review research that supports the idea that higher-level construals promote consideration of the abstract, global considerations of events in judgment, decision, and action. This research suggests that higher-level construals might promote not only consideration of the environmental implications of one's decisions and actions, but that they might also increase the likelihood of actually engaging in environmentally friendly behavior through a number of psychological mechanisms. We then discuss how such work may inform intervention and policy designed to promote pro-environment decisions and actions.

THINKING GLOBALLY PROMOTES ACTING LOCALLY

As noted above, a particularly vexing challenge for changing environmentally relevant behaviors is that the rewards of selecting environment-sustaining options often are quite abstract and far removed from present experience. Global warming, for instance, is a planetwide phenomenon, hypothesized to have its strongest impacts on human life decades into the future. In contrast, driving a gasoline-consuming, carbon-emitting automobile along California's Pacific Coast Highway, overlooking the cliffs and rolling surf of the Pacific Ocean en route from Los Angeles to San Francisco, can be intensely exhilarating. How can an individual be persuaded to forgo this unique, concrete experience in the service of averting decades-away costs of global warming? When might an individual weight the distal, abstract costs of global warming more strongly than the tangible pleasures and conveniences of air conditioning and ice-cold drinks in disposable bottles on a hot, muggy day? Next we review evidence that higher-level construals increase the weighting of high-level decision features such as desirability, abstract goals, values, and self-standards.

Desirability versus Feasibility

The decision to engage in any behavior must take into account both the desirability and feasibility of the action. What is most desirable, however, is not always most feasible, and what is most feasible is not always most desirable. For example, although complete independence from fossil fuels may be desirable, it is not yet feasible given current technology. Similarly, although throwing a plastic bottle in a nearby trash receptacle can be the most feasible way to dispose of it, committing that bottle to a landfill would hardly appear desirable. Research suggests that how people construe events systematically affects the weighting of desirability versus feasibility concerns (e.g., Fujita, Eyal, Chaiken, Trope, & Liberman, 2008; Liberman & Trope, 1998; Sagristano, Trope, & Liberman, 2002; Liviatan et al., 2008; Todorov et al., 2007). Whereas feasibility considerations reference the specific and concrete means by which an act is performed (*how* one performs a particular act), desirability considerations reference the general and abstract ends that the act achieves (*why* one performs a particular act). Accordingly, higher-level construals, relative to lower-level construals, increase the weight placed on desirability rather than feasibility considerations. For example, when making decisions about the distant versus near future (and thus construing events abstractly versus concretely), people are more concerned about the value of possible rewards and are less sensitive to the likelihood that such rewards will actually materialize (e.g.,

Sagristano et al., 2002). Higher-level construals also prompt people to be less sensitive to how difficult an action is to accomplish and more sensitive to what that action achieves (e.g., Fujita et al., 2008; Liberman & Trope, 1998). For example, when purchasing a new DVD player, higher-level construals prompted people to be more concerned about whether the product was constructed of environment-friendly materials (a desirability concern) rather than how easy the user manual was to read (a feasibility concern; Fujita et al., 2008).

Abstract versus Concrete Goals

Many of the goals that people strive to attain, such as conserving the environment, cannot be accomplished by a particular act in a single moment (e.g., Rachlin, 1995). Rather, such abstract goals are achieved by a myriad of different behaviors across diverse circumstances. The goal to reduce one's carbon footprint, for example, cannot be completely and fully attained simply by taking public transportation to work one single morning. Instead, this goal requires multiple behaviors (e.g., driving a fuel-efficient car, unplugging unused appliances, buying local foods, etc.) across multiple situations (e.g., on the road, in the house, in the supermarket). Appreciating that these heterogeneous behaviors in diverse contexts all serve the same end requires abstraction. Specific, concrete considerations that appear in the moment, however, often tempt people to behave in ways that are contrary to those abstract goals. For example, the allure of a ride in a high-powered sports car may tempt one to abandon one's goal of reducing one's carbon footprint. When situations present concrete rewards that threaten abstract goals, higher-level construals should help people "see the forest beyond" and adhere to their abstract goals.

Initial evidence for this prediction comes from research on self-relevant information search. The opportunity to receive feedback about one's self may constitute a conflict between more abstract self-improvement goals and more concrete self-enhancement concerns (e.g., Butler, 1993; Dweck & Leggett, 1988; Trope, 1986, Trope & Neter, 1994). Positive feedback is affectively pleasant in the moment, yet does little to diagnose one's deficiencies. Negative feedback, on the other hand, has affective costs in the moment, but provides the necessary information to better oneself over time. Which feedback one prefers thus represents a self-regulatory trade-off between seeking the more concrete affective rewards afforded by positive feedback versus the more abstract epistemic rewards afforded by negative feedback. These considerations suggest that higher-level construals should foster more abstract self-assessment and self-improvement goals over more concrete self-enhancement considerations. Irrespective of the methods by which construal levels were induced or measured, research has demonstrated that higher-level construals promote preference for negative rather than positive feedback across diverse domains ranging from social intelligence to career aptitude (Freitas et al., 2001). For example, those who chronically construe events more abstractly evidence less interest in downward social comparison and greater interest in liabilities-focused feedback.

Similar results have been found in studies of self-control decision making. One does not become *healthier* or *thinner* by a single action in a particular moment.

One must sustain these efforts across a number of different circumstances. Our daily lives, however, frequently entail situations that present concrete rewards that threaten to undermine these admirable abstract goals. For example, a decadent candy bar may tempt dieters to abandon their weight-loss goals. In these situations, higher-level construals should promote decisions that favor more abstract goals. Indeed, research has shown that among college-age female undergraduates, inducing higher-level construals experimentally promoted preferences for apples over candy bars as a snack (Fujita & Han, 2009). Similarly, students committed to academic achievement evaluate objects and activities that undermine studying more negatively when induced to construe events more abstractly (Fujita, Trope, et al., 2006). Thus higher-level construals protect one's abstract goals from competing concrete, situation-specific rewards. They keep people cognizant of those aims that transcend any particular moment and are realized only through sustained effort across varied situations.

Value–Behavior Correspondence

For many people, concern for the environment stems from personal values. Values are principles that not only serve as guides for behavior but also serve a central role in people's sense of identity. Research suggests that people's behavior corresponds to their values to a greater extent when they construe events in higher- rather than lower-level terms (e.g., Eyal, Sagristano, Trope, Liberman, & Chaiken, 2009; Torelli & Kaikati, 2009). For example, endorsement of environmental values on Schwartz's (1992) value questionnaire predicted stronger behavioral intentions to engage in future pro-environmental behaviors to the extent that participants construed events abstractly (Eyal et al., 2009). Higher-level construals, moreover, have also been shown to promote greater correspondence between values and actual behavior (Torrelli & Kaikati, 2009).

Beyond promoting value–behavior correspondence, research also suggests that people are likely to judge the actions of others in terms of moral values when construing events more abstractly (e.g., Eyal, Liberman, & Trope, 2008). People are much more punitive for moral value transgressions when construing events in higher-level terms. They also praise and think more positively of moral value successes when those successes are construed more abstractly. Judgments of others' success or failure at behaviors that promote environmental conservation values thus may depend on level of construal.

Self-Standards

Among the most abstract purposes people pursue is being the kind of person each of us aspires to be. Cybernetic models thus place desired self-concepts at the very top of goal hierarchies, with more concrete subgoals serving as means of realizing those abstract self-standards (e.g., Carver & Scheier, 1999, Figure 1.5; Powers, 1973). People typically strive to behave consistently with their desired self-concepts, such that even relatively mundane actions can come to be viewed in relation to them (e.g., James, 1890; Kim & Markus, 1999; Snyder & Fromkin, 1980).

Accordingly, construing events more abstractly (e.g., "joining the army") should lead one to consider not only its anticipated outcomes (e.g., promoting the nation's defense), but also its relations to one's own important self-guides (e.g., being strong, being brave, or being responsible). When focused on immediate, low-level details of action, in contrast, behaviors and decisions should be more likely to be viewed as compartmentalized within the domain or task at hand, rendering them less pertinent to one's self-views (see also Baumeister, 1990; Emmons, 1992), as has been speculated to be true of individuals who commit atrocities while focusing exclusively on the low-level details of their behavior (Lifton, 1986).

Examining these predictions, one set of studies tested the hypothesis that higher-level construals would increase the extent to which one relates one's present decisions to one's self-standards (Freitas, Langsam, Clark, & Moeller, 2008). When evaluating or deciding between political candidates or consumer products, for instance, construing action in higher-level terms should increase attraction to candidates and products that embody the characteristics one strives to realize oneself. One's choice then would be viewed as pertinent to how one sees oneself, rather than as a discrete, compartmentalized decision with little bearing on one's self-views. Indeed, desiring for oneself a political candidate's personal qualities predicted evaluating favorably and voting for that candidate to a greater extent among participants focused on the distal future (and presumably construing action in higher-level terms) than the proximal future (and presumably construing action in lower-level terms). Similarly, individuals who chronically construe action in higher-level terms responded more favorably to advertisements appealing to their desired self-concept (e.g., How do you define yourself? Buy a hybrid. Be part of the solution) than to product quality (e.g., High performance. What could be better? Buy a hybrid and add horsepower).

Further clarifying which aspects of self are most salient as a function of level of action construal, a recent series of studies contrasted individuals' focus on their relatively idealistic and pragmatic senses of self. Following research on distributive justice (Lind & Tyler, 1988), which indicates that being treated with dignity and respect are among individuals' core self-referential concerns, Kivetz and Tyler (2007) hypothesized that construing events more abstractly would increase individuals' focus on action opportunities' implications for their more idealized senses of self than their more pragmatic concerns. Supporting this reasoning, individuals anticipating distant (abstract) versus near-future (concrete) events (such as college courses or banking institutions) judged dignity-related features (e.g., the professor/institution usually treats students/customers with respect and dignity) to be more important than pragmatic features (e.g., the course looks good on the resumé or good interest rates on credit cards). Beyond demonstrating that level of construal increases the perceived self-relevance of actions and decisions (Freitas et al., 2008), Kivetz and Tyler's (2007) findings suggest that specific self-conceptual concerns with attaining an idealized sense of self are of particularly heightened salience with higher-level construals.

HOW THINKING GLOBALLY
FACILITATES ACTING LOCALLY

Enhancing concern for the environment in decision making and behavior requires understanding not only whether various factors might promote environmentally responsible choices and action, but also how those factors produce their effects. Without a proper understanding of mechanism, well-intentioned interventionists may inadvertently undo the very results that they wish to promote. Fortunately, research findings have not only demonstrated that higher- versus lower-level construals promote the weighting of more abstract, global concerns, but they have also illuminated some of the underlying psychological mechanisms.

Cognitive Accessibility

As noted earlier, different construals highlight different features of one's social environment. Cognitively, this suggests that higher- and lower-level construals should render different features of events more or less accessible, activating and rendering it easier to think about various thought content (Freitas et al., 2004; see also Herzog, Hansen, & Wänke, 2005). Whereas higher-level construals should promote the accessibility of one's abstract goals and values, lower-level construals should enhance the accessibility of more immediate, context-specific concerns. Indeed, empirical studies support this assertion. As noted earlier, diagnostic feedback presents a choice dilemma between the more concrete affective rewards afforded by positive feedback versus the more abstract epistemic rewards afforded by negative feedback (e.g., Butler, 1993; Dweck & Leggett, 1988; Trope, 1986, Trope & Neter, 1994). Feedback recipients are not alone in experiencing this dilemma; so too do those who must provide the feedback. The latter must decide whether to indulge recipients' immediate self-enhancement concerns by providing positive feedback, or promote recipients' more general self-assessment and self-improvement concerns by providing more critical, negative feedback. Indeed, as is the case with feedback recipients, research suggests that higher-level construals prompt feedback providers to prefer negative over positive feedback (Freitas et al., 2004). Moreover, when prompted to consider the recipients' motives, feedback providers at higher-level construals found it easier to think about recipients' abstract, more distal goals rather than their more immediate emotional concerns, as indicated by the amount of time required to list each respective type of thought. Increased cognitive accessibility of more abstract and distal goals thus appears to be one mechanism by which higher-level construals impact decision making and behavior.

Information Search

Beyond cognitive accessibility, different construals also prompt searches for different types of information. Research indicates that higher-level construals prompt people to search for information relevant to one's more abstract and global concerns (Sagristano et al., 2002; Torelli & Kaikati, 2009). For example, Torelli and Kaikati (2009) presented participants with a consumer product and gave them an opportunity to learn about its various features. They found that higher-level construals prompted people with environmentalism values to seek out more information about the consumer product's environment-friendly features to a greater degree than lower-level construals. Thus, not only do higher-level construals render more accessible one's higher-order concerns, but they also lead people to gather additional information that speaks to these concerns.

Attention

Different construals can also change to what degree people attend to information that they have collected and is cognitively accessible. Research suggests that people more carefully attend to information that is consistent with their subjective construal of a situation. Such attention can be assessed by the scrutiny with which people process various arguments. For example, a study by Fujita and colleagues (2008) presented participants with strong versus weak persuasive arguments in favor of donating to a wildlife charity. They found that people were more sensitive to the strength of the arguments (i.e., they were persuaded by strong rather than weak arguments) to the extent that the content of those arguments was relevant to those features of the situation highlighted by their respective construals. When the content of a persuasive appeal and the concerns raised by a particular construal match, people scrutinize and carefully attend to the message. Those at higher-level construals more carefully process higher-level information, whereas those at lower-level construals more carefully process lower-level information. When there is a mismatch, however, people are more cursory in their processing, giving less attention to what the persuasive message actually says.

On the Nonnecessity of Effortful Processing

Although higher-level (versus lower-level) construals can prompt greater attention to and deeper processing of information pertaining to one's more abstract and global (versus concrete and local) concerns, this elaborative and effortful processing is not a necessary condition to observe changes in construal-dependent decisions and behavior. Research demonstrates that levels of construal can change people's decisions and behavior even without their engaging in any effortful processing of information. A recent investigation of self-control conducted among female college students, who generally can be expected to experience self-control dilemmas pertaining to eating healthful versus unhealthful foods, showed that level of construal modulates the ease with which people associate low-level rewards (i.e., temptations such as high-calorie foods) with negative concepts (Fujita & Han, 2009). In one study, to induce higher- versus lower-level construals, participants were provided with a series of objects (e.g., a dog) and were asked to generate general category labels versus specific examples of each (e.g., *animal* versus *poodle*), respectively (see Fujita, Trope, et al., 2006). Participants next completed the "apples versus candy bars" version of the Implicit Association Test (IAT), a reaction time-based measure that assesses the degree to which people associate apples and candy bars with positivity versus negativity (Karpinski & Hilton, 2001). Importantly, the IAT assesses participants' evaluations of objects without requiring any effortful or deliberative processing (Fazio & Olson, 2003; Greenwald, McGhee, & Schwartz, 1998). Participants induced to higher-level construals more readily associated candy bars with negativity. These implicit evaluations, moreover, explained the effect of the construal levels on participants' choices between healthy (apples) and unhealthy (candy bars) food. Specifically, the stronger preference for apples over candy bars among those induced to higher-level construals was mediated by these implicit evaluative associations. Accordingly, construal levels may not require any extensive effortful processing of information to impact people's decisions and behavior; those effects emerge even when people are not compelled to think deeply about their options.

Perceived Goal Conflict

One powerful barrier to translating one's abstract goals into action is overcoming conflict between competing motivations. Even the best of environment-sustaining intentions and motivations may fail to result in action when conflicted by powerful competing goals, as in the example of the land owner who cares about her environment but who considers clearing a small patch of forest in pursuit of an agricultural goal. Research suggests that higher-level construals may promote goal-directed decisions and behavior by reducing the perceived conflict between potentially competing goals. Higher-level construals tend to prompt more abstract categorization of objects and events. Adopting more general, superordinate conceptualizations can reduce discrepancies noted at more specific and subordinate conceptualizations (e.g., Medin & Smith, 1984; Rosch, 1975; see also Levy, Freitas, & Salovey, 2002). For example, ostriches, penguins, and vultures on the surface have many important differences that set them apart from each other (e.g., where they live, what they eat, what they look like), differences that are highlighted by the use of lower-level categories. These differences, however, become less evident if one were to consider all three more abstractly as birds. The same might be true of the various goals people pursue. Consider, for example, different ongoing goals one might have of "excelling at work" and of "avoiding unhealthy foods." On their surface, these goals are quite distinct from one another, given their different content domains as well as their different strategic emphases (Higgins, 1998). When construed in higher-level terms, however, both goals can be related to broader aims one may hold of exercising self-discipline, of achieving competence, or of being generally successful in one's endeavors. To the extent that one construes one's actions in terms of their relatively abstract purposes, then, one may be more likely to perceive one's different life endeavors as related coherently to one another, thereby promoting the perception that one's efforts toward those endeavors sustain rather than conflict with one another.

Testing the above reasoning, a recent study (Freitas, Clark, Kim, & Levy, 2009) assessed individual differences in level of construal and the extent to which participants experienced their ongoing goals as concordant or discordant with one another. Subjective experiences of goal pursuit have proved amenable to study via the personal strivings approach (for review, see Emmons, 1996), which examines individuals' perceived underlying motivations for their goals and perceived conflicts among their goals. Of greatest relevance here, the latter of those two phenomena is assessed via a matrix in which participants rate the facilitative versus inhibitory impact of each of their goal pursuits on each of their other goal pursuits, yielding a single summary score reflecting the amount of concordance each participant perceives across all of his or her ongoing goals (Emmons & King, 1988). Using this measure, more abstract construals were indeed found to relate to greater perceived concordance among one's ongoing goals, such that individual, specific goals appear related to a broader, coherent construal of one's self-regulatory efforts (Freitas et al., 2009). These results remained significant when controlling for participants' self-esteem, perceived meaning in life, and overall goal focus. Conceptually similar results have also been found when people's construals are manipulated rather than measured as individual differences (Clark & Freitas, 2012). Accordingly, adopting more abstract, higher-level construals may reduce the perceived conflict between one's potentially competing goals and motivations.

IMPLICATIONS FOR ENVIRONMENTALLY ORIENTED PERSUASIVE APPEALS

The research reviewed above converges on the notion that more abstract, higher-level construals of objects and events should promote greater consideration of high-level (abstract, goal-related) rather than low-level (concrete, procedure-related) features and concerns. The effect of these construals on decisions and behavior have been demonstrated irrespective of whether opportunities pertain to oneself directly (e.g., Freitas et al., 2001) or someone else (Freitas et al., 2004), with direct implications for evaluation, preferences, and actual goal-relevant behaviors. Moreover, these effects cumulatively have been observed whether level of action construal was measured as a chronic individual-differences variable (e.g., Freitas et al., 2001) or manipulated as a function of the psychological distance of events (e.g., Eyal et al., 2009; Fujita et al., 2008; Liberman & Trope, 1998), or as a function of how previous unrelated events were construed (e.g., Freitas et al., 2004; Fujita, Trope, et al., 2006; Torelli & Kaikati, 2009).

These findings suggest that a primary challenge for encouraging environmentally responsible decisions and actions is to change the way people tend to construe events in the moment of choice. Although in principle many people would espouse environmentalism-compatible values and goals, the pushes and pulls of everyday life prompt lower-level construals that lead people to focus on more concrete, immediate concerns. Thus, a key problem is to bring people's local decisions into greater accordance with their more global concerns, thereby permitting them to *think globally, act locally*. The research reviewed above indicates that to accomplish this objective, one can adopt one of two strategies. One strategy is to promote more distanced or abstract construals of immediate environment-relevant decisions and actions. The second strategy is to take the abstract aim of conserving the environment, and find a way to present environment-friendly options more concretely. We discuss each of these possibilities in the following sections.

Inducing More Abstract Construals to Promote Environmental Concerns

Although common sense might suggest that environmental dilemmas would be conveyed most urgently and therefore compellingly in reference to the immediate future, the findings reviewed above instead strongly imply the opposite suggestion. Increasing rather than decreasing psychological distance is associated with higher-level construals (e.g., Liberman & Trope, 1998; Trope & Liberman, 2003, 2010). Accordingly, environmental dilemmas may be conveyed most effectively, for example, in reference to the distal future (e.g., anticipated rising sea levels) rather than the proximal future (e.g., current habitat encroachment). In this way, costs and benefits pertaining to relatively low-level features of decisions, such as those entailing inconveniences, may be less salient than costs and benefits pertaining to high-level features of decisions, such as those entailing broader environmental benefits. Distancing need not be limited to the dimension of time; removing an event along any dimension of distance (e.g., temporal, spatial, social, hypothetical) should promote greater consideration of issues relevant to the environment. For example, asking people what they would have others do rather than what they themselves should do (a social distance intervention) should promote greater environmental consideration. Similarly, one can expect those who live farther from a particular area to be more supportive of pro-environmental policies than those who live closer.

Beyond distance, as reviewed earlier, research has suggested numerous other ways to induce higher-level construals to promote environmental decisions and action. For example, as more positive moods promote higher-level construals (Beukeboom & Semin, 2005, 2006; Gasper & Clore, 2002; Isen & Daubman, 1984; Mikulincer, Kedem, & Paz, 1990; Mikulincer, Paz, & Kedem, 1990), rather than portray the doom and gloom of global warming, it may make more sense to encourage people to strive for a positive, verdant, and bright future. Research also indicates that visualizing events from a third-person rather than first-person perspective enhances abstract construals (e.g., Libby, Shaeffer, & Eibach, 2009), suggesting that mundane cues such as camera angle may play a powerful role in the way people process environment-relevant information. Situational features as incidental as ceiling height (e.g., Meyers-Levy & Zhu, 2007) and temperature (e.g., IJzerman & Semin, 2009), moreover, have been shown to impact the manner in which people construe events, thus suggesting additional potential means of increasing concern for the environment.

On Precommitment

One concern that some might have about applying research on construal levels to promote environmental decisions and actions might be the ease with which people might reconstrue events. Unless a decision is irreversible, there is little to prevent people from changing their minds and undoing the decision after an alternate construal is adopted. The potential for such a problem is highlighted by Rogers and Bazerman (2008). Their research indicates that in the distant future, people are supportive of policies that highlight what they *should* do rather than what they *want* to do. As the distant future becomes more proximal, however, people are less supportive of these policies. For example, Rogers and Bazerman (2008) found that people support a tax on automotive gasoline and bans on fishing to allow fish stocks to replenish when such programs were to be instituted in the distant future (e.g., four years from now). Support for these programs, however, diminished when they were to be instituted in the proximal future (e.g., next month). Importantly, Rogers and Bazerman (2008) found that these preference reversals were mediated by changes in construals. They note that without something to bind these decisions, people will simply undue these policies at the very moment they are to be initiated and implemented.

Fortunately, research suggests that people are to some degree aware that they will change their minds and engage in processes to protect their initial decisions. They take steps to ensure that their decision cannot be undone at some later time in the future. That is, people are willing to *precommit* their decisions. The most famous example of precommitment is the story of Odysseus, who, wanting to hear the Siren's call without endangering his ship, had himself bound to the mast so as to be powerless in directing his ship to its doom. Research suggests that nonmythical people also engage in a variety of precommitment strategies to prevent anticipated future temptations from undermining their goals (e.g., Thaler & Shefrin, 1981; Trope & Fishbach, 2005; Wertenbroch, 1998). For example, people volunteer to pay higher cancellation fees the more likely it is that they will miss a diagnostic but uncomfortable health screening (e.g., Trope & Fishbach, 2000). Such financially counternormative behavior decreases the likelihood that people will change their minds and choose not to go.

Recent research by Fujita and Roberts (2010), moreover, indicates that people are more likely to capitalize on such precommitment strategies when construing events at higher- rather than lower-level construals. By prompting greater concern for one's abstract goals and values, higher-level construals also encourage efforts to protect those goals from anticipated future threats. In one study, for example, participants were presented with various objects (e.g., a sedan, a dump truck, a boat, and a convertible) and asked to explain how each object represented the same superordinate category versus distinct, subordinate categories. This categorization task induces a tendency to respectively construe subsequent, unrelated events more abstractly versus concretely (Lin, Murphy, & Shoben, 1997; Fujita & Roberts, 2010). Participants were then presented with an opportunity to participate in a future psychology study that promised valuable feedback on their cognitive abilities, although scheduled at an inconvenient time (e.g., 2 a.m.). As an assessment of precommitment, they were asked how much they would pay as a cancellation fee if they failed to attend their scheduled appointment. As expected, to the degree that the feedback was perceived as valuable, higher-level construals led participants to be willing to pay higher cancellation fees as a means of precommitting their decision to participate in the future study. Thus, not only might higher-level construals lead people to make decisions that favor their environmental goals and values, but they may also motivate people to adopt strategies rendering those decisions less reversible. Those wishing to promote environmental decisions and actions might then not only strive to induce higher-level construals, but also to provide opportunities to utilize precommitment strategies.

Making the Abstract Concrete

The strategy discussed above focuses on transforming one's concrete experiences to be more reflective of one's abstract goals and values through higher-level construals to promote environmental decisions and behavior. Rather than encourage higher-level construals, however, an alternate strategy might be to capitalize on the knowledge that people tend to construe immediate choice contexts more concretely rather than abstractly, and to tailor accordingly one's persuasive efforts to make more salient those concrete rewards that ultimately promote environmental causes. Thus, rather than try to change the way people think, one might instead change the immediate, local situation with which people are confronted. In most of the examples that we have discussed in this chapter, the concrete features of a situation lead people to make decisions that are contrary to their abstract objectives. Those interested in promoting consideration of environmental concerns might restructure those local choice contexts to direct people's attention not to the goal-undermining concrete aspects of a situation, but rather to the concrete goal-promoting aspects. For example, research indicates that highlighting what one's donation might do to save a particular, specific killer whale encourages donation behavior in the immediate future to a greater extent than donations to a more general "save the whales" campaign (e.g., Fujita et al., 2008). Presumably, the appeal to a specific killer whale rather than to whales more generally resonated with people's lower-level construal of the event. Structuring choice contexts so that apparent concrete rewards are consistent, rather than inconsistent, with abstract goals and values in this way may ultimately promote environmental decisions and behavior.

Caveats and Clarifications

Although we propose that research on construal levels may help promote environmental decision making, it is important to consider several important caveats. First, we propose that higher-level construals will promote increased consideration of environmental goals and values. Though higher-level construals may lead people to think more about how a decision may reflect their views on environmentalism, this thinking may not necessarily translate to environmental decisions or actions. There are a number of intervening steps from translating thought to action (for extensive review, see Gollwitzer & Bargh, 1996), much of which may be outside the purview of research on the level of abstraction of people's subjective construals.

Much of what we have discussed also assumes that people value and think positively about environmentalism as an abstract aim. That is, given that people have adopted environmental goals and consider environmentalism to be a desirable value, higher-level construals should promote greater weighting of environment-relevant features in decisions and behavior. However, if people do not value environmentalism as an abstract concern, then construal levels should be expected to have little effect. Indeed, someone who denies the impact of humans on the welfare of the environment might even be more anti-environmental when construing events in higher-level terms. Thus, any attempt to incorporate research on construal levels to promote environmentalism needs to be explicitly dovetailed with efforts to persuade people that environmentalism is worthy and desirable as a central goal and value.

CONCLUSION

In addressing the need to elucidate those psychological principles of greatest relevance to promoting environmentally relevant decision making, research must attend to how to overcome conflict among competing goals, how to insure that individuals connect their concrete experiences to their abstract environmental goals and values, and how the abstract rewards of deciding in favor of environment-sustaining options can be conveyed most compellingly. We have argued that research on levels of construal (Liberman & Trope, 2008; Trope & Liberman, 2003, 2010; Vallacher & Wegner, 1987) provides important insights for addressing these challenges. The evidence reviewed above shows that a number of situational and individual-difference factors can promote construing events in terms of high-level, abstract aims, rather than in terms of more low-level, concrete situation-specific features. In turn, these higher-level construals promote greater accessibility of abstract goal-related thought, greater search for goal-relevant information, increased attention to and processing of goal-relevant stimuli, and reduced perceptions of conflicts between goals. Collectively, this research indicates that variability in level of action construal can be a powerful determinant of the extent to which individual decision makers *want* to select environment-sustaining options. More abstract construals promote a tighter connection between *thinking globally* and *acting locally*. To capitalize on these research findings, those wishing to promote environmentalism should focus either on promoting higher-level construals of immediate environmentally relevant decisions and action or on restructuring choice situations such that the concrete rewards are consistent with relatively abstract environmental goals and values. We noted that environmentally oriented persuasive appeals also might make use of well-known principles of precommitting decisions while people's motivation to select environment-sustaining options is at its highest. In this way, people can more effectively think globally, act locally. We look forward to future work examining these applications of basic psychological research and theory to the pressing issue of encouraging individual decision makers to provide active stewardship of the Earth's environment.

REFERENCES

Bar-Anan, Y., Liberman, N., & Trope, Y. (2006). The association between psychological distance and construal level: Evidence from an implicit association test. *Journal of Experimental Psychology: General, 135*(4), 609–622.

Baumeister, R. F. (1990). Suicide as escape from self. *Psychological Review, 97*(1), 90–113.

Beukeboom, C. J., & Semin, G. R. (2005). Mood and representations of behaviour: The how and why. *Cognition and Emotion, 19*(8), 1242–1251.

Beukeboom, C. J., & Semin, G. R. (2006). How mood turns on language. *Journal of Experimental Social Psychology, 42*(5), 553–566.

Bruner, J. S. (1957). On perceptual readiness. *Psychological Review, 64*(2), 123–152.

Butler, R. (1993). Effects of task and ego-achievement goals on information seeking during task engagement. *Journal of Personality and Social Psychology, 65* (1), 13–31.

Carver, C. S., & Scheier, M. F. (1982). Control theory: A useful conceptual framework for personality—Social, clinical, and health psychology. *Psychological Bulletin, 92*(1), 111–135.

Carver, C. S., & Scheier, M. F. (1990). Origins and functions of positive and negative affect: A control-process view. *Psychological Review, 97*(1), 19–35.

Carver, C. S., & Scheier, M. F. (1999). Themes and issues in the self-regulation of behavior. In R. S. Wyer (Ed.), *Advances in social cognition* (Vol. 12, pp. 1–107). Mahwah, NJ: Erlbaum.

Clark, S. L., & Freitas, A. L. (2012). [Construing action abstractly and perceiving correspondence among goals.] Unpublished data.

Dweck, C. S., & Leggett, L. (1988). A social-cognitive approach to motivation and personality. *Psychological Review, 95*, 256–273.

Emmons, R. A. (1992). Abstract versus concrete goals: Personal striving level, physical illness, and psychological well-being. *Journal of Personality and Social Psychology, 62*(2), 292–300.

Emmons, R. A. (1996). Striving and feeling: Personal goals and subjective well-being. *The psychology of action: Linking cognition and motivation to behavior* (pp. 313–337). New York: Guilford Press.

Emmons, R. A., & King, L. (1988). Conflict among personal strivings: Immediate and long-term implications for psychological and physical well-being. *Journal of Personality and Social Psychology, 54*, 1040–1048.

Eyal, T., Liberman, N., & Trope, Y. (2008). Judging near and distant virtue and vice. *Journal of Experimental Social Psychology, 44*(4), 1204–1209.

Eyal, T., Sagristano, M. D., Trope, Y., Liberman, N., & Chaiken, S. (2009). When values matter: Expressing values in behavioral intentions for the near versus distant future. *Journal of Experimental Social Psychology, 45*(1), 35–43.

Fazio, R. H., & Olson, M. A. (2003). Implicit measures in social cognition research: The meaning and use. *Annual Review of Psychology, 54*(1), 297–327.

Förster, J., Friedman, R. S., & Liberman, N. (2004). Temporal construal effects on abstract and concrete thinking: Consequences for insight and creative cognition. *Journal of Personality and Social Psychology, 87*(2), 177–189.

Freitas, A., Clark, S., Kim, J., & Levy, S. (2009). Action-construal levels and perceived conflict among ongoing goals: Implications for positive affect. *Journal of Research in Personality, 43*(5), 938–941.

Freitas, A., Gollwitzer, P., & Trope, Y. (2004). The influence of abstract and concrete mind-sets on anticipating and guiding others' self-regulatory efforts. *Journal of Experimental Social Psychology, 40*, 739–752.

Freitas, A., Langsam, K., Clark, S., & Moeller, S. (2008). Seeing oneself in one's choices: Construal level and self-pertinence of electoral and consumer decisions. *Journal of Experimental Social Psychology, 44*(4), 1174–1179.

Freitas, A. L., Salovey, P., & Liberman, N. (2001). Abstract and concrete self-evaluative goals. *Journal of Personality and Social Psychology*, 80(3), 410–424.

Fujita, K., Eyal, T., Chaiken, S., Trope, Y., & Liberman, N. (2008). Influencing attitudes toward near and distant objects. *Journal of Experimental Social Psychology*, 44, 562–572.

Fujita, K., & Han, H. (2009). Moving beyond deliberative control of impulses: The effect of construal levels on evaluative associations in self-control conflicts. *Psychological Science*, 20(7), 799–804.

Fujita, K., Henderson, M., Eng, J., Trope, Y., & Liberman, N. (2006). Spatial distance and mental construal of social events. *Psychological Science*, 17(4), 278–282.

Fujita, K., & Roberts, J. C. (2010). Promoting prospective self-control through abstraction. *Journal of Experimental Social Psychology*, 46(6), 1049–1054.

Fujita, K., Trope, Y., Liberman, N., & Levin-Sagi, M. (2006). Construal levels and self-control. *Journal of Personality and Social Psychology*, 90(3), 351–367.

Gasper, K., & Clore, G. L. (2002). Attending to the big picture: Mood and global versus local processing of visual information. *Psychological Science*, 13(1), 34–40.

Gollwitzer, P. M., & Bargh, J. A. (1996). *The psychology of action: Linking cognition and motivation to behavior.* New York: Guilford Press.

Greenwald, A., McGhee, D., & Schwartz, J. (1998). Measuring individual differences in implicit cognition: The implicit association test. *Journal of Personality and Social Psychology*, 74(6), 1464–1480.

Griffin D. W., & Ross, L. (1991). Subjective construal, social inference, and human misunderstanding. In M. P. Zanna (Ed.), *Advances in experimental social psychology* (Vol. 24, pp. 319–359). New York: Academic Press.

Hastorf, A. H., & Cantril, H. (1954). They saw a game; A case study. *The Journal of Abnormal and Social Psychology*, 49(1), 129–134.

Henderson, M. D., Fujita, K., Trope, Y., & Liberman, N. (2006). Transcending the "here": The effects of spatial distance on social judgment. *Journal of Personality and Social Psychology*, 91, 845–856.

Herzog, S. M., Hansen, J., & Wänke, M. (2005). Temporal distance and ease of retrieval. *Journal of Experimental Social Psychology*, 43, 483–488.

Higgins, E. T. (1998). Promotion and prevention: Regulatory focus as a motivational principle. In M. P. Zanna (Ed.). *Advances in experimental social psychology Vol. 30*, (pp. 1–46). New York: Academic Press.

Ijzerman, H., & Semin, G. R. (2009). The thermometer of social relations: Mapping social proximity on temperature. *Psychological Science*, 20(10), 1214–1220.

Isen, A. M., & Daubman, K. A. (1984). The influence of affect on categorization. *Journal of Personality and Social Psychology*, 47(6), 1206–1217.

James, W. (1890). *The principles of psychology, vol. 1.* New York: Henry Holt.

Karpinski, A., & Hilton, J. L. (2001). Attitudes and the implicit association test. *Journal of Personality and Social Psychology*, 81(5), 774–788.

Kim, H., & Markus, H. R. (1999). Deviance or uniqueness, harmony or conformity? A cultural analysis. *Journal of Personality and Social Psychology*, 77(4), 785–800.

Kivetz, Y., & Tyler, T. (2007). Tomorrow I'll be me: The effect of time perspective on the activation of idealistic versus pragmatic selves. *Organizational Behavior and Human Decision Processes*, 102(2), 193–211.

Kross, E., Ayduk, O., & Mischel, W. (2005). When asking "why" does not hurt: Distinguishing rumination from reflective processing of negative emotions. *Psychological Science*, 16(9), 709–715.

Kruglanski, A. W., Shah, J. Y., Fishbach, A., Friedman, R., Chun, W. Y., & Sleeth-Keppler, D. (2002). A theory of goal systems. In *Advances in experimental social psychology, vol. 34* (pp. 331–378). San Diego, CA: Academic Press,.

Kunda, Z. (1990). The case for motivated reasoning. *Psychological Bulletin*, 108(3), 480–498.

Levy, S., Freitas, A., & Salovey, P. (2002). Construing action abstractly and blurring social distinctions: Implications for perceiving homogeneity among, but also empathizing with and helping, others. *Journal of Personality and Social Psychology*, 83(5), 1224–1238.

Libby, L. K., Shaeffer, E. M., & Eibach, R. P. (2009). Seeing meaning in action: A bidirectional link between visual perspective and action identification level. *Journal of Experimental Psychology: General*, 138(4), 503–516.

Libby, L. K., Shaeffer, E. M., Eibach, R. P., & Slemmer, J. A. (2007). Picture yourself at the polls: Visual perspective in mental imagery affects self-perception and behavior. *Psychological Science*, 18(3), 199–203.

Liberman, N., Sagristano, M., & Trope, Y. (2002). The effect of temporal distance on level of mental construal. *Journal of Experimental Social Psychology*, 38, 523–534.

Liberman, N., & Trope, Y. (1998). The role of feasibility and desirability considerations in near and distant future decisions: A test of temporal construal theory. *Journal of Personality and Social Psychology*, 75(1), 5–18.

Liberman, N., & Trope, Y. (2008). The psychology of transcending the here and now. *Science*, 322(5905), 1201–1205.

Liberman, N., Trope, Y., McCrea, S., & Sherman, S. (2007). The effect of level of construal on the temporal distance of activity enactment. *Journal of Experimental Social Psychology*, 43(1), 143–149.

Lifton, R. J. (1986). *The Nazi doctors: Medical killing and the psychology of genocide*. New York: Basic Books.

Lin, E. L., Murphy, G. L., & Shoben, E. J. (1997). The effects of prior processing episodes on basic-level superiority. *The Quarterly Journal of Experimental Psychology A: Human Experimental Psychology*, 50A(1), 25–48.

Lind, E., & Tyler, T. (1988). *The social psychology of procedural justice*. New York: Plenum Press.

Liviatan, I., Trope, Y., & Liberman, N. (2008). Interpersonal similarity as a social distance dimension: Implications for perception of others' actions. *Journal of Experimental Social Psychology*, 44(5), 1256–1269.

Medin, D. L., & Smith, E. E. (1984). Concepts and concept formation. *Annual Reviews in Psychology*, 35, 113–138.

Meyers-Levy, J., & Zhu, R. (2007). The influence of ceiling height: The effect of priming on the type of processing that people use. *Journal of Consumer Research*, 34(2), 174–186.

Mikulincer, M., Kedem, P., & Paz, D. (1990). Anxiety and categorization: I. The structure and boundaries of mental categories. *Personality and Individual Differences*, 11(8), 805–814.

Mikulincer, M., Paz, D., & Kedem, P. (1990). Anxiety and categorization: II. Hierarchical levels of mental categories. *Personality and Individual Differences*, 11(8), 815–821.

Powers, W. T. (1973). *Behavior: The control of perception*. Chicago: Aldine.

Rachlin, H. (1995). Self-control: Beyond commitment. *Behavioral and Brain Sciences*, 18(1), 109–159.

Rogers, T., & Bazerman, M. H. (2008). Future lock-in: Future implementation increases selection of "should" choices. *Organizational Behavior and Human Decision Processes*, 106(1), 1–20.

Rosch, E. (1975). Cognitive representations of semantic categories. *Journal of Experimental Psychology: General*, 104(3), 192–233.

Sagristano, M., Trope, Y., & Liberman, N. (2002). Time-dependent gambling: Odds now, money later. *Journal of Experimental Psychology: General*, 131(3), 364–376.

Schmeichel, B. J., & Vohs, K. (2009). Self-affirmation and self-control: Affirming core values counteracts ego depletion. *Journal of Personality and Social Psychology*, 96(4), 770–782.

Schwartz, S. H. (1992). Universals in the content and structure of values: Theoretical advances and empirical tests in 20 countries. In M. P. Zanna (Ed.), *Advances in Experimental Social Psychology,* Vol. 25 (pp. 1–65). San Diego, CA: Academic Press.

Semin, G. R., & Smith, E. R. (1999). Revisiting the past and back to the future: Memory systems and the linguistic representation of social events. *Journal of Personality and Social Psychology,* 76(6), 877–892.

Smith, P. K., & Trope, Y. (2006). You focus on the forest when you're in charge of the trees: Power priming and abstract information processing. *Journal of Personality and Social Psychology,* 90(4), 578–596.

Snyder, C. L., & Fromkin, H. L. (1980). *Uniqueness: The human pursuit of difference.* New York: Plenum.

Thaler, R. H., & Shefrin, H. M. (1981). An economic theory of self-control. *Journal of Political Economy,* 89(2), 392–406.

Todorov, A., Goren, A., & Trope, Y. (2007). Probability as a psychological distance: Construal and preferences. *Journal of Experimental Social Psychology,* 43(3), 473–482.

Torelli, C., & Kaikati, A. (2009). Values as predictors of judgments and behaviors: The role of abstract and concrete mindsets. *Journal of Personality and Social Psychology,* 96(1), 231–247.

Trope, Y. (1986). Self-enhancement and self-assessment in achievement motivation. In R. M. Sorrentino & E. T. Higgins (Eds.), *Handbook of motivation and cognition: Foundations of social behavior* Vol. 1 (pp. 350–378). New York: Guilford Press.

Trope, Y., & Fishbach, A. (2000). Counteractive self-control in overcoming temptation. *Journal of Personality and Social Psychology,* 79(4), 493–506.

Trope, Y., & Fishbach, A. (2005). Going beyond the motivation given: Self-control and situational control over behavior. In R. R. Hassin, & J. S. Uleman (Eds.), *The new unconscious* (pp. 537–563). New York: Oxford University Press.

Trope, Y., & Liberman, N. (2003). Temporal construal. *Psychological Review,* 110(3), 403–421.

Trope, Y., & Liberman, N. (2010). Construal level theory of psychological distance. *Psychological Review,* 117(2), 440–463.

Trope, Y., & Neter, E. (1994). Reconciling competing motives in self-evaluation: The role of self-control in feedback seeking. *Journal of Personality and Social Psychology,* 66(4), 646–657.

Vallacher, R. R., & Wegner, D. M. (1987). What do people think they're doing? Action identification and human behavior. *Psychological Review,* 94(1), 3–15.

Vallacher, R. R., & Wegner, D.M. (1989). Levels of personal agency: Individual variation in action identification. *Journal of Personality and Social Psychology,* 57(4), 660–671.

Wakslak, C. J., & Trope, Y. (2009). Cognitive consequences of affirming the self: The relationship between self-affirmation and object construal. *Journal of Experimental Social Psychology,* 45(4), 927–932.

Wakslak, C. J., Trope, Y., Liberman, N., & Alony, R. (2006). Seeing the forest when entry is unlikely: Probability and the mental representation of events. *Journal of Experimental Psychology: General,* 135(4), 641–653.

Wegner, D. M., Vallacher, R. R., Macomber, G., Wood R., & Arps, K. (1984). The emergence of action. *Journal of Personality and Social Psychology,* 46(2), 269–279.

Wertenbroch, K. (1998). Consumption self-control by rationing purchase quantities of virtue and vice. *Marketing Science,* 17(4), 317.

8

Is the Sky Falling?
The Notion of the Absurd Versus the Feeling of the Absurd

TRAVIS PROULX

*P*eople are saying that the sky is starting to fall. We're consuming the Earth's resources faster than they can be renewed or replaced. We're pumping more greenhouse gases into the atmosphere; the planet's already warmer than it's been for millennia. The coral reefs are bleaching and the big fish that filled our oceans have been fished away. Fresh water is increasingly scarce. Human populations grow exponentially; other species disappear at the same pace. Our global petroleum reserves are running out; the economies they fuel are running out of time to find an alternative. And the people who are saying all of this aren't just a flock of Chicken Littles. They're respected scientists* holding charts and graphs, whose broad consensus has informed the reports and recommendations that intergovernmental bodies have been issuing for the past three decades. The evidence is overwhelming and converges at the same conclusion: the actions we're taking to benefit ourselves in the present are not sustainable into the future.

Given the scale of the crisis and the severity of the consequences, people must be alarmed—terrified even. The dinner tables, boardrooms, and governmental chambers of the industrialized world are no doubt hosting the same lively debate: How do we best solve this crisis? What steps should we take first? Who will be most affected by these decisions? Citizens are organizing en masse to meet these challenges. Voters are marching through their nation's capitals demanding that elected leaders take action. Politicians are clearing their legislative agendas to navigate this existential crossroads of the human race.

---

* (and Al Gore)

A series of recent polls reflects the sheer magnitude of public concern. A CNN/ Opinion Research Poll (March 19–21, 2010) revealed that a full 2% of American adults ranked "Energy and Environmental Policies" as "the most important issue when you decide how to vote for Congress this year"—dead last among the issues they were asked to rank.

However, this apparent low level of concern lay in contrast to an earlier CBS News/*New York Times* poll (February 5–10, 2010). When asked the open-ended question "What do you think is the most important problem facing this country today?" roughly 20% of respondents reported anything that could be categorized as relevant to environmental sustainability—an indication of no concern whatsoever.

OK. LET'S START AGAIN

People are saying that the sky is starting to fall. Two decades of low interest rates are overheating the economy. Easy money is looking for somewhere to grow. Irrational exuberance is blowing bubble after bubble. The dotcom bubble grows and bursts. Then the commodities market surges and implodes. Now, the biggest bust of all is looming over the financial landscape—a housing market built on sub-prime mortgages built on worthless paper, packaged into securities that no one understands, valued on the basis of mathematical formulas with no basis in reality, given AAA ratings and sold to banks all over the globe. And the people who are saying all of this aren't just a flock of Chicken Littles. They're respected economists and investors, holding charts and graphs and making their case from the nation's newsstands and bestseller lists. The evidence is overwhelming and converges at the same conclusion: the actions we're taking to benefit ourselves in the present are not sustainable into the future.

AND THEN THE SKY FALLS

Overnight, the potentially worthless subprime paper is recognized as actually worthless. Along with the houses built on the paper, and the banks and brokerage houses that bought it all up. The stock market collapses. People stop buying houses and the people who build them don't have jobs anymore. Borrowing from the banks isn't an option; they're not lending anymore. Credit freezes and contracts. The economy shrivels. Unemployment and underemployment reach levels not seen since the Great Depression. The US government begins to borrow to bail out the banks and put people to work. This adds to a decade of massive debt, projected to reach 90% of gross domestic product (GDP) in the coming year.

Given the scale of the crisis and the severity of the consequences, people *are* alarmed and terrified and it really is all anyone is talking about and citizens are taking action and marching on capitals and politicians are desperately trying to sort it all out.

It appears that we do care, so some extent, about the short-term and long-term survival of our species. Depending upon the nature of the crisis, we may be goaded into taking action. What, then, are the central differences between the looming environmental crisis (general apathy), and the looming economic crisis (genuine panic)? And what might these differences tell us about turning apathy into healthy concern?

The direct consequences of the economic crisis are here, being experienced in very real ways, every day, by everyday people. Mass unemployment, vanishing retirement funds, and soaring taxes are all acute and salient threats. In contrast, the crisis of environmental sustainability is experienced by most people as a potentiality rather than an actuality—in much the same way as the economic crisis was experienced before the bottom fell out in the fall of 2008. While it is sometimes unacknowledged, most people in the Western, industrialized world aren't experiencing as much as a slap on the wrist in terms of salient sustainability threat. Are we running out of food and raw materials? Our grocery stores are filled with abundant, cheap food. Our retail stores are filled with abundant, cheap manufactured goods. Inflation isn't an issue. Energy is cheap—even if we're paying a little more for gas than we'd like. If species are going extinct, we've yet to notice an absence of Egyptian Barbary Sheep. Manhattan remains above sea level, and most people in the Western hemisphere would have welcomed global warming this past winter. None of this diminishes an undeniable trend toward the increasing scarcity and expense of every essential resource, or the inevitably disastrous consequences of manmade global warming. It only points out the difference between two experiences—speeding toward a brick wall at 100 mph (economic or environmental sustainability), and hitting that wall (economic or environmental collapse).

It doesn't take an academic to distinguish the experiences of potential crisis and actual crisis—you don't need an existential psychologist to explain why people flinch when they are punched in the face. However, an existential psychologist may come in handy when you want to understand the broader, cognitive implications of these differing crises. In particular, the differing implications for those basic theories that determine how we understand our world, ourselves, and our relation to the world. We call these theories *meaning frameworks*, and a good deal of the research that we conduct in social psychology deals with experiences that violate these frameworks and the ways that we respond to these violations.

Over the course of the next few pages, two general propositions will be argued. First, it will be suggested that the evidence called up for environmental (un)sustainability—while "objectively" compelling, does not constitute an acute meaning threat for the vast majority of people in the Western world. It is largely for this reason that matters of environmental sustainability are generally ignored by the general population. In contrast, the nature of the current economic crisis constitutes an acute meaning threat, in addition to the hardships it has invoked.

Second, it will be argued that to the extent environmental (un)sustainability is experienced as a meaning threat, the psychological mechanisms we often engage in following these experiences have allowed us to avoid addressing this threat directly; that is, in a manner that actually attempts to solve the crisis.

In general, social psychologists have spend the past 30 years demonstrating the following social psychological phenomena—when people have experiences that threaten their belief systems, this makes them feel funny, and this funny feeling generally motivates them to affirm these belief systems far more strongly. This phenomenon has two primary components that constitute the cause and effect, respectively. On the one hand, we have the experience that violates belief systems and evokes the funny feeling. On the other hand, we have the behaviors that people engage in to make that funny feeling go away. When it comes to matters of environmental sustainability, it may be the case that there is no relevant threat to most people's belief systems—and to the extent that there is, people tend to respond by affirming the status quo. Let's examine both of these possibilities in turn.

WHAT SORTS OF EXPERIENCES ARE MEANING THREATS?

People maintain systems of expected associations that help them understand themselves, their world, and their relation to this world. Broadly, these expected associations can be called *meaning frameworks*, insofar as they are formed and maintained in largely the same ways regardless of their content. Through experience and reflection, we expect snow to be cold, friends to be helpful, and good things to happen to good people (while bad people get what they deserve). When we have experiences that violate these expected associations, we may experience a unique form of psychological arousal—that feeling you get when things don't seem quite right.

Existentialist philosophers called this the *feeling of the absurd*, and claimed that it resulted from any violation of expected associations, that is, meaning frameworks. Beginning with Kierkegaard in the mid-19th century, existentialists were the first to imagine that we experienced our reality as a series of relationships, and that these relationships allow us to understand our world and our place within it. According to Camus, the creation and maintenance of meaning frameworks constituted the "fundamental impulse of the human drama" (1955, p.10), whether they represented our scientific beliefs, religious systems, or plans for a weekend dinner party. According to Heidegger, experiences that violated these systems of relations (1996/1956. p. 13), simply called *nonrelations*, evoked a unique mode of anxiety that he called *angst*. When discussing this mode of anxiety close to a century earlier, Kierkegaard underscored the variety of meaning violations that could elicit this unpleasant feeling, from being reminded of his ultimate mortality to finishing a beer and finding a live frog at the bottom of the mug—neither of these experiences makes any sense.

However, simply contemplating a state of affairs that does not make sense is not the same thing as an *experience* of meaninglessness. As Camus put it, "the notion of the absurd is not the same as the feeling of the absurd" (1955, p. 5). Only direct experiences that violate our meaning frameworks have the effect of eliciting that angst we experience when things don't make sense. As Camus concedes, if you read his lament at the arbitrary nature of existence in an unfeeling universe you may actually find that it makes a lot of sense; finding out that the kindest person you know has cancer may not make sense—and the feeling of the absurd ensues.

So what do we do when we feel a twinge of angst? For the most part, we avoid resolving the absurdity altogether. *Inauthentic* is the adjective that Heidegger uses to describe our general strategy to deal with meaning threats—the anomalies that bombard our understanding of the world are unending and often irresolvable; rather than allow ourselves to be undermined—or dedicate our lives to existential philosophy—we generally cover the anomalies of life by heightening our commitment to the very meaning frameworks that were violated. After all, there's nothing unjust about your kind friend getting cancer. Won't overcoming this illness serve to make them stronger? And if you're Kierkegaard, you may affirm an entirely unrelated meaning framework. Why not make a trip to Konigsberg to see that play you've seen a dozen times before? You can mouth along with the dialogue and laugh at the same jokes and make that feeling of the absurd fade away, lost in a world of the familiar and predictable.

WHAT DOES PSYCHOLOGY HAVE TO SAY ABOUT ANY OF THIS?

As is often the case with science and philosophy, psychologists have found new words and ways to tell very much the same story—offering broad empirical justifications for nodding one's head while one reads Camus. As it turns out, people do form expected associations by reflecting on their experiences, and these mental representations allow us to understand ourselves (self-schemas, Markus, 1977), our world (perceptual paradigms, Bruner & Postman, 1949; causal scripts, Nelson, 1981) and our relation to this world (social schemas, Kuethe, 1962; cultural worldviews, Greenberg et al., 1994). Occasionally, these mental representations are even referred to as meaning frameworks (Baumeister, 1991). When these frameworks are violated by contradictory experiences, we experience a funny felling that tells us something isn't quite right. This feeling has been called *uncanniness* (Freud, 1919), imbalance (Heider, 1914), disequilibrium (Piaget, 1937), cognitive dissonance (Festinger, 1957), and more recently, uncertainty (McGregor, 2001).

So what do we do when we feel this twinge of uncertainty? Given the choice, we'll address this unpleasant feeling in a way that avoids dealing with the anomalous experience directly—often by affirming the very meaning framework that was threatened. Did getting unexpectedly dumped threaten your sense of self-worth? Well, you were amazing on the basketball court yesterday (Tesser, 2001). Getting screwed over by The Man? That doesn't mean the world isn't fair—you probably deserved it (Jost et al., 1994). Don't feel like you're in control of your life? Of course you are! Or at least *something* is in control (Kay et al., 2008). Alternatively, you could affirm a meaning framework that isn't even related to the framework that was threatened. Did that Franz Kafka short story weird you out? Why not affirm your national identity? (Proulx and Heine, 2010). Did you find that Monty Python parody disturbing? You can always affirm your moral values and punish that criminal.

As the *threat-compensation* literature grows in social psychology, this general phenomenon is demonstrated again and again—when committed meaning frameworks are violated by unexpected experiences, we will affirm meaning frameworks that we remain committed to. In each of these (hundreds) of studies, it's a direct experience of some kind that elicits the presumed feeling that something isn't quite right, and prompts the subsequent affirmation efforts to make this feeling go away—efforts that Heidegger would deem *inauthentic* insofar as they are attempts to *cover over*, rather than address the experience itself. But what of Camus' claim that only direct experiences will elicit the requisite *feeling of the absurd* that provokes these compensatory affirmation efforts? Will the mere contemplation of something that doesn't make sense, that is, *the notion of the absurd*, also evoke these compensatory efforts?

HOW DO WE DISTINGUISH THE FEELING OF THE ABSURD FROM THE NOTION OF THE ABSURD?

A threat-compensation study conducted by Baldwin and Wesley (1996) suggests that the mere contemplation of a meaning threat isn't enough to initiate these behavioral consequences. As noted, experiences that violate people's meaning frameworks evoke compensatory affirmation of related or unrelated meaning frameworks. One of the most common meaning threat experiences used by social psychologists is a mortality salience experimental manipulation: participants enter the lab and are told that they will be filling out a series of questionnaires. One of these questionnaires asks them to "Please briefly describe the emotions that the thought of your own death arouses in you. Jot down, as specifically as you can, what you think will happen to you as you physically die, and once you are physically dead." Being presented with the reality of one's impending death is not something most undergraduates expect to do on a given day—and they reliably respond by affirming any aspect of their cultural worldview that the experimenter puts under their nose (for a review, see Pyszczynski et al., 2004). In the Baldwin and Welsey study, people were also exposed to this *mortality salience* manipulation, with the assumption that they would respond by affirming their cultural worldview by viewing criminals more negatively. However, they wanted to compare the effect of mortality salience with another potential meaning threat—reading a passage that expressed a belief that life is meaningless:

> I don't know what it means to live this life. Things seem so isolated and distant from me when I just sit down and consider what this world means. And every time I try to make sense of what's going on down here I find things not quite the same as they were before. Each day the world is different and I just get confused and lost in all of this change. The world seems to be this huge contradictory mess. Then I realize that I'm only looking at this tiny piece of reality that I deal with myself daily and that there is a whole universe of "things" which is infinite going on out there which I can't even think about coming to terms with. I'm like a speck of sand but even the whole beach doesn't come close to showing how small I am in the universe. I try to find some sense and meaning in reality to answer why I'm here but I just come up blank. (Baldwin and Wesley, 1996 p. 95)

Of no surprise to Camus, this sensible passage, cogently expressing the notion of the absurd, failed to provoke the same meaning-affirmation behaviors as the unexpected reminder of one's imminent death.

Following from this study, we aimed to compare the ability of an unexpected, meaning-violating *experience* to elicit compensatory affirmation moral belief efforts that were equivalent to reminding people of their own death (Proulx & Heine, 2008). In our study, we chose a potential meaning threat that was maximally unrelated to a moral meaning framework—the violation of an unconscious perceptual meaning framework. As our participants entered our lab, they were greeted by a female experimenter, Megan, who was conducting the study. Participants were then seated and asked to fill out a series of questionnaires. As they did so, Megan made her way to a filing cabinet and stepped out of sight for a moment—replaced by another experimenter who looked nothing like Megan but who was dressed in the same clothes. Remarkably, 95% of the participants didn't consciously notice the switch in experimenters; they continued with the study as though nothing was amiss. Nevertheless, we expected that participants would unconsciously experience this anomaly, and would deal with the *feeling of the absurd* by affirming a moral meaning framework (punishing a criminal) more strongly than participants who had experienced no experimenter switch. As it turned out, this is exactly what we found, where the affirmation of a moral meaning framework was on par with another experimental condition where we reminded people of their own mortality.

SO WHAT DOES ALL OF THIS HAVE TO DO WITH ENVIRONMENTAL SUSTAINABILITY?

Simply put: The contemplation of trends toward environmental catastrophe is not a concrete, meaning-violating experience. As such, it is not treated by most people as a meaning threat. To the extent that a small number of people treat this information as a meaning threat (between 0% and 2%, if the polls are correct), the common response is to affirm a committed meaning framework rather than actually deal with the problem. So how do we get regular folks to treat this information as a meaning threat, and actually engage in sustainable behaviors? Rather than closing with a litany of potential solutions, I'll make two predictions:

First: Whether due to dwindling petroleum reserves or the impact of speculation on global markets, energy prices will rise. Specifically, oil will once again climb to over $100 a barrel and people will find that the prices of everything flown and driven to their local marketplace have spiked—not to mention the price at the pump. When this happens—and when it persists for weeks and months and years—people will experience this turn of events as a salient violation of their current understanding of how the world works.

Second: When this happens, they will look to affirm a meaning framework to which they are firmly committed. Eventually, the respected scientists (and Al Gore) who point at the charts and graphs will figure out that meaning affirmation can take the form of environmental sustainability—if environmental sustainability is framed as a meaning framework to which North Americans, in particular, are committed.

As Nietzsche pointed out long ago (1887/1996), the Western mindset is the expectation of endless growth and the pursuit of happiness over the avoidance of unhappiness. Some might call this mindset the *Myth* of Infinite Growth, but myth or not, it's what we Westerners tacitly believe, and we'll affirm this commitment when it is threatened by contradictory information such as charts and graphs (and Al Gore) telling us that these expectations must be tempered. Framed as *sustainable living*, environmental sustainability can be taken as an admission of defeat—an acknowledgment that our ambitions were folly, and that our pursuit of happiness must be replaced with the avoidance of misery—the tragic consequences of a depleted ecosystem and flooded eastern seaboard.

And yet, sustainability in other domains is not understood as admissions of defeat and an abandonment of positive striving. In fact, *economic* sustainability is understood as a prerequisite for continued growth and happiness. As such, the streets of Washington DC have been flooded with folks who are protesting a relative abstraction—the national debt—insofar as it may threaten their own prosperity and that of future generations. At some point, the experience of environmental unsustainably will provoke a *feeling of the absurd* among those in the industrialized West. Rather than abandon their expectation in infinite growth, they will be given the opportunity to *affirm it* by engaging in sustainable behaviors that will allow this growth to continue. The scientists and politicians will eventually figure this out (and Al Gore, too).

REFERENCES

Baldwin, M. W., & Wesley, R. (1996). Effects of existential anxiety and self-esteem on the perception of others. *Basic And Applied Social Psychology, 18*(1), 75–95.

Baumeister, R. F. (1991). *Meanings of life.* New York: Guilford Press.

Bruner, J., & Postman, L. (1949). On the perception of incongruity: A paradigm. *Journal of Personality, 18*(2), 206–223.

Camus, A. (1955). *An absurd reasoning: The Myth of Sisyphus and other essays.* New York: Knopf.

Festinger, L. (1957). *A theory of cognitive dissonance.* Stanford, CA: Stanford University Press.

Frankl, V. E. (1946). *Man's search for meaning.* New York: Washington Square Press.

Freud, S. (1919/1990). The Uncanny. In A. Dickson (Ed.), *Sigmund Freud: 14. Art and literature* (pp. 335–376). New York: Penguin Books.

Greenberg, J., Pyszczynski, T., Solomon, S., Simon, L., & Breus, M. (1994). Role of consciousness and accessibility of death-related thoughts in mortality salience effects. *Journal of Personality and Social Psychology, 67*(4), 627–637.

Heidegger, M. (1996/1956). *Being and time.* Albany: State University of New York Press.

Heider, F. (1958). *The psychology of interpersonal relations.* New York: John Wiley & Sons.

Inzlicht, M., McGregor, I., Hirsh, J., & Nash, K. (2009). Neural markers of religious conviction. *Psychological Science, 20,* 385–392.

Jost, J. T., & Banaji, M. R. (1994). The role of stereotyping in system-justification and the production of false consciousness. *British Journal of Social Psychology, 33*(1), 1–27.

Kay, A., Gaucher, D., Napier, L., Callan, M., & Laurin K. (2008). God and the government: Testing a compensatory control mechanism for the support of external systems. *Journal of Personality and Social Psychology, 95*(1), 18–35.

Kierkegaard, S. (1846/1997). Concluding unscientific postscript to philosophical fragments. In H. Hong & E. Hong (Eds.), *The essential Kierkegaard* (pp.187–246). Princeton, NJ: Princeton University Press.

Kuethe, J. (1962). Social schemas. *Journal of Abnormal and Social Psychology, 64*(1), 31–38.

Markus, H. (1977). Self-schemata and processing information about the self. *Journal of Personality and Social Psychology, 35*(2), 63–78.

McGregor, I., Zanna, M. P., Holmes, J. G., & Spencer, S. J. (2001). Compensatory conviction in the face of personal uncertainty: Going to extremes and being oneself. *Journal of Personality and Social Psychology, 80*(3), 472–488.

Nelson, K. (1981). Social cognition in a script framework. In J. H. Flavell & L. Ross (Eds.), *Social cognitive development: Frontiers and possible futures* (pp. 97–118). Cambridge, UK: Cambridge University Press.

Nietzsche, F. (1887/1996). *On the genealogy of morals*. Oxford: Oxford World's Classics.

Piaget, J. (1937/1954). *The construction of reality in the child*. New York: Basic Books.

Proulx, T., & Heine, S. J. (2008). The case of the transmogrifying experimenter: Affirmation of a moral schema following implicit change detection. *Psychological Science, 19*(12), 1294–1300.

Proulx, T., & Heine, S. J. (2010). The frog in Kierkegaard's beer: Finding meaning in the violation-compensation literature. *Social and Personality Psychology Compass, 4*(10), 889–905.

Pyszczynski, T., Greenberg, J., Solomon, S., Arndt, J., & Schimel, J. (2004). Why do people need self-esteem? A theoretical and empirical review. *Psychological Bulletin, 130*(3), 435–468.

Tesser, A. (2000). On the confluence of self-esteem maintenance mechanisms. *Personality and Social Psychology Review, 4*, 290–299.

9

Consequences of System Defense Motivations for Individuals' Willingness to Act Sustainably

JILLIAN C. BANFIELD, STEVEN
SHEPHERD, and AARON C. KAY

*P*eople in developed nations are content to watch *An Inconvenient Truth,* *Food, Inc.,* or *No Impact Man* and bemoan the problems highlighted by these films. We discuss climate change, lament the ubiquity of factory farms, and perhaps even turn off our lights during Earth Hour. In short, the current zeitgeist is one of concern for environmental sustainability. The rhetoric around the issues, however, often fails to translate into real behavioral change. Despite the urgency of the problems and our recognition of the need for change, very little substantive change occurs (Van Vugt, 2009).

Few people deny that our very unsustainable ways of living are problematic. We emit greenhouse gases at rates that are already affecting our planet in dramatic ways. Daily newspapers abound with dire stories about the impact of climate change, such as record heatwaves that claim hundreds of lives (Burke, 2010). Climate change is perhaps the most easily accessible example of our struggle as a species to live sustainably, but we abuse the planet and its resources in many other ways. For example, because of the way the federal government subsidizes farmers in the United States, valuable farm land is dedicated to growing corn at a much higher rate than is necessary to meet demand, which has encouraged food manufacturers to continually find new ways to inject corn into food products. We now find corn in everything from soft drinks and breakfast cereals to feed for cattle that are more appropriately raised on grass (Pollan, 2007). The fact that we use our vanishing supply of fossil fuels to produce a crop that we do not need would seem absurd, save for the fact that we sometimes waste fossil fuels even more directly. When an oil well in the Gulf of Mexico recently burst open, British

111

Petroleum conducted a series of inept interventions meant to stem the flow, making it astoundingly clear that BP was ill-prepared to contain such a spill and protect the surrounding ecosystems.

Although government and industry have enormous impact on the environment, individual actions also reflect a lack of sustainability. For example, people rely on their cars to take them virtually everywhere, despite the fact that more than half of their journeys cover less than a mile (Sutherland, 2003). We focus on the price of food—demanding cheap tomatoes year round, for example—and do not worry about whether the farmers and migrant workers receive living wages (Schlosser, 2007). We complain about the hassles of delays and security searches when we fly, rather than considering the vast amount of carbon the plane pumps into the atmosphere (Doyle, 2010). Governments, industry, and individuals all contribute to the overall sustainability of our way of life.

The purpose of this chapter is not to provide a laundry list of humanity's failures to live sustainability. Instead, we are interested in contributing to an understanding of why people do not change their behavior, despite recognizing that our current use of resources is unsustainable. Behavior change is necessary to ensure a sustainable future (McKenzie-Mohr, 2000), so understanding the barriers to change is imperative. To overcome climate change and other problems wrought by our unsustainable use of the Earth requires change from everyone. As a species, we need to evolve to meet the challenge of sustainability (Cascio, 2009). Although governments can regulate some aspects of our individual behavior, to truly improve the sustainability of the way we inhabit this planet, all of us will have to change. Individual action has enormous potential for promoting sustainability (Stern, 1992; Winter & Koger, 2004). We may have to forgo a plane trip, pay more for organic vegetables, eat less sushi, buy smaller homes, or have fewer children. With respect to energy use, Stern (1992, 2000) notes that many individual behaviors may seem insignificant, but can have enormous impact on greenhouse gas emissions when aggregated across millions of people. Indeed, energy use by homes accounts for 38% of carbon dioxide emissions in the United States, and 8% of all emissions in the world (Gardner & Stern, 2008). Thus, changing individuals' behavior can go a long way toward improving sustainability.

The Intergovernmental Panel on Climate Change (IPCC, 2007) concurs that individual action is necessary for adapting to climate change and that policy makers need to be aware of barriers to behavior change. The IPCC report identified four main cognitive and informational barriers to behavior change, such as the difficulty of translating attitudes into behavior. The report focuses on errors in perception, suggesting that behavior will change if people have the right information and enough cognitive resources. The IPCC report contains little discussion of the role of motivation in fostering or inhibiting behavior change, aside from noting that appeals to fear and guilt do not motivate behavior change. Without more discussion of motivation, our understanding of why behavior change fails to occur is necessarily impoverished. In what follows, we explore the role of two related motivational processes—system justification and compensatory control—in promoting unsustainable behaviors at the individual level. Specifically, we consider how, ironically, recognizing the severity of environmental problems may decrease the likelihood of individual behavior change.

IMPLICATIONS OF SYSTEM JUSTIFICATION AND COMPENSATORY CONTROL MOTIVES FOR SUSTAINABLE BEHAVIOR

Why is it that despite recognizing the dire situation facing our planet, individual behavior change is sorely lacking? According to system justification theory (Jost & Banaji, 1994), people are strongly motivated to believe their systems are functioning legitimately, properly, and as they "ought to be" (Kay et al., 2009). Doing so, it is argued, helps people cope with the numerous existential and epistemic threats that would accompany acknowledging one is governed by an illegitimate, disorderly, or unfair system (Jost & Hunyady, 2002). Although this motive is not always or uniformly active, there are numerous contexts that tend to increase the likelihood of its expression (Kay & Zanna, 2009). A well-accepted principle of motivated behavior and cognition is that blockages to goal pursuit, or a specific motivational end, tend to strengthen the pursuit of that particular goal (Atkinson, 1964). The system justification motive is no different. Generally labeled as *system threat manipulations*, numerous experiments have demonstrated the impact of challenging people's belief in the legitimacy of their system on the expression of system-justifying behaviors and judgments.

A long line of research in system justification theory (Jost & Banaji, 1994) has documented that, when the system justification motive is threatened, people tend to bolster and defend the status quo (Kay, Jimenez, & Jost, 2002; Lau, Kay, & Spencer, 2008; Napier, Mandisodza, Anderson, & Jost, 2006). It has been observed, for example, that a threat to the legitimacy of the social system—in the form of a newspaper article that laments the eroding social and economic conditions of one's system—increases the extent to which people endorse stereotypes that legitimize inequality, casting it as not unfair but due to individual differences in skill and talent (Kay, Jost, & Young, 2005). System threat also leads people to increasingly believe that the way things *are* is the way they *should* be. Following the presentation of system-threatening information, for example, participants become more likely to report that extant gender and status inequalities (such as the overrepresentation of men in CEO positions or the overrepresentation of the wealthy in political positions) are representative of how things *should* ideally be (Kay et al., 2009). Aside from contributing to system-justifying beliefs, system threats have also been shown to contribute to the stability of the sociopolitical system. Using survey data, Willer (2004) showed that approval ratings of President Bush increased every time the terror alert in the United States was raised between 2001 and 2004. Despite the fact that terror alerts indicate that the system is objectively disordered, they appear to have led citizens to increase their endorsement of the man in charge of that system. In a similar vein, Ullrich and Cohrs (2007) showed that reminders of terrorist attacks increased scores on a general measure of system justification (Kay & Jost, 2003). In short, then, there is good evidence that system threat begets system defense. Although these various experimental and correlational paradigms employ a range of system threat manipulations and a diverse set of system justification measures, common to all of them is the observation that information that challenges people's belief in a just, legitimate, and orderly system strengthens their motive to justify it.

What are the implications of this threat and defense tendency for sustainable behavior? What might it suggest about the nature of people's reactions to information about environmental crises? The answer to these questions is rather straightforward: Given that system threats tend to foster attempts at defending the legitimacy of the status quo (rather than attempts to change it), it is very feasible that information about the system's failings in coping with environmental issues may decrease, rather than increase, individual effort at change. That is, to the extent information about pending environmental crises serves to threaten the system, this information may engender increased reliance on and defense of the system—a tendency correlated with decreased interest in acting for change (Gaucher, Kay, & Laurin, 2010; Wakslak, Jost, Tyler, & Chen, 2007)—rather than individual action aimed at rectifying problems. Supporting this, Feygina, Jost, and Goldsmith (2010) have suggested that the fear induced by evidence of environmental degradation causes resistance to change. Thus, according to system justification theory, threatening people with evidence about the harm being done to the environment can be counterproductive to the goal of achieving sustainability. Instead of motivating change, we suggest, such threats will cause people to look to the broader social system to solve the problem.

This proposition—that the dire and threatening nature of environmental problems may cause people to rely more on the system and less on themselves—is also supported by recent research on processes of compensatory control (Kay et al., 2008; Kay, Gaucher, McGregor, & Nash, 2010; Kay, Whitson, Gaucher, & Galinsky, 2009), a psychological model that was itself inspired by, and builds upon, system justification theory. According to the model of compensatory control, people flexibly and interchangeably rely on the self and on their external systems (e.g., governments, organizations, religions) to satisfy the motive to believe that the world is orderly and controlled. When feelings of personal control (which are important means of preserving the belief in an orderly and nonrandom world) are restricted, limited or reduced, it is argued, people increasingly place their faith in external systems that maintain control (Kay et al., 2008). Doing so provides people with the ability to maintain the cherished belief that the world is orderly and nonrandom, even in the face of information that personal control is limited.

There are several empirical examples of this process. When personal control is experimentally lowered, for example, people report increased belief in the existence of controlling religious deities (Kay et al., 2008; Kay, Moscovitch, & Laurin, 2010; Laurin, Kay, & Moscovitch, 2008), increased defense and support of governmental institutions (Kay et al., 2008), and increased faith in societal progress (Rutjens, van Harreveld, & van der Pligt, 2010). In addition, correlational data demonstrates that, across the world, lower reports of feelings of personal control are associated with increased support for governmental intervention (Kay et al., 2008). In short, then, when people feel personal control is challenged, the natural response is not necessarily to battle to overcome this challenge and regain personal control, but to defensively bolster faith in external systems to compensate for this lack of control.

How can this perspective explain (the lack of) sustainable behavior, especially in light of the clear public awareness of the severity of environmental problems? Like system justification theory, the model of compensatory control also answers this question through suggesting a defensive overreliance upon external social systems. This latter perspective differs from system justification theory, however, in its emphasis on one specific psychological need driving this overreliance. To the extent that environmental issues are communicated to the larger population as particularly dire or severe, people may feel as though the ability for any one individual to solve these problems is nearly nil. As a consequence of this restricted feeling of personal control, the model of compensatory control would suggest that people may then compensate by placing increased faith in the system's ability to assert control in this domain. Thus, much like processes of system justification, processes of compensatory control may lead people to cope with information of potential environmental catastrophes not by working harder for change, but by placing more faith in the abilities of the system.

Both of these theoretical perspectives can, therefore, shed light on why, despite the widespread acknowledgment of the risks environmental issues pose, societies have a particularly difficult time motivating sustainable behavior at the individual level. Both system justification theory (Jost & Banaji, 1994) and the model of compensatory control (Kay et al., 2008) suggest that people often defensively bolster their faith in external systems (at the expense of faith in the self), and both suggest this heightened faith in external systems can be caused by factors commonly included in the communication of environmental information. As an example of how these processes may play out in everyday life, imagine someone viewing Al Gore's Academy Award–winning documentary about climate change, *An Inconvenient Truth*. In one memorable scene, Mr. Gore attempts to portray, as dramatically as possible, the Earth's changing levels of carbon dioxide emissions and average temperature over time. To do so, Mr. Gore climbs upon an elevating device, which raises him to the ceiling of the auditorium, to emphasize the point that carbon dioxide emissions are currently far higher than any time in history. Clearly, Mr. Gore included this prop in his presentation to convince people of the gravity of the situation and motivate environmental behavior. His tactic, though, if it threatens perceptions of the system's legitimacy or perceptions of personal control, might actually motivate the opposite—a defensive bolstering of faith in the system to tackle this problem. We now turn to a description of very recent research that, while not designed to address sustainable behavior specifically, nicely illustrates how the presentation of complex and severe social problems that require individual action to solve can, in fact, promote increased reliance on the system.

SOCIAL PROBLEMS AND DEFENSIVE RELIANCE ON THE SYSTEM

We have conducted a series of recent studies to explore the antecedents and consequences of trusting the government to manage the environment, as well as other social domains, such as the economy, that are plagued by unsustainability (Shepherd & Kay, 2012). In this program of research—which is still in its infancy—we have attempted to demonstrate that the increased perceptions of important social issues as complex and/or difficult to resolve leads not to increased individual efforts at understanding, addressing, and solving them, but instead to the unintended consequence of increased faith in the government to solve these issues and decreased interest in personally engaging them. We now describe four experimental studies that, when considered together, empirically demonstrate this phenomenon (Shepherd & Kay, 2012).

In the first of these studies, we sought simply to demonstrate that increased perceptions of complexity, within an environmental context, lead to increased faith in the government. In this study, participants read about two different sources of energy, neither of which the participants knew anything about beforehand. Participants were randomly assigned to one of two conditions that varied how the energy sources were described. In one condition, we simplified the description of how these energy sources work, whereas in another condition, participants read complex descriptions. Importantly, manipulation checks confirmed that participants who read complex descriptions of the two energy sources believed the sources to be more complex than did those who read the simpler description. Afterward, participants were asked questions gauging their trust in the government to manage these energy sources. What was the effect of this manipulation on participants' faith in government? Although it would be logical to assume that people would be more worried about the government's ability to manage the energy source when it is described as more complex, the exact opposite occurred. Those in the complex description condition trusted the government more to manage these energy sources and to deal with any problems that could arise than did those in the simple description condition. It is noteworthy that this increased trust did not come about because of a familiarity with the energy source, or any existing precedent that the government actually can manage these energy sources. The participants were told that these sources were developed by private industry, not by the government. Nonetheless, the more complex the participants believed the energy sources to be, and the less they personally understood them, the more they blindly trusted the government to efficiently manage them.

Why did this happen? That is, why did the increased complexity lead participants to report more faith in the government, rather than less? According to both system justification theory and the model of compensatory control, when people feel as though they themselves cannot cope with certain issues, they feel dependent on their external systems (such as the government) to address the issues for them. This feeling of system dependence, in turn, is thought to promote system trust and support (Kay et al., 2009; Laurin, Shepherd, & Kay, 2010; Van der Toorn, Tyler, & Jost, 2011). By bolstering support for the status quo, the decisions that governments make, and the processes by which they make those decisions, people can feel confident that those with power are making decisions that are in one's best interests. We thought it likely, therefore, that feelings of system dependence may mediate the relationship between perceptions of an issue's complexity and faith in the government to manage it.

To test this hypothesis, we conducted an experiment similar to the one described previously, but with a different and more mainstream energy source (biofuel). This time, however, we measured feelings of dependence as well as faith in the government. As with the previous study, participants who read a complex description of how biofuel works did indeed deem it more complex and reported more faith in the government to manage it. Furthermore, those participants who read the complex description also reported feeling more dependent on the government in this domain than those who read a simpler description of how biofuel works. As predicted, this increased sense of dependence mediated the effect of the complexity manipulation on government trust. In this experiment, we also assessed the extent to which the complexity manipulation led participants to defend the government's handling of the energy source, even when it was made explicit that the government is not composed of scientists who understand the energy source. Specifically, participants were told that while scientists *inform* politicians when it comes to making decisions regarding the country's energy plans, the final decision is made by government officials. Participants were then asked the extent to which this is a desirable way for decisions regarding energy to be made, and whether or not changes should occur (e.g., scientists and panels of experts should make the decisions instead). Similar to the results for trust in the government, we found that feeling unknowledgeable led to an increase in the feeling that the current decision-making process is appropriate, and that the status quo is desirable. This relationship between feeling unknowledgeable and preferring the status quo was again mediated by perceived dependence on the government.

These two studies suggest that at times when people should be engaged in learning about various social issues, such as energy, they are instead more likely to defer responsibility to those in power. The studies also suggest that this process is driven, at least in part, by feelings of dependence and that that this process influences not only blanket, generalized faith in the government but also specific support for the government's decision-making procedures. Although such a process may help people psychologically to cope—by alleviating the stress associated with knowing important social issues are potentially too complex or dire to manage personally—this support for the government's decision-making processes can have detrimental effects. Governments are not immune to making mistakes, or putting their own interests over those of the public. But because people trust that the government will solve problems that arise, especially those that appear most complex, people may want to entirely avoid learning about these issues, since doing so may make people aware that the issues are not being perfectly managed by the government or some other external system. If so, then we should observe that issues that are complex not only beget increased feelings of dependence upon and faith in the government to manage them, but also cause a decreased willingness to expose the self to in-depth information about the issue. Moreover, not only should people be demotivated to learn about these issues, but, if they believe the government is adequately managing them, they should show less interest in doing so themselves. In other words, once people feel more dependent on and place more faith in their government to deal with a complex, important social problem, they should become less motivated to address these issues themselves, and more motivated to avoid them altogether. This process should occur for two reasons: (i) because people have placed an increased level of trust in the government to manage an issue, thus putting less onus on the individual; and (ii) because exposing the self to information about the issue risks disrupting the psychologically comforting perceptions of the government as capable and in control of a given issue.

A pair of experiments provides evidence for this extension of the basic phenomenon. In one such study, we specifically tested the effects of faith in the government to cope with a particular issue on willingness to learn about that issue. Participants, who had enrolled in a study on task performance and preferences, were told that they had up to 12 minutes to work on three different computer tasks. The instructions stated that they could spend as long as they wanted on any one task, and did not have to do all of them. In actuality, we were only interested in one particular task, which always appeared first in the sequence. The first part of this task served as a manipulation of government trust. Participants were randomly assigned to read a short article stating either (i) that the government can be trusted to manage the economy; or (ii) that the government is incapable of managing the economy. Following the article was a much longer, educational article that explained how the economy entered a recession in the autumn of 2008, whether or not it would get worse, and if the government could do anything about it. The beginning of the article made it clear that while the article would be informative, it would also contain a lot of negative news. Our dependent measure of interest was the time participants spent reading this article before moving on to another task. As predicted, those participants who trusted the government's ability to manage the economy spent significantly less time (25% less) reading the informative article about the economy, as compared to those in the other condition. Thus, simply feeling that the government is in control of a social issue has detrimental effects on people's willingness to educate themselves about the issues at hand.

Of course, it is entirely reasonable that people who believe the government can adequately manage an issue will feel less of a need to learn about the issue themselves. That, in and of itself, is not a problem. This tendency becomes more problematic, however, when we consider the fact that people can develop a specific faith in the government not necessarily because of any information they have about the government's competencies, but because of efforts at coping with existential or epistemic threats. Furthermore, it is important to distinguish between a simple lack of interest in learning about a specific social issue, and a motivation to actively *avoid* learning about those issues. The latter is obviously more problematic than the former. But do people actually develop a motivation to avoid this type of information, rather than just a lack of motivation to approach it? We sought to answer this question in an experiment in which participants completed one of two tests about how the economy operates: either an easy test or a difficult one. After participants completed one of these two tests, they were explicitly asked about their attempts to avoid information about the economy and the merits of an "ignorance is bliss" approach. Those who completed the test containing difficult questions about the economy increasingly reported and defended a motivation to avoid information pertinent to the economy.

But, does increased faith in government and decreased interest in exposure to relevant information actually translate into decreased proactive behavior? To test this possibility, as well as the entire causal chain in one single experiment, participants were presented with one of two descriptions of the economy: either a simple or a complex description. Afterward, they were given a checklist of individual behaviors that are recommended to help alleviate the problems associated with the economy. Participants were asked to place a check beside any in which they thought they could engage. Measures of government dependence, government trust, and motivation to avoid information about the economy were also included. The results tell a powerful story: those participants who read the more complex description of the economy felt less able to engage in behaviors that could help them cope with the recession, increased feelings of government dependence (within the context of the economy), increased trust in the government's ability to manage the economy, and finally, an increased desire to avoid hearing or learning about the economy. In addition, a path analysis indicated a causal chain, such that the increased complexity predicted decreased behavioral intentions, which predicted increased feelings of dependence, which predicted increased feelings of trust and motivation to avoid information. In other words, when people felt less able to understand the economy or navigate through the recession, they felt more dependent on the government, and showed an increased desire to avoid learning about economic issues.

Across these four studies, then, we see clear evidence of a tendency to psychologically defer to the system when social problems appear overly complex. This tendency not only undermines current engagement with social issues, but prevents people from educating themselves about these issues, potentially perpetuating a cycle of complacency and inaction that ultimately limits the development of a sustainable society. When individuals feel an issue is exceptionally complex and dire, rather than seeking out more information or feeling even more of a need to alter their behavior, they may instead engage defensive processes, causing them to defer to governments and institutions that they believe are equipped to manage the problems for them. Instead of changing their own behaviors, people avoid learning about the issues and what they can do to solve them. Rather than proactively trying to change things for the better, people cope with threat by leaving their fate in the hands of external systems that may or may not have their best interests at heart.

Of course, we are not arguing that all people will always fail to act. Some people are simply more prone to changing their behavior, and some situations are so undeniably serious that people feel they must change their behavior. The recent global recession, for example, was sudden and drastic enough that some people changed their behavior, such as by improving their money management skills. Especially severe threats, though, are relatively rare, so rapid behavioral change in response to threat is also uncommon. We argue, instead, that the system justification and compensatory control motivations make inaction and system defense the dominant response among most people. The kinds of threats that people encounter on a daily basis should typically evoke the responses we have illustrated in this chapter.

MOTIVATING SUSTAINABLE BEHAVIOR

In this chapter, we have focused on the ways through which psychological motivations that promote reliance upon external systems can be activated in environmental contexts and inhibit behavior change. Although processes of system justification and compensatory control can make sustainability more difficult to achieve, these same motivations should also theoretically be possible to harness to promote change. For example, framing change as a way of demonstrating commitment to the system may be an effective method of tapping the system justification motive for the better. Consistent with this, Feygina and colleagues (2010) demonstrated that participants who highly endorsed the sociopolitical system indicated more willingness to do pro-environment behaviors when environmental sustainability was framed as patriotic, as compared to when no framing was used. In other words, the typical negative relationship, such that greater endorsement of the system leads to less willingness to do pro-environment behaviors was eliminated by reframing sustainability in a way that appealed to people who highly endorse the system. Thus, small changes in the wording of promotional materials can channel underlying motivations into desired behaviors.

Similarly, motivations to perceive a controlled and orderly world can be channeled to promote sustainable behavior. Banfield, Nadolny, and Kay (2012) have demonstrated that, when prosocial behavior is cast as a way to reestablish order in the world, people will increasingly engage in prosocial behavior following control threats. This reasoning can also be applied to fostering sustainability-oriented behaviors. For example, curbside recycling and composting could be portrayed as a way of affecting one's environment. By sorting their waste, people literally impose order on a situation that would otherwise be more chaotic, and thus can feel a sense of agency over the outcomes around them. This idea echoes Clayton and Brook (2005), who suggested that some unsustainable behaviors are the result of a desire to control the environment (e.g., applying pesticides to achieve uniformity). They suggested highlighting the lack of control over chemicals in the environment when pesticides are used. By framing unsustainable behaviors as reducing control over the environment, and sustainable behaviors as increasing control, policy makers can harness people's basic compensatory control processes for the ultimate goal of achieving sustainability.

Finally, the work reported previously by Shepherd and Kay (2012) also suggests possible interventions, especially in how environmental issues are described and communicated to the public. Because people turn to the government when issues seem complex, threatening, and beyond personal control, scare tactics that attempt to hammer home the gravity of the situation are likely to backfire. They are more likely to engender reliance on the system than the self. To reduce people's reliance on the system, and motivate them to act, literature about environmental sustainability should be written in plain language that emphasizes the individual's ability to effect change. If information is communicated in a way that emphasizes the individual's role in fixing the problem and reasons for not giving up hope, as opposed to reasons why hope is nearly lost, we are more likely to circumvent defensive reliance on the system. Information about the environment need not necessarily evoke deference to external systems. Information, when presented in a psychologically digestible way, can empower people to confront pressing social issues, and to acknowledge that the government is not solely responsible for solving problems.

CONCLUSION

A surge of research over the past two decades has made it clear that people turn to their external systems—legitimizing them as just, appropriate, desirable, and as they ought to be—when confronted with a number of existential and epistemic threats. Unfortunately, two of the most potent causes of this tendency to justify and defend external systems often accompany messages of environmental awareness. These messages, which tend to include information about the catastrophic point we have reached and the dire consequences of our current trajectory, are fraught with undertones that challenge the legitimacy of the system that has allowed us to arrive here (i.e., system threats) and one's ability to fix the problem (i.e., personal control threat). As a result, although people are well aware of the severity of these problems, they may often react to reminders of them by defending their system and its ability to address the problem, rather than changing their own behavior. The research reviewed in this chapter suggests, albeit somewhat indirectly, that such a process can occur. Thus, although adaptive for our daily lives, these motivational tendencies may stifle our ability to adapt to a changing environment, making sustainable behaviors relatively elusive. But as we learn more about the operation of these motivational systems, it may be possible to circumvent, and even channel, these motivations to achieve greater sustainability.

REFERENCES

Atkinson, J. W. (1964). *An introduction to motivation*. New York: Van Nostrand.

Banfield, J. C., Nadolny, D., & Kay, A. C. (2012). *Helping in a random world: Prosocial intentions and behavior can satiate compensatory control needs.* Manuscript in preparation.

Burke, J. (2010). Hundreds die in Indian heatwave. *Guardian*. Retrieved July 27, 2010 from http://www.guardian.co.uk/world/2010/may/30/india-heatwave-deaths.

Cascio, J. (2009). Get smarter. *The Atlantic*. Retrieved July 27, 2010 from http://www.the-atlantic.com/magazine/archive/_2009/07/get-smarter/7548/.

Clayton, S., & Brook, A. (2005). Can psychology help save the world? A model for conservation psychology. *Analyses of Social Issues and Public Policy*, 5, 87–102. doi: 10.1111/j.1530-2415.2005.00057.x.

Doyle, A. (2010). Like Sept. 11, volcano plane ban may hold climate clue. Reuters. Retrieved July 27, 2010 from http://www.reuters.com/article/idUSTRE63M1PH20100423.

Feygina, I., Jost, J. T., & Goldsmith, R. E. (2010). System justification, the denial of global warming, and the possibility of "system-sanctioned change. *Personality and Social Psychology Bulletin*, 36(3), 326–338.

Gardner, G. T., & Stern, P. C. (2008). The short list: The most effective actions U.S. households can take to curb climate change. *Environment*. Retrieved July 27, 2010 from http://www.environmentmagazine.org/Archives/Back%20Issues/September-October%202008/gardner-stern-full.html.

Gaucher, D., Kay, A. C., & Laurin, K. (2010). The power of the status quo: Consequences for maintaining and perpetuating inequality. In D. R. Bobocel, A. C. Kay, M. P. Zanna, & J. M. Olson (Eds.), *The psychology of justice and legitimacy (Vol. 11)* (pp. 109–118). Philadelphia: Psychology Press.

International Panel on Climate Change. (2007). 17.4.2.4 Informational and cognitive barriers. Retrieved July 27, 2010 from http://www.ipcc.ch/publications_and_data/ar4/wg2/en/ch17s17-4-2-4.html.

Jost, J. T., & Banaji, M. R. (1994). The role of stereotyping in system justification and the production of false consciousness. *British Journal of Social Psychology, 33*(1), 1–27.

Jost, J. T., & Hunyady, O. (2002). *The psychology of system justification and the palliative function of ideology*. Hove, England: Psychology Press/Taylor & Francis (UK).

Kay, A. C., Gaucher, D., McGregor, I., & Nash, K. (2010). Religious belief as compensatory control. *Personality and Social Psychology Review, 14*(1), 37–48.

Kay, A. C., Gaucher, D., Napier, J. L., Callan, M. J., & Laurin, K. (2008). God and the government: Testing a compensatory control mechanism for the support of external systems of control. *Journal of Personality and Social Psychology, 95*(1), 18–35.

Kay, A. C., Gaucher, D., Peach, J. M., Laurin, K., Friesen, J., Zanna, M. P., & Spencer, S. J. (2009). Inequality, discrimination, and the power of the status quo: Direct evidence for a motivation to see the way things are as the way they should be. *Journal of Personality and Social Psychology, 97*(3), 421–434.

Kay A. C., Jimenez, M. C., & Jost, J. T. (2002). Sour grapes, sweet lemons, and the anticipatory rationalization of the status quo. *Personality and Social Psychology Bulletin, 28*(9), 1300–1312.

Kay, A. C., & Jost, J. T. (2003). Complementary Justice: Effects of "poor but happy" and "poor but honest" stereotype exemplars on system justification and implicit activation of the justice motive. *Journal of Personality and Social Psychology, 85*(5), 823–837.

Kay, A. C., Jost, J. T., & Young, S. (2005). Victim-derogation and victim-enhancement as alternate routes to system-justification. *Psychological Science, 16*(3), 240–246.

Kay, A. C., Moscovitch, D., & Laurin, K. (2010). Randomness, attributions of arousal, and belief in God. *Psychological Science, 21*(2), 216–218.

Kay, A. C., Whitson, J. A., Gaucher, D., & Galinsky, A. D. (2009). Compensatory control: Achieving order through the mind, our institutions, and the heavens. *Current Directions in Psychological Science, 18*, 264–268.

Kay, A. C., & Zanna, M. P. (2009). A contextual analysis of the system justification motive and its societal consequences. In J. T. Jost, A. C. Kay, & H. Thorisdottir (Eds.), *Social and psychological bases of ideology and system justification* (pp. 158–181). New York: Oxford University Press.

Lau, G. P., Kay, A. C., & Spencer, S. J. (2008). Loving those who justify inequality: The effects of system threat on attraction to women who embody benevolent sexist ideals. *Psychological Science, 19*(1), 20–21.

Laurin, K., Kay, A. C., & Moscovitch, D. M. (2008). On the belief in God: Towards an understanding of the emotional substrates of compensatory control. *Journal of Experimental Social Psychology, 44*, 1559–1562.

Laurin, K., Shepherd, S., & Kay, A. C. (2010). Restricted emigration, system inescapability, and defense of the status quo: System-justifying consequences of restricted exit opportunities. *Psychological Science, 21*(8), 1075–1082. doi: 10.1177/0956797610375448.

McKenzie-Mohr, D. (2000). Fostering sustainable behavior through community-based social marketing. *American Psychologist, 55*(5), 531–537.

Napier, J. L., Mandisodza, A. N., Anderson, S. M., & Jost, J. T. (2006). System justification in responding to the poor and displaced in the aftermath of hurricane Katrina. *Analyses of Social Issues and Public Policy, 6*(1), 57–73.

Pollan, M. (2006). *The omnivore's dilemma: A natural history of food.* New York: Penguin Press.

Rutjens, B. T., van Harreveld, F., & van der Pligt, J. (2010). Yes we can: Belief in progress as compensatory control. *Social Psychological and Personality Science, 1,* 246–252.

Schlosser, E. (2007). Penny foolish. *New York Times.* Retrieved July 27, 2010 from http://www.nytimes.com/2007/11/29/opinion/29schlosser.html.

Shepherd, S., & Kay, A. C. (2012). On the perpetuation of ignorance: System dependence, system justification, and the motivated avoidance of sociopolitical information. *Journal of Personality and Social Psychology, 102*(2), 264–280. doi: 10.1037/a0026272.

Stern, P. C. (1992). Psychological dimensions of global environmental change. *Annual Review of Psychology, 43,* 269–302.

Stern, P. C. (2000). Toward a coherent theory of environmentally significant behavior. *Journal of Social Issues, 56*(3), 407–424.

Sutherland, J. (2003). A word of advice to Ken Livingstone. *Guardian.* Retrieved July 27, 2010, from http://www.guardian.co.uk/environment/2003/oct/27/congestioncharging.politics.

Ullrich, J., & Cohrs, J. C. (2007). Terrorism salience increases system justification: Experimental evidence. *Social Justice Research, 20*(2), 117–139.

van der Toorn, J., Tyler, T. R., & Jost, J. T. (2011). More than fair: Outcome dependence, system justification, and the perceived legitimacy of authority figures. *Journal of Experimental Social Psychology, 47,* 127–138. doi:10.1016/j.jesp.2010.09.003.

Van Vugt, M. (2009). Averting the tragedy of the commons: Using psychological science to protect the environment. *Current Directions in Psychological Science, 18*(3), 169–173.

Wakslak, C., Jost, J. T., Tyler, T. R., & Chen, E. (2007). Moral outrage mediates the dampening effect of system justification on support for redistributive social policies. *Psychological Science, 18*(3), 267–274.

Willer, R. (2004). The effects of government-issued terror warnings on presidential approval ratings. *Current Research in Social Psychology, 10*(1), 1–12.

Winter, D. D. N., & Koger, S. M. (2004). *The psychology of environmental problems.* Mahwah, NJ: Lawrence Erlbaum Associates.

Section 4

Exploiting Self-Control in Sustainable Behavior

10

From Weakness to Strength
Low Self-Control Can Be Good for Sustainability

KATHLEEN D. VOHS and BOB M. FENNIS

UNDERSTANDING SELF-CONTROL: A BRIEF OVERVIEW

*T*he study of self-control in the field of psychology has concentrated mainly on how people pursue personal goals and the intrapsychic work that goes toward reaching those goals. Classic work on self-awareness and self-standards (Duval & Wicklund, 1971), the notion that people have self-guides that organize their behavior (Higgins, 1987), and conceptualizing emotional states as indicators of goal progress (Carver & Scheier, 1990) has focused on both the inner processes that make goal pursuit possible as well as individualistic goals that people seek to achieve.

Recently, work in the areas of self-regulation and self-control (we use the terms indistinguishably) has integrated the interpersonal function of the self into theorizing about self-control. Self-control is a costly process, which means that for it to be here today it had to bring ample survival and reproductive benefits.

SELF-CONTROL AS GOVERNED BY A LIMITED SUPPLY OF RESOURCES

In our view, the engine that drives self-regulation is a limited and depletable set of resources. Acts of self-control use this resource and drain it, which means that people sometimes become temporarily taxed of their self-control abilities. When this happens, so-called depleted people behave quite similarly to people with chronically low self-control.

Similar to the functioning of a muscle, the limited resource model of self-regulation (Baumeister, Bratslavsky, Muraven, & Tice, 1998; Vohs & Heatherton, 2000) posits that all manner of self-control behaviors draw on a limited resource, which can be thought of as a strength or energy. Therefore, each act of active volition will have a detrimental impact on subsequent acts of volition, due to the fact that they draw from the same resource. This state is called self-control depletion and in it, people are relatively less capable or motivated to function effectively, which results in behavior based on habit, routine, and automatic processes (Baumeister, Muraven, & Tice, 2000; Baumeister, Schmeichel, & Vohs, 2007; Vohs & Schmeichel, 2007; Vohs, Baumeister & Ciarocco, 2005).

Research using the self-regulatory resource model typically uses a paradigm involving two resource-taxing tasks. In the first phase, participants are either requested to perform a task that is thought to require self-regulatory resources, or they perform a version of the experimental task that ought not to require much if any of the resource. Later, performance on a second and often unrelated resource-consuming task is measured, which is the dependent measure. A state of self-regulatory resource depletion is inferred if performance on the second task is worse due to having completed a demanding task initially. In short, being depleted of one's self-control resources is a bit like a self-control hangover (Vohs, 2006). A body of findings across diverse domains, including over 130 published studies, suggests support for the model.

WHY ARE PEOPLE LOW IN SELF-CONTROL?

To understand the proposal for how to promote sustainable behavior through low self-control, it is important to outline what circumstances likely lead to low self-control. It is relatively straightforward to detail what is known about chronic low self-control, and that is genetics. There are strong genetic effects for a variety of characteristics that indicate low self-control, including low conscientiousness, impulsivity, and attention deficit and hyperactivity disorder (ADHD). To give readers a sense of the magnitude of these effects, the heritability quotient for conscientiousness ranges from .40 to .49 (Bouchard & McGue, 2003). One review of the literature concluded that the heritability component of ADHD is .80 (Stevenson, 1994, as cited in Barkley, 1997). That there is a strong genetic and therefore trait component to self-control (Tangney, Baumeister, & Boone, 2004) means that a person who exhibits poor self-control in one domain will likely exhibit poor self-control in another.

Predicting when people are likely to become depleted of their self-regulatory resources rests on understanding the basic fact that people must first engage in self-control. Therefore, circumstances that are known to elicit temptations, urges, or impulses will be those likely to deplete the self-regulatory resources within some segment of people in those settings.

One common impetus for impulses is the urge to spend. Not only do over one-third of consumers self-identify as compulsive buyers (as reported in Vohs & Faber, 2007), recent analyses by *Sports Illustrated* found that almost 80% of NFL players are broke or near bankruptcy within two years after retirement (Torre, 2009). In short, the urge to buy is a strong one that many people experience.

In a series of studies, Vohs and Faber (2007) showed that regulatory resource depletion may affect this type of indulgence: the desire to impulsively spend. In their research, Vohs and Faber demonstrated that depleting consumers of their self-regulatory resources by attentional, mental, or emotional self-control tasks resulted in increases on several indexes of impulsivity in the marketplace.

We predicted that not only would being depleted of self-control resources lead to more impulsive spending but that people who already have tendencies to overspend would be the most affected in their spending patterns when they are depleted. As expected, we found this pattern: a significant effect of being depleted and interaction of depletion condition with trait impulsive buying habits, which represented the need to regulate one's spending. One experiment, for instance, asked participants in the depletion condition to write down their thoughts for several minutes, with the exception that they were not allowed to think thoughts of a white bear—a task that is known to be a self-control endeavor (Wegner, Carter, Schneider, & White, 1987). Other participants were allowed to think anything they wanted for the thought-listing task, including a white bear. Hence, the former group was given a thought suppression goal, whereas the latter was not. After the thought-listing task, participants were shown 22 products that were said might be carried in the near future at the university bookstore. We gave them $10 to spend in the mock bookstore or take with them. The dependent measure was spending in this spontaneous purchasing situation. As expected, participants who had been in the self-regulatory resource depletion condition spent more money and bought more items than participants in the no depletion condition. Moreover, participants with chronic problems with overspending spent more than other participants when they had been depleted of their self-regulation resources. Hence, controlling one's spending requires self-regulation, and when self-regulatory resources run low, unnecessary spending is likely to occur.

Another temptation that sometimes requires active self-regulation to withstand is that presented by the lure of attractive and enjoyable (but often unhealthy and fattening) food. For people attempting to control their food intake, the availability and proximity of tempting food may exert a strong impact on their ability to curb the urge to eat. Vohs and Heatherton (2000) examined the impact of the temptation of tasty food on self-regulatory resources. In one study, the authors had dieters and nondieters watch a (boring) movie about the daily life of bighorn sheep. In the room in which they watched the movie, snacks and candy were placed. Those snacks were either within close reach of the participant or across the room. In addition, participants were either instructed to refrain from eating the food, or were told they were free to do so. It was expected that being close to tempting food items that were free for the taking presented a formidable temptation that needed considerable amounts of regulatory resources to resist, especially for dieters. Because dieters are regulating with respect to an eating goal (i.e., they are controlling their behavior toward food)—but nondieters are not—dieters were expected to become more depleted than nondieters in the same condition. The results were in accordance with this prediction. After watching the sheep movie, both dieters and nondieters were asked to taste and rate ice cream. Dieters ate significantly more ice cream than nondieters when they had been seated next to the available snacks and candy. Furthermore, Vohs and Heatherton (2000) found that depletion effects for dieters were not only restricted to eating-related behaviors, but extended to nonfood-related self-regulatory behaviors as well (persistence at solving impossible puzzles), thus pointing to the fact that once depleted, people will exhibit reduced performance at a variety of subsequent acts of self-control.

Another demonstration of when people become depleted of self-control was provided by the work of Schmeichel, Vohs, and Baumeister (2003) who demonstrated that intellectual functioning uses self-regulatory resources. Specifically, logical reasoning and higher-order reflective processes seem to tap into self-control resources (Strack & Deutsch, 2004; Vohs, 2006). In one of their studies, Schmeichel et al. (2003) requested participants to watch a video of a woman being interviewed. On the bottom portion of the screen appeared unrelated words that participants in the depletion condition were asked to actively ignore. Nondepletion participants also saw the irrelevant words but were not asked to ignore them. The results showed that depletion condition participants subsequently performed worse than nondepletion participants on logical reasoning problems from the Graduate Record Exam (GRE), and they attempted to solve fewer items. Hence, attentional control during the video task resulted in a decrement in complex cognitive functioning as measured by the GRE test.

Apart from these studies, the limited-resource model of self-control has been supported by research on such domains as active decision making (Vohs et al., 2008), persuasion (Wheeler, Briñol, & Hermann, 2007) and stereotype suppression (Richeson & Shelton, 2003).

THE INTERPLAY BETWEEN SELF-CONTROL AND PUBLIC SOCIAL BEHAVIORS

Because self-control is a costly process, people use it for those outcomes that offer them the most rewards, which in many cases is social belonging and acceptance. Hence, the desire to be socially acceptable likely underlies much of why people endeavor to engage in self-control (Baumeister & Leary, 1995; Heatherton & Vohs, 1998).

To be sure, another reason that people use self-control is to enact the difficult behaviors that reflect their core values. People who believe in a higher power, God, or who believe in the goodness of the church harness their self-control in order to adhere to those values (McCullough & Willoughby, 2009). Similarly, people who place a high value on behaving in sustainable ways will mostly certainly use some of their precious self-control resources toward being environmentally friendly in their actions. However, we think that they are not the only ones whose behavior, via the process of self-control, can be attuned to sustainable actions.

Low-Self-Control People Are Easily Persuaded
by Social Influence Tactics

The key to the current plan in which low self-control is seen as a possible advantage for promoters of sustainable action is this finding: When people are low in self-control (temporarily or dispositionally), they are more easily affected by social influence techniques than they would be otherwise. A series of experiments by Fennis, Janssen, and Vohs (2009a, 2009b; also Janssen, Fennis, Pruyn, & Vohs, 2008) demonstrates this point.

The compliance-gaining procedures that influence professionals' use have in common the presence of multiple decision moments or sequential requests (Cialdini, 1993). One of the most famous of these is the foot-in-the-door technique (Freedman & Fraser, 1966), in which the influence agent starts with a small request and follows with a larger target request. The door-in-the-face technique (Cialdini et al., 1975) starts with a larger request, followed by a smaller request. Fennis et al. (2009a) argued that consciously attending and responding to these initial requests drains self-regulatory resources. The resulting state of regulatory resource depletion then increases the chances of compliance through the use of decisional heuristics that are embedded in the influence context. Six field and lab studies supported this idea.

For example, participants in one study were exposed to the opening stage of a typical foot-in-the-door ploy by presenting participants with a few introductory questions that either prompted active self-presentation (Experiment 1) or higher-order cognitive processing (Experiment 2). Next, compliance with a target request was measured (Experiment 1) as well as performance on an unrelated task to assess resource depletion. In addition to increased compliance with the target request, both studies showed evidence of self-regulatory resource depletion in that participants who had been given the scripted influence treatment performed worse on the subsequent self-regulation task than other participants. In addition, the authors showed that a state of self-regulatory failure increases susceptibility to the influence attempt by fostering the use of norms to guide decision making. Compliance among depleted participants increased as a function of employing the reciprocity norm (Experiment 4) or the liking norm (Experiment 5). Finally, and in line with the perspective of this chapter, Fennis et al. (2009a) tested whether individual differences in trait self-control in combination with a technique called the *lowball technique* (Cialdini, 1993) produced parallel effects on compliance as was found among people who were differentially depleted of their self-regulatory resources. Indeed, low- but not high-self-control people were more compliant after the lowball technique.

In summary, people who engage in self-control or have low trait self-control are more easily influenced than are others because low-self-control people rely on superficial cues that direct them how to behave. One particularly notable aspect of the Fennis et al. (2009a) experiments is that the cues could lead people toward good ends as easily as bad ones. For instance, the experiment that used the lowball technique cued compliance in the context of prosocial behavior—namely, donating money to an organization for children. As seen in Figure 10.1, low-self-control

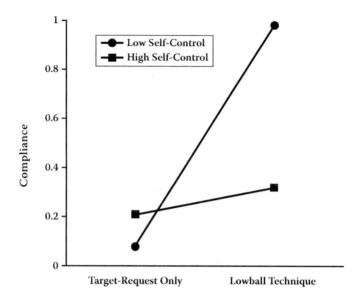

Figure 10.1   Average amount of money donated to charity as a function of influence technique and trait self-control, Experiment 6

people actually donated more money than high-self-control people when earlier exposed to the lowball technique.

NEW PERSPECTIVES ON MAKING SUSTAINABLE BEHAVIOR HAPPEN

People who are (temporarily or chronically) low in self-control are good targets for cues promoting sustainable actions—if those cues make use of social influence tactics (Cialdini, 1993). The social aspect of the influence tactics is key because as outlined earlier in this chapter, social acceptance was almost surely the reason that costly self-control capacities emerged in early humans. Hence, the benefits of using social influence techniques instead of the trickier ploys that dastardly influence agents use—not only are social influence techniques likelier to work because they cue the collective, but they are far more ethical as well.

Imagine a city in which there is a city center that most people go to for work. One idea would be to have billboards or signage posted facing the city center because it would be viewable as people leave work after having presumably spent much of the day engaging in self-control (e.g., emotion regulation, attention control). This sign would make use of social influence techniques such as social proof, which works to influence people by showing how many other people are engaging in sustainable actions. Even better would be to have different signs for different places that featured actors that matched the demographics of the people who would be exposed to the sign. A sign facing San Jose, California—aka Silicon Valley—could feature 35- to 50-year-old white and Asian men, which would match the demographics of that city. Similarly, signs facing urban centers such as Atlanta, Georgia could feature black professionals. Signs in Hispanic communities could feature Hispanic families. People feel compelled to comply when they believe that their in-group endorses the norm (Cialdini, 1993).

Prior research has shown that engaging in logical reasoning and higher-order thinking involves self-control resources (Schmeichel et al., 2003). Teenagers must perform mathematical problems and sharpen their reasoning skills as part of their education process, which means that they too are likely to be depleted at the end of a school day. In addition, teens are known to be especially influenced by aspirational reference groups, which include celebrities, athletes, and musicians. Hence, public service announcements (PSAs) could be aired on television in the afternoon and early evening when teens are finished with the school day and likely watching television. They would feature aspirational group members that fit the target market for the television show. A football game would feature famous athletes, musicians could promote sustainable behavior on MTV and other music channels, and gossip shows could air PSAs with celebrities.

It is common to see volunteers for a cause out on the streets or sidewalks, asking for passersby to stop and sign a petition. The low-self-control perspective would say that it would be best to approach consumers after they have exited a store rather than before. Prior research has not only shown that resisting the temptation of an impulse purchase requires self-control (Vohs & Faber, 2007), as discussed previously, but also that the act of making choices requires self-control (Vohs et al., 2008). In combination, then, this suggests that when people leave a grocery store or a superstore (such as IKEA), which offer a vast array of options, they would be more open to signing a petition for sustainable action than if the request came before they entered the store. So too with customers leaving a store with sweets, chocolates, or other highly tempting items. The petition, however, is typically not the central request of the cause promoter. Signing the petition is a classic foot-in-the-door tactic, which works off of the principle of commitment and consistency. Hence, the next step after securing the signature would be to follow up with a request to donate time or money to the cause of sustainability. According to the current approach, asking for signatures and donations after customers have resisted their impulses to buy or made a series of choices would be highly effective.

A different tack comes from considerations of where people with low self-control are likely to be. Knowing that people indulge in their impulses when they are depleted and that chronically low-self-control people have myriad problems with behavioral control, places that cater to (for lack of a better term) "addicts" would be good targets for cues toward sustainability. Bars, casinos, racetracks, strip clubs, and all-you-can-eat restaurants might be worthy candidates for consideration. We suggest using aspirational groups here too as models of sustainable action, as well as attractive others, to encourage guests of these establishments.

CONCLUDING REMARKS

Authors who have commented on the implementation of research from psychology on sustainable actions have bemoaned the effects (few and far between) and the tactics (too complicated, too sophisticated) used thus far (McKenzie-Mohr, 2000). Our approach, however, is quite different. One could argue that low self-control is the number one underlying process that unites worldwide epidemics in waste, obesity, medicinal noncompliance, violence, and lack of initiative. We propose to take advantage of this state, and to turn what is typically considered bad (poor self-control) into a process that could shore up sustainable behavior.

Our prior work suggests that these people are prime targets for social influence cues, which work to offer low-self-control people a guide for behavior. Several possible ideas for which tactics would work most effectively under which circumstances were reviewed, although readers likely can think of many other creative ideas too. We welcome those ideas and comments as we build a theory on how something that is typically considered to be a bane to society (i.e., low self-control) can be put to good use. Tactics that transform a weakness to a strength have the potential to be mighty impactful.

REFERENCES

Barkley, R. A. (1997). *ADHD and the nature of self-control.* New York: Guilford.

Baumeister, R. F., Bratlavsky, E., Muraven, M., & Tice, D. M. (1998). Ego depletion: Is the active self a limited resource? *Journal of Personality and Social Psychology, 74,* 1252–1265.

Baumeister, R. F., & Leary, M. R. (1995). The need to belong: Desire for interpersonal attachments as a fundamental human motivation. *Psychological Bulletin, 117,* 497–529.

Baumeister, R. F., Muraven, M., & Tice, D. M. (2000). Ego depletion: A resource model of volition, self-regulation, and controlled processing. *Social Cognition, 18,* 130–150.

Baumeister, R. F., Schmeichel, B. J., & Vohs, K. D. (2007). Self-regulation and the executive function: The self as controlling agent. In A. W. Kruglanski & E. T. Higgins (Eds.), *Social psychology: Handbook of basic principles (2nd Edition)* (pp. 516–539). New York: Guilford.

Bouchard, T. J. Jr., & McGue, M. (2003). Genetic and environmental influences on human psychological differences. *Journal of Neurobiology, 54,* 4–45.

Carver, C. S., & Scheier, M. F. (1990). Origins and functions of positive and negative affect: A control-process view. *Psychological Review, 97,* 19–35.

Cialdini, R. B. (1993). *Influence: The psychology of persuasion.* New York: Morrow.

Cialdini, R. B., Vincent, J. E., Lewis, S. K., Catalan, J., Wheeler, D., & Darby, B. L. (1975). Reciprocal concessions procedure for inducing compliance: The door-in-the-face technique. *Journal of Personality and Social Psychology, 31,* 206–215.

Duval, S., & Wicklund, R. A. (1972). *A theory of objective self-awareness.* New York: Academic Press.

Fennis, B. M., Janssen, L., & Vohs, K. D. (2009a). Acts of benevolence: A limited-resource account of compliance with charitable requests. *Journal of Consumer Research, 35,* 906–924.

Fennis, B. M., Janssen, L., & Vohs, K. D. (2009b). Impaired self-control can promote pro-social and health-fostering behavior. *Psychology and Health, 24,* 25.

Freedman, J., & Fraser, S. (1966). Compliance without pressure: The foot-in-the-door technique. *Journal of Personality and Social Psychology, 4,* 195–202.

Heatherton, T. F., & Vohs, K. D. (1998). Why is it so difficult to inhibit behavior? *Psychological Inquiry, 9,* 212–215.

Higgins, E. T. (1987). Self-discrepancy: A theory relating self and affect. *Psychological Review, 94,* 319–340.

Janssen, L., Fennis, B. M., Pruyn, A. Th. H., & Vohs, K. D. (2008). The role of regulatory resource depletion in the effectiveness of social influence techniques. *Journal of Business Research, 61,* 1041–1045.

McCullough, M. E., & Willoughby, B. L. B. (2009). Religion, self-regulation, and self-control: Associations, explanations, and implications. *Psychological Bulletin, 135,* 69–93.

McKenzie-Mohr, D. (2000). Promoting *sustainable* behavior: An introduction to community-based social marketing. *Journal of Social Issues, 56,* 543–554.

Richeson, J. A., & Shelton, J. N. (2003). When prejudice does not pay: Effects of interracial contact on executive function. *Psychological Science, 14,* 287–290.

Schmeichel, B. J., Vohs, K. D., & Baumeister, R .F. (2003). Intellectual performance and ego depletion: Role of the self in logical reasoning and other information processing. *Journal of Personality and Social Psychology, 85,* 33–46.

Stevenson, J. (1994, June). Genetics of ADHD. Paper presented at the Professional Group for ADD and Related Disorders, London.

Strack, F., & Deutsch, R. (2004). Reflective and impulsive determinants of social behaviour. *Personality and Social Psychology Review, 8,* 220–247.

Tangney, J. P., Baumeister, R. F., & Boone, A. L. (2004). High self-control predicts good adjustment, less pathology, better grades, and interpersonal success. *Journal of Personality, 72,* 271–324.

Torre, P. S. (2009). How (and why) athletes go broke. *Sports Illustrated.* Retrieved April 9, 2010, from http://sportsillustrated.cnn.com/vault/article/magazine/MAG1153364/index.htm.

Vohs, K. D. (2006). Self-regulatory resources power the Reflective System: Evidence from five domains. *Journal of Consumer Psychology, 16,* 215–223.

Vohs, K. D., Baumeister, R. F., & Ciarocco, N.J. (2005). Self-regulation and self-presentation: Regulatory resource depletion impairs impression management and effortful self-presentation depletes regulatory resources. *Journal of Personality and Social Psychology, 88,* 632–657.

Vohs, K. D., Baumeister, R. F., Schmeichel, B. J., Twenge, J. M., Nelson, N. M., & Tice, D. M. (2008). Making choices impairs subsequent self-control: A limited resource account of decision making, self-regulation, and active initiative. *Journal of Personality and Social Psychology, 94,* 883–898.

Vohs, K. D., & Faber, R. J. (2007). Spent resources: Self-regulatory resource availability affects impulse buying. *Journal of Consumer Research, 33,* 537–547.

Vohs, K. D., & Heatherton, T. F. (2000). Self-regulatory failure: A resource-depletion approach. *Psychological Science, 11,* 249–254.

Vohs, K. D., & Schmeichel, B. J. (2007). Self-regulation: How and why do people reach (and fail to reach) their goals. In C. Sedikides & S. J. Spencer (Eds.), *Frontiers in social psychology: The self* (pp. 139–163). New York: Psychology Press.

Wegner, D. M., Schneider, S. J., Carter, D. J., & White, T. L. (1987). Paradoxical effects of thought suppression. *Journal of Personality and Social Psychology, 53,* 5–13.

Wheeler, S. C., Briñol, P., & Hermann, A .D. (2007). Resistance to persuasion as self-regulation: Ego-depletion and its effects on attitude change processes. *Journal of Experimental Social Psychology, 43,* 150–156.

11

A Neuroaffective Perspective on Why People Fail to Live a Sustainable Lifestyle

JENNIFER N. GUTSELL and MICHAEL INZLICHT

A sustainable and environmentally friendly lifestyle provides a never-ending supply of everyday decisions: Do I leave the tap on or off while I shave? Should I buy the expensive energy-saving light bulbs? Should I drive to work or take the bike? Should I become a vegetarian? Although seemingly easy and minor, the mere number of decisions requires us to constantly be on guard; a sustainable lifestyle asks for strong self-control. When we are interested in whether or not a particular individual will act according to sustainable and pro-environmental standards, we need to ask two important questions. First, does this person have strong enough pro-environmental values required to motivate pro-environmental behavior? Second, does this person have the capacity to suppress their egoistic needs and change their behavior to act according to their pro-environmental values?

THE NATURE OF SELF-CONTROL

Although many people care about the environment and adopt goals to act in a sustainable and pro-environmental way, only a few people actually follow through with their good intentions. What is it that enables these people to overcome their selfish and immediate needs, such as enjoying the comfort of driving, experiencing the thrill of consuming, or running the air conditioning at full blast? Most likely, what distinguishes those who follow through with their good intentions as opposed to those who do not is the effectiveness of their self-control mechanisms.

Self-control refers to the mental effort individuals use to bring their own behavior in line with a preferred state—a goal (Muraven & Baumeister, 2000). When we engage in self-control, we effortfully override a predominant response, such as the urge to eat the steak, with another behavior, such as choosing the veggie stir fry, in order to attain a goal, such as maintaining a vegetarian diet. According to cybernetic models of self-control (Wiener, 1948; see also Carver & Scheier, 1981), the goal serves as a reference value to which a monitoring process compares the current state. If this comparison detects a discrepancy between the goal and the current state, an error signal is sent out to an operating system, and attempts to change the current state are initiated. The new state is then again compared to the goal and, if necessary, further change is initiated. As long as this process reduces the discrepancy fast and efficiently, it runs smoothly and automatically. However, if the discrepancy remains and the goal is blocked, for example, when there are no vegetarian options on the menu, negative emotions arise and the process soon becomes conscious and effortful (Carver, 2004). In the same way, when the process reduces the discrepancy at a pace faster than expected, we feel positive emotions. Therefore, emotions are an essential part of self-control. Their general purpose is to help the organism to meet challenges and opportunities (Levenson, 1994). Emotions, in other words, are for acting; we experience emotions when something important is at stake; they are what motivates us to strive for a goal in the first place, and we become painfully aware of them when a goal is blocked (Lewis & Todd, 2005).

Effective self-control, therefore, requires four components. First, we need a clear and specific goal; second, we need emotions to energize and motivate self-control; third, we need an intact monitoring system that is vigilant and can correctly identify any differences between the goal and the current state; and finally, we need an intact operating system that can initiate the necessary changes.

In this chapter we propose that strong moral values are beneficial to self-control because violations of moral values result in strong emotional reactions, motivating people to engage in self-control in order to correct the situation. Moreover, strong moral values can automate the self-control process, thus saving resources and making the process more efficient. We further propose that our brains evolved in a way that certain kinds of moral values elicit stronger emotional reactions than others, and thus can motivate sustainable behavior better. Finally, we propose that one particular kind of moral value—the values related to purity and sanctity and the associated emotion of disgust—is an especially powerful motivator for sustainable behavior. We will begin by taking a closer look at the neural processes underlying self-control in order to gain a deeper understanding of how emotions influence it.

SELF-CONTROL IN THE BRAIN

To learn about the neural mechanisms of self-control, we take a look at the four components of self-control—the goal, the emotions, the operating process, and the monitoring process. Goals are represented in memory and therefore depend on the brain structures involved in semantic memory such as the hippocampus and its surrounding areas, the medial temporal lobe, the diencephalon, and the basal forebrain (Zola-Morgan & Squire, 1993). Since the specifics of the neural mechanisms involved in memory would not provide any further insight into self-control, we will not elaborate on these mechanisms further.

The functional neuroanatomy of emotions is complex and includes evolutionarily very old regions, such as the brain stem and hypothalamus, and relatively new and more flexible structures in the cerebral cortex (Todd & Lewis, 2008). The brain stem, the evolutionarily oldest part of the brain, includes nuclei that are responsible for our most basic motivational drives. These drives can be organized in four basic systems (Panksepp, 1998): the seeking system, which underlies appetitive approach behaviors; the rage system, which is triggered by frustrated goals; the fear system, which is associated with avoidance behavior; and the panic system, which underlies attachment behaviors. The brain stem produces neurochemicals, such as dopamine and norepinephrine, which allow the drives to influence other, higher-order brain areas including the hypothalamus that might trigger a stress response and release stress hormones into the bloodstream (Panksepp, 1998), and the limbic system that modulates behavioral responses and is involved in memory and learning (Tucker, Derryberry, & Luu, 2000). Finally the cortex is also involved in emotional processing. Especially the paralimbic structures, such as the anterior cingulate cortex (ACC) and the ventral prefrontal cortex (V-PFC), receive emotional signals from the brain stem and the limbic system and use this information to modulate attention, perception, and action (Bechara, Damasio, & Damasio, 2000). Through the paralimbic system, the subcortical structures can subtly influence cognitive processing such as decision making and behavioral control in service of the ancient basic drives that set the agendas for behavior. This bottom-up flow of emotional action tendencies provides the energy and direction for behavior and, at the same time, the top-down control processes ensure that we do not inflexibly follow our impulses and basic reflexive behavior (Tucker et al., 2000).

The monitoring and control of behavior is associated with activation in the dorsolateral prefrontal cortex (DLPFC; Spence & Frith, 1999)—predominantly associated with control processes—and two paralimbic cortical regions: the orbitofrontal cortex (OFC) and the ACC (Bechara, Damasio, Tranel, & Damasio, 1997; Botvinick et al., 2001; Kerns, Cohen, MacDonald, Cho, Stenger, & Carter, 2004; Ochsner et al., 2004), predominantly associated with monitoring processes.

The DLPFC has been associated with planning, working memory, selective attention (Chao & Knight, 1998), and most importantly, the selection and initiation of action (Spence & Frith, 1999). Consequently, damage to the DLPFC results in apathy (Dimitrov et al., 1999). As paralimbic structures, the ACC and the OFC receive input from subcortical brain areas, such the limbic system and the brain stem (Paus, 2001) and are also connected to prefrontal areas. The OFC is implicated in reward and inhibition processes (Elliott, Dolan, & Frith, 2000), specifically in monitoring reward values and suppressing previously rewarding responses that no longer are associated with reward (Elliott et al., 2000). The ACC is involved in conflict monitoring and error detection and is part of a circuit that regulates both cognitive and emotional processing (Bush, Luu, & Posner, 2000). Moreover, it is involved in the generation of intention, and signals the command for execution to other brain areas, such as the DLPFC (Luu, Tucker, & Derryberry, 1998). It is this signal for behavioral intentions to which we now turn.

In electroencephalographic (EEG) studies, activation of the monitoring system is associated with a component of the event-related potential (ERP) called the *error-related negativity* (ERN) (Falkenstein, Hohnsbein, Hoorman, & Blanke, 1990; Gehring, Goss, Coles, Meyer, & Donchin, 1993). The ERN is a negative voltage deflection in the ERP after an incorrect response in reaction time tasks. It originates in the ACC (Van Veen & Carter, 2002) and is said to reflect the affective reaction to discrepancies between the actual and the correct response. Therefore, we can describe the ERN as the signal for behavioral control sent by the monitoring system to the operating system. Interestingly, ERN amplitude decreases when people's ability to self-control is reduced. In a study investigating the neural processes involved in self-control failure, Inzlicht and Gutsell (2007) found that after people engaged in self-control in an initial task, their ERN amplitude was decreased in a subsequent self-control reaction-time task. Interestingly, this decrease in ERN amplitude was correlated with, and in fact mediated by, subsequent decreases in task performance on a Stroop task (Inzlicht & Gutsell, 2007).

These findings suggest that a state of reduced self-control ability is associated with reduced affective reactions to one's own errors. Could it be that people stopped caring about their bad performance? Did they fail the subsequent self-control task because they did not feel the "pain" of failure? The results of this one study (Inzlicht & Gutsell, 2007) and that of others (e.g., Gutsell & Inzlicht, 2012a; Moser, Most, & Simons, 2010) suggests yes. Emotions are indeed an essential part of self-control. In terms of maintaining sustainable behavior, this indicates the following: even if we have a clear environmental goal and even if we realize that going to a fast food chain after a stressful day is not in line with our goal, as long as we do not feel strongly about the goal and feel the pain induced by deviating from it, we will not have the energy to overcome our urge to have a yummy burger.

In the remainder of the chapter we propose that pro-environmental issues are not emotionally charged enough to motivate people to act in a sustainable way. We need salient goals and powerful motivation to engage in self-control, but when it comes to abstract environmental goals, people often lack one essential component of self-control—emotion.

STRONG MORAL INTUITIONS PROVIDE THE EMOTIONS TO FUEL SELF-CONTROL

People's strongest values are their moral values. Moral values predict intentions to act and actual behavior (Schwartz, 1977), and they do so better than mere attitudes without the moral connotation (Godin, Conner, & Sheeran, 2005). The reason for this superiority seems to lie in the strengths of the emotional reactions elicited by violations of moral values.

The rationalist tradition, evolved from theorists such as Kohlberg (1969), Piaget (1932), and Turiel (1983), emphasizes the role of deliberate cognitive processes; when people decide how one should act in a certain situation, they reach the solution primarily by a process of reasoning and reflection (Haidt, 2001). Recently the rationalist model has been challenged by the idea that our moral decisions result from strong emotional reactions to the moral subject in question. When people make decisions that concern their moral values, they get very emotional and feel strong implicit tendencies to act according to their values. These moral intuitions (Haidt, 2001) guide moral behavior in an automatic and effortless way.

Indeed, moral intuitions often express themselves through strong affective reactions—something that is generally called a gut feeling—and people often use their gut feelings as a source of information when they make decisions (Batson et al., 2007; Haidt, 2007). For example, when people receive false feedback on how strong their body's psychophysiological reaction to certain moral issues are, they later give more priority to the moral issue that they thought their body reacted to the most (Haidt, 2001). Thus, the participants relied on their body's psychophysiological reactions—their gut feelings—to judge moral issues. Moreover, using fMRI, Greene, Sommerville, Nystrom, Darley, and Cohen (2001) showed that when people are confronted with moral dilemmas in which the rationally correct response would be to act against strong intuitive emotional response tendencies, they have a harder time solving the dilemma as indicated by longer response times. For example, when Greene and colleagues' participants judged a personal dilemma—for example, whether it would be OK to push a person in front of a trolley in order to save the lives of five other people—they were less likely to agree than when they would merely have to press a button that would direct the trolley to another track where it would kill one person instead of five—a more impersonal dilemma. Interestingly, the only differences in brain activity for the personal and the impersonal dilemmas were found in the medial frontal gyrus, the angular gyrus, and the posterior cingulate gyrus—all areas previously associated with emotional processing (Harenski, Antonenko, Shane, & Kiehl, 2010). Moreover, those few who actually decided that pushing the person was appropriate took much longer to respond, possibly indicating interference of the strong emotional response with the deliberate, rational judgment. Therefore, the degree to which a moral issue engages our emotions determines the strength of our moral intuitions and the ease of those decisions.

The implication is that strong moral values elicit strong emotional reactions when violated. This makes moral values potential powerful motivators for sustainable behavior. If sustainability became a moral issue, people should feel these strong emotional reactions whenever they engage in nonsustainable behavior, motivating them to change their behavior and to take action.

Because of the strong influence that emotions have on our moral decisions, moral values that elicit very strong emotional reactions when violated can be almost inviolable—the individual feels so strongly about these values that a violation would cause a sudden very strong feeling of repulsion just by the thought of such a violation. People are extremely reluctant to make trade-offs when such "sacred" values are at stake (Tanner, 2009). In other words, they do not apply the same criteria of costs versus benefits to their most sacred moral values.

Research on prejudice reduction has shown that people for whom egalitarian values are self-determined, internalized, and sacred, and for whom these values have strong personal significance, can automatically suppress prejudice (Legault, Green-Demers, & Eadie, 2009). Thus it seems that strong, emotionally charged, moral values—our sacred values—have the capacity to automate our behavior, thereby making willful control of moral behavior unnecessary. In the same way, strong, emotionally charged, pro-sustainability values could facilitate sustainable behavior by automating it, thereby circumventing the necessity of constant, active behavioral control.

Providing people with strong moral values that have the potential to elicit strong emotional reactions when violated could boost people's capability to self-control in three important ways. First, having pro-environmental moral values would make behavioral goals, such as recycling, salient and easily accessible and would therefore facilitate monitoring the progress in goal attainment. Second, strong moral intuitions associated with pro-environmental values would elicit a strong affective reaction to any failure to act according to these values—most likely associated with an increased activity in the ACC, therefore providing a strong signal for behavioral change to the prefrontal operating system. Finally, moral pro-environmental values might even be central and important enough for the person to automate sustainable behavior and thus might facilitate the operating process in self-control. Once sustainable behavior becomes auto-matic, effortful self-control would be unnecessary, thereby saving people's self-control resources.

PROMOTING THE "RIGHT KIND" OF MORAL VALUES

How strongly we feel about an issue depends to a large degree on why we think it is important. We know that strong emotional reactions are necessary for good self-control, and strong moral values can elicit such strong emotional reactions when violated. The question now is whether all types of moral values are equally well suited to motivate sustainable behavior.

Research on morality has long been almost exclusively focused on two impor-tant moral domains. The first is empathy-related moral concern, where the cen-tral criterion to discern right from wrong is whether another person or entity gets hurt—people care for the environment because they feel with and for the plants, animals, and people. The second is fairness-related moral concern, which is pri-marily concerned with whether or not someone is treated fairly—people care for the environment because it's not fair to future generations to destroy natural resources (Haidt & Graham, 2007).

According to Haidt and Graham's (2007) five-foundation model of morality, the empathy-related domain (harm/care) evolved from our natural instinct to protect and nurture our children and relatives. It is based on altruism and our capacity to feel the emotion of compassion. The fairness-related moral domain (fairness/justice) evolved from the need to have a functional community and is based on ide-als of reciprocity and equal respect. Although harm/care and fairness/justice seem to have evolved based on distinct evolutionary selection pressures, they are both part of our social behavioral repertoire. When we decide to buy an environmen-tally friendly laundry detergent, we might do that because we do not want other people or animals to get hurt by toxins in the rivers and drinking water—a harm/care value. Alternatively, we might choose the detergent because we think it's not fair for future generations if we keep on destroying our natural resources—a fairness/justice value. In both cases it is about others; our behavior is driven by social concerns about protecting individuals (Haidt & Graham, 2007) and most likely depends on our social abilities.

Showing that the moral domains of harm/care and fairness/justice indeed rely on social abilities such as cognitive and emotional perspective taking and empathy, Robertson (2006) demonstrated that sensitivity to moral issues is associated with activity in many brain areas that are involved in social processing. While participants looked at pictures depicting harm/care-related and fairness/justice-related moral issues, the polar medial prefrontal cortex, the dorsal posterior cingulated cortex, and the posterior superior temporal sulcus where active—areas that, among other functions, have been previously related to cognitive and emotional perspective taking (Frith & Frith, 2001, Ruby & Decety, 2001), imitation (Chaminade, Meltzoff, & Decety, 2002), and monitoring of one's own and others' mental states (Frith & Frith, 2001). Thus, both harm/care and fairness/justice rely on people's ability to empathize with those affected by our moral decisions.

However, such a focus on a social morality that is based on empathy for individuals becomes problematic when the issue at hand is not about individuals, such as the destruction of pristine and remote natural environments, or if it concerns people who are very much distinct or unfamiliar to the person who makes the moral decision. Research on empathy suggests that empathy is limited to close others and those who are similar to us and are familiar to us (e.g., Gutsell & Inzlicht, 2010a). Thus harm/care and fairness/justice might be insufficient to motivate people when the problem at hand extends outside of this closed circle of close familiar and similar others.

THE LIMITATIONS OF THE HARM/CARE AND FAIRNESS/JUSTICE MORAL DOMAINS

The individual-focused morality in Western societies is based on psychological and biological systems that evolved from life in small groups. Our ability to empathize particularly well with those to whom we feel connected, therefore, may have been biologically hardwired through natural selection. According to the concept of inclusive fitness, empathy and prosocial behavior are determined by their contribution to reproductive success in ancestral environments (Hamilton, 1964). From an evolutionary perspective, it makes much more sense to help those who share our genes or who are phenotypically similar to us—a sign of genetic similarity (Hamilton, 1964). Moreover, it makes sense to help those who are part of our group and with whom we are familiar (Krebs, 1991). This selection pressure seems to have shaped us in such a way that our neural networks for empathy are specifically responsive to people to whom, for one reason or another, we feel a strong connection.

According to the action–perception model of empathy (Preston & de Waal, 2002), people understand others' emotions by simulating these emotions. When someone (the subject) observes another (the object) experiencing emotions, the object's body and facial expressions activate the subject's neural networks for the same expressions (Dimberg, Thunberg, & Elmehed, 2000). Expressing the emo-tion elicits the associated autonomic and somatic responses, which then generate the emotional experience (Decety & Jackson, 2004). Hence, the subject has access to the object's inner states because the mere perception activates the same neural networks in the subject. By adopting the object's inner states, the subject experi-ences these states and emotions firsthand and thus lays the foundation for empathy. This simulation in shared neural networks for action and perception is essential for all subsequent stages of empathy.

The system of neurons building these shared networks is called the *mirror neuron system* (Carr, Iacoboni, Dubeau, Mazziotta, & Lenzi, 2003) because dur-ing observation, this system "mirrors" the activation patterns that produce the action. This mirror system is a cortical network that consists of sensory motor areas in parts of the premotor cortex, the caudal part of the inferior frontal cor-tex, and the rostral part of the inferior parietal lobule (Decety & Lamm, 2007). However, this neural simulation mechanism extends to other areas of the brain depending on the specific nature of the mirrored stimulus. It is, thus, not limited to simple motor behavior but can pick up more abstract intentions and emotional states. Research using fMRI identified shared networks of observation and expe-rience for disgust (Wicker, Keysers, Plailly, Royet, Gallese, & Rizzolatti, 2003), pain (Singer, Seymour, O'Doherty, Kaube, Dolan, & Frith, 2006), touch (Keysers, Wicker, Gazzola, Anton, Fogassi, & Gallese, 2004), and facial expressions (Carr et al., 2003). For example, the observation of someone in pain activates the somato-sensory cortex, the anterior medial cingulated cortex, the cerebellum, and the anterior insula—areas also active when the observer experiences pain themselves (Singer et al., 2004). Thus, the perceiver "catches" the emotions and experiences of the object, and thereby automatically derives an intuitive understanding of the other. This process is automatic, without intention or conscious control. Yet our emotional networks are not triggered in every situation and for everyone.

From behavioral research we know that whether we empathize with someone or not depends on perceived similarity, familiarity (Wilson & Sober, 1998: 21), and affiliation with the target (Vignemont & Singer, 2006). Apes also empathize more with familiar apes who received electric shocks than with unfamiliar apes (Miller, Murphy, & Mirky, 1959). Moreover, in humans, emphatic concern for others is eliminated when one controls for "oneness"—the degree to which participants per-ceive themselves in the other (Cialdini, Brown, Lewis, Luce, & Neuberg, 1997). These biases seem to exist even on a neural level. Research on empathy for pain found that the observation of another person receiving painful stimuli activated the same networks as the experience of pain, but only when the observer liked the other person or was somehow affiliated with him or her (Singer et al., 2006; Xu, Zuo, Wang, & Han, 2009).

The neural simulation process is also constrained by our social categories and social attitudes. A recent fMRI study, for example, found that people show more neural activation in pain circuits when observing the painful penetration of the hands of ethnic in-group members than of out-group members (Xu, Zuo, Wang, & Han, 2009; see also Mathur, Harada, Lipke, & Chiao, 2010). Similarly, using transcranial magnetic simulation (TMS), Avenanti, Sirigu, & Aglioti (2010) found less corticospinal muscle inhibition when participants observed ethnic out-group members receiving painful stimuli than when observing the same thing happening to in-group members. Finally, using the electroencephalogram (EEG) to measure vicarious activations of motor cortex during observation of action, Gutsell and Inzlicht (2010) found that people simulate actions of ethnic out-group members less than those from ethnic in-group members and the degree of simulation decreases the more prejudiced people are toward out-groups. Based on these findings it seems that empathy is limited to close, familiar, and similar others and that the more distant the other is, the less empathy we feel.

WHERE DOES THAT LEAVE THE ENVIRONMENT?

If we do not intuitively catch the emotions of those who do not belong to our inner social circle, then we will have a harder time empathizing with them and, importantly, their suffering will not elicit the same strong emotional reactions that would the suffering of someone to whom we feel more connected. Therefore, because the individual-focused moral domains of harm/care and fairness/justice depend on those emotional reactions to others' suffering, they might be insufficient to elicit strong enough moral emotions to motivate sustainable behavior. Sustainable behavior often is targeted toward alleviating relatively abstract environmental problems. For example, when we recycle, we often do not see a direct relation to our own well-being or the well-being of close others. Most likely it is hard for people to relate to abstract constructs such as biodiversity or the climate. Although easier, it will also be problematic to relate to the millions suffering from the lack of natural resources in faraway countries, or to animal species people have never seen.

Generally, most people would agree that they care for the environment and probably most people have at least some goals that are related to a sustainable lifestyle, but for most people, the problems that sustainable behavior aims to alleviate are rather abstract. For example, more than 50% of the people in the United States agree with the statement that climate change is a very serious problem (United Nations Development Program, 2007). However, when asked what they worry most about when thinking about climate change, people were most concerned about the impact on people around the world and nature. Only a minority was actually concerned about the impacts on themselves, their families, and their communities. This might explain why people often do not act in a sustainable way to prevent climate change although they agree that it is a serious problem. When people do not see how climate change would affect them personally, or close others, their empathic brains might simply shut down leaving them without the necessary emotional "fuel" for self-control. Although they might have good intentions, those people will fall back into their old nonsustainable habits the minute being green becomes effortful and requires them to restrain their selfish impulses.

Given that environmental issues are likely excluded from our inner social circle and empathy toward entities of the environment does not come to us naturally, a possible solution could be to actively foster empathy for the environment. Cognitive perspective taking, for example, has been shown to increase interpersonal sensitivity and understanding (Galinsky & Moskowitz, 2000). It can also increase helping (Batson, Chang, & Orr, 2002) and foster self–other merging (Galinsky, Ku, & Wang, 2005)—the individual feels more connected and similar to another person or object. Research on environmentalism suggests that inducing empathy through cognitive perspective taking is indeed a potent technique for increasing environmental concern and promoting pro-environmental behavior (Berenguer, 2007; Schultz, 2000). For example, research participants who took the perspective of an animal or a tree being harmed by human activity allocated more funding to environmental projects as opposed to other prosocial causes (Berenguer, 2007). Interestingly, perspective taking seems to exert its beneficial effects on empathy not simply by making people care enough to compensate for their lack of empathy, but by targeting the very basis of empathy—the neural simulation process itself. In a recent study, Gutsell and Inzlicht (2012b) had participants either take the perspective of a person while writing about a day in this person's life or try to be as objective as possible and to avoid taking the perspective while writing. Participants who took the perspective later showed more motor neuron activity while watching videos of strangers performing simple actions. These findings suggest, that perspective taking can facilitate the mirroring process and could, therefore, be a powerful tool to increase empathy for the environment. However, perspective taking seems to have its limits: Although, participants in Berenguer's (2007) study did show more pro-environmental behavior after having taken the perspective of a harmed bird or harmed trees, perspective taking was less effective when the targets were trees. Thus, although empathy-related biases could be alleviated through interventions that foster perspective taking, it might be comparatively harder when plants or the nonliving environment are concerned. Particularly for very abstract environmental issues it might, thus, be necessary to take a different approach.

DISGUST—AN ALTERNATIVE FUEL FOR SUSTAINABLE BEHAVIOR

As described above, most researchers have seen and still see morality as essentially concerned with protecting individuals. Human morality, however, does not end with harm/care and justice/fairness. Haidt and Joseph (2004) proposed that there are actually five psychological systems or moral foundations that each evolved independently and provide every human with a preparedness that creates affective reactions to certain patterns in the social environment. Cultures build their individual sets of moral virtues and vices on these universal and fundamental moral foundations and thus in different cultures, each moral foundation might be differently pronounced.

The individual-based foundations of harm/care and fairness/justice are only two of these five foundations. In addition the model includes two group-based moral foundations: (1) in-group/ loyalty, which evolved from living in kin-based groups, is concerned with the welfare of the in-group and promotes virtues such as loyalty, patriotism, and conformity; and (2) authority/respect, which evolved from life in hierarchically structured in-groups, promotes virtues such as respect, duty, and obedience. Finally, the model includes purity/sanctity. In contrast to all four other domains, purity/sanctity did not evolve from selection pressures posed by life in small groups, but from food selection. When humans started to include meat in their diet at the same time as their brains started to grow rapidly, they developed the uniquely human emotions of disgust (Rozin, Haidt, & McCauley, 2000). Although disgust initially served to facilitate the oral rejection of harmful or distasteful substances (Rozin & Fallon, 1987), during our evolutionary history, it evolved to extend to social and moral domains. Consequently, disgust not only guides our food preferences but also shapes our moral values and judgments.

People report finding immoral acts disgusting (Rozin et al., 2000) and they punish people when they are disgusted by their unfair behavior (Chapman, Kim, Susskind, & Anderson, 2009). Due to their evolutionary origin, social and moral disgust still function very much like physical disgust. For example, immoral behavior elicits the typical facial disgust expression (Chapman et al., 2009) and the same neural structures are involved in the experience of physical and moral disgust (Moll et al., 2005). Research participants who read scenarios designed to evoke pure disgust versus moral disgust or indignation show similar activity in the lateral and medial orbitofrontal cortex, areas involved in diverse reward and food-related processing.

Because disgust—a powerful moral emotion—did not evolve from life in small groups, but from an entirely nonsocial domain, it likely is not restricted to our immediate social environment. Therefore, purity/sanctity—the moral foundation strongly associated with disgust—is likely a moral value that could include those abstract environmental issues that do not immediately concern other people or focus on nonliving concepts such as pristine mountain lakes or the climate.

Disgust evolved from the concern that objects are pure, clean, and not contaminated. When it evolved to a moral emotion, it seems to have maintained this focus on objects and extended to include abstract concepts. In many cultures, purity/sanctity and the related disgust support a set of virtues and vices that aim to keep the body clean and the soul pure. Common purity/sanctity concerns are about chastity and spirituality. One should not engage in carnal passions such as lust or gluttony, because that would taint the body and thereby taint the soul (Haidt & Joseph, 2005). These concerns work similarly with objects; most people would be horrified if someone would spit on a church floor or on a flag, because this physical taint is strongly associated with the taint of something spiritual and sacred. Disgust is a powerful motivator, and because it is not social in nature, it may not be limited by the same social boundaries as the individual-focused moral emotions, such as compassion and a sense of fairness. Therefore, by making the environment a sacred place, by giving it a soul that needs to be protected and kept pure, we may be able to create powerful motivations to protect the environment.

CONCLUSION

If people would start to treat nature as something sacred, as something that cannot simply be used, but must remain pure, people would feel a strong moral obligation to protect the environment. This moral obligation would lead to a pang of disgust whenever people would see or think about the destruction of our planet, and most importantly, this disgust might make people truly care about whether they act according to their pro-environmental beliefs. A person with the purity/ sanctity moral value of "the earth is sacred and must not be destroyed" could adapt a behavioral goal such as "I will recycle." Should she fail to follow through with her intentions, throwing a whole pile of paper into the garbage because the recycling container is a few steps further down the street, she will literally feel disgusted by her behavior and this strong emotion will make her go those extra few steps. When not recycling represents a violation of something sacred, engaging in sustainable behavior becomes easy and almost automatic, therefore saving cognitive rescores and making a sustainable lifestyle possible, even under stress or other constraints.

REFERENCES

Avenanti, A., Sirigu, A., & Aglioti, S. M. (2010). Racial bias reduces empathic sensorimotor resonance with other-race pain. *Current Biology, 20,* 1028–1022.

Batson, C. D., Chang, J., & Orr, R. (2002). Empathy, attitudes, and action: Can feeling for a member of a stigmatized group motivate one to help the group? *Personality and Social Psychology Bulletin, 28,* 1656–1666.

Batson, C. D., Eklund, J. H, Chermok, V. L., Hoyt, J. L., & Ortiz, B. G., (2007). An additional antecedent of empathic concern: Valuing the welfare of the person in need. *Journal of Personality and Social Psychology, 93,* 65–74.

Bechara, A., Damasio, H., & Damasio, A. R. (2000). Emotion, decision making, and the orbitofrontal cortex. *Cerebral Cortex, 10,* 295–307.

Bechara, A., Damasio, H., Tranel, D., & Damasio, A. R. (1997). Deciding advantageously before knowing the advantageous strategy. *Science, 275,* 1293–1294.

Berenguer, J. (2007). The effects of empathy in proenvironmental attitudes and behaviors. *Environment and Behavior, 39,* 269–283.

Botvinick, M. M., Braver, T. S., Barch, D. M., Carter, C. S., & Cohen, J. D. (2001). Conflict monitoring and cognitive control. *Psychological Review, 108,* 624–652.

Bush, G., Luu, P., & Posner, M. I. (2000). Cognitive and emotional influences in anterior cingulate cortex. *Trends in Cognitive Sciences, 4,* 215–222.

Carr, L., Iacoboni, M., Dubeau, M., Mazziotta, J. C., & Lenzi, G. L. (2003). Neural mechanisms of empathy in humans: A relay from neural systems for imitation to limbic areas. *Proceedings of the National Academy of Sciences, 100,* 5497–5502.

Carver, C. S. (2004). Self-regulation of action and affect. In R. F. Baumeister & K. D. Vohs (Eds.), *Handbook of self-regulation: Research, theory, and applications* (pp. 62–83). New York: Guilford Press.

Carver, C. S., & Scheier, M. F. (1981). The self-attention-induced feedback loop and social facilitation. *Journal of Experimental Social Psychology, 17,* 545–568.

Chaminade, T., Meltzoff, A. N., & Decety, J. (2002) Does the end justify the means? A PET exploration of the mechanisms involved in human imitation. *NeuroImage 15,* 318–328.

Chao, L. L., & Knight, R. T. (1998). Contribution of human prefrontal cortex to delay performance. *Journal of Cognitive Neuroscience, 10,* 167–177.

Chapman H. A., Kim D. A., Susskind J. M., & Anderson A. K. (2009). In bad taste: Evidence for the oral origins of moral disgust. *Science, 323,* 1222–1226.

Cialdini, R. B., Brown, S. L., Lewis, B. P., Luce, C., & Neuberg, S. L. (1997). Reinterpreting the empathy–altruism relationship: When one into one equals oneness. *Journal of Personality and Social Psychology, 73,* 481–494.

Decety, J., & Jackson, P. (2004). The functional architecture of human empathy. *Behavioral and Cognitive Neuroscience Reviews, 3,* 71–100.

Decety, J. & Lamm, C. (2007). The role of the right temporoparietal junction in social interaction: How low-level computational processes contribute to meta-cognition. *The Neuroscientist, 13*, 580–593.

Dimberg, U., Thunberg, M., & Elmehed, K. (2000).Unconscious facial reactions to emotional facial expressions. *Psychological Science, 11*, 86–89.

Dimitrov, M., Granetz, J., Peterson, M., Hollnagel, C., Alexander, G., & Grafman, J. (1999). Associative learning impairments in patients with frontal lobe damage. *Brain and Cognition, 41*, 213–230.

Elliot, R., Dolan, R. J., & Frith, C. D. (2000). Dissociable functions in the medial and lateral orbitofrontal cortex: Evidence from human neuroimaging studies. *Cerebral Cortex, 10*, 308–317.

Falkenstein, M., Hohnsbein, J., Hoormann, J., & Blanke, L. (1990). Effects of errors in choice reaction tasks on the ERP under focused and divided attention. In C. H. M. Brunia, A. W. K. Gaillard, & A. Kok (Eds.), *Psychophysiological Brain Research, 1*, 192–195.

Frith, U., & Frith, C. (2001). The biological basis of social interaction. *Current Directions in Psychological Science, 10*, 151–155.

Galinsky, A. D., Ku, G., & Wang, C. S. (2005). Perspective-taking and self–other overlap: Fostering social bonds and facilitating social coordination. *Group Processes and Intergroup Relations, 8*, 109–124.

Galinsky, A. D., & Moskowitz, G. B. (2000). Perspective-taking: Decreasing stereotype expression, stereotype accessibility, and in-group favoritism. *Journal of Personality and Social Psychology, 78*, 708–724.

Gehring, W. J., Goss, B., Coles, M. G., Meyer, D. E., & Donchin, E. (1993). A neural system for error detection and compensation. *Psychological Science, 4*, 385–390.

Godin, G., Conner, M., & Sheeran, P. (2005). Bridging the intention–behaviour "gap": The role of moral norm. *British Journal of Social Psychology, 44*, 497–512.

Greene, J. D., Sommerville, R. B., Nystrom, L. E., Darley, J. M., & Cohen, J. D. (2001). An fMRI investigation of emotional engagement in moral judgment. *Science, 293*, 2105–2108.

Gutsell, J. N., & Inzlicht, M. (2010). Empathy constrained: Prejudice predicts reduced mental simulation of actions during observation of outgroups. *Journal of Experimental Social Psychology, 46*, 841–845.

Gutsell, J. N., & Inzlicht, M. (2012a). Cognitive resource depletion reduces negative affect. Unpublished manuscript.

Gutsell, J. N., & Inzlicht, M. (2012b). Perspective taking reduces group biases in neural motor resonance. Unpublished manuscript.

Haidt, J. (2001). The emotional dog and its rational tail: A social intuitionist approach to moral judgment. *Psychological Review, 108*, 814–834.

Haidt, J. (2007). The new synthesis in moral psychology. *Science, 31*, 998–1002.

Haidt, J., & Graham, J. (2007). When morality opposes justice: Conservatives have moral intuitions that liberals may not recognize. *Social Justice Research, 20*, 98–116.

Haidt, J., & Joseph, C. (2004). Intuitive ethics: How innately prepared intuitions generate culturally variable virtues. *Daedalus: Special Issue on Human Nature, 133*, 55–66.

Hamilton, W. D. (1964). The genetical evolution of social behavior. *Journal of Theoretical Biology, 7*, 17–52.

Harenski, C. L., Antonenko, O., Shane, M. S., & Kiehl, K. A. (2010). A functional imaging investigation of moral deliberation and moral intuition. *NeuroImage, 49*, 2707–2716.

Inzlicht, M., & Gutsell, J. N. (2007). Running on empty: Neural signals for self-control failure. *Psychological Science, 18*, 933–937.

Kerns, J. G., Cohen, J. D., MacDonald, A. W. III., Cho, R. Y., Stenger, V. A., & Carter, C. S. (2004). Anterior cingulate conflict monitoring and adjustments in control. *Science, 303*, 1023–1026.

Keysers, C., Wicker, B., Gazzola, V., Anton, J. L., Fogassi, L., & Gallese, V. (2004). A touching sight: SII/PV activation during the observation and experience of touch. *Neuron, 42*, 335–346.

Kohlberg. L. (1969). Stage and sequence: The cognitive-developmental approach to socialization. In D. A. Goslin (Ed.), *Handbook of socialization theory and research* (pp. 347–480). Chicago: Rand McNally.

Krebs, D. L. (1991). Altruism and egoism: A false dichotomy? *Psychological Inquiry, 2*, 137–139.

Legault, L., Green-Demers, I., & Eadie, A. L. (2009). When internalization leads to automatization: The role of self-determination in automatic stereotype suppression and implicit prejudice regulation. *Motivation and Emotion, 33*, 10–24.

Levenson, R. W. (1994). Human emotions: A functional view. In P. Ekman & R. J. Davidson (Eds.), *The nature of emotion: Fundamental questions* (pp. 123–126). New York: Oxford University Press.

Lewis, M. D., & Todd, R. M. (2005). Getting emotional: A neural perspective on emotion, intention, and consciousness. *Journal of Consciousness Studies, 12*, 210–235.

Luu, P., Tucker, D.M., & Derryberry, D. (1998). Anxiety and the motivational basis of working memory. *Cognitive Therapy and Research, 22*, 577–594.

Mathur, V. A., Harada, T., Lipke, T., & Chiao, J. Y. (2010). Neural basis of extraordinary empathy and altruistic motivation. *NeuroImage, 51*, 1468–1475.

Miller, R. E., Murphy, J. V., & Mirky, I. A. (1959). Non-verbal communication of affect. *Journal of Clinical Psychology, 15*, 155–158.

Moll, J., de Oliveira-Souza, R., Moll, F. T., Ignácio, F. A., Bramati, I. E., Caparelli-Dáquer, E. M., et al. (2005). The moral affiliations of disgust. *Cognitive and Behavioral Neurology, 18*, 68–78.

Moser, J. S., Most, S. B., & Simons, R. F. (2010). Increasing negative emotions by reappraisal enhances subsequent cognitive control: A combined behavioral and electrophysiological study. *Cognitive, Affective, & Behavioral Neuroscience, 10*, 195–207.

Muraven, M., & Baumeister, R. F. (2000). Self-regulation and depletion of limited resources. Does self-control resemble a muscle? *Psychological Bulletin, 126*, 247–259.

Ochsner, K. N., Ray, R. D., Cooper, J. C., Robertson, E. R., Chopra, S., Gabrieli, J. D. E., & Gross, J. J. (2004). For better or for worse: Neural systems supporting the cognitive down- and up-regulation of negative emotion. *Neuroimage, 23*, 483–499.

Panksepp, J. (1998). *Affective neuroscience: The foundations of human and animal emotions.* New York: Oxford University Press.

Paus, T. (2001). Primate anterior cingulate cortex: Where motor control, drive and cognition interface. *Nature Reviews Neuroscience, 2*, 417–424.

Piaget, J. (1965). *The moral judgement of the child* (M. Gabain, Trans.). New York: Free Press. (Original work published 1932).

Preston, S. D., & de Waal, F. B. M., (2002). Empathy: Its ultimate and proximate bases. *Behavioral and Brain Science, 25*, 1–72.

Robertson, D., Snarey, J., Ousley, O., Harenski, K., Bowman, F.D., Gilkey, R., & Kilts, C. (2007). The neural processing of moral sensitivity to issues of justice and care. *Neuropsychologia, 45*, 755–766.

Rozin P., & Fallon A. E. (1987) A perspective on disgust. *Psychological Review, 94*, 23–41.

Rozin, P., Haidt, J., & McCauley, C. R. (2000). Disgust. In M. Lewis & J. M. Haviland-Jones (Eds.), *Handbook of emotions* (2nd ed., pp. 637–653). New York: Guilford Press.

Ruby, P., & Decety, J. (2001). Effect of subjective perspective taking during simulation of action: A PET investigation of agency. *Nature Neuroscience, 4*, 546–550.

Schultz, P. W. (2000). Empathizing with nature: The effects of perspective taking on concern for environmental issues. *Journal of Social Issues, 56,* 391–406.

Schwartz, S. H. (1977). Normative influences on altruism. In L. Berkowitz (Ed.), *Advances in experimental social psychology* (Vol. 10, pp. 221–279). New York: Academic Press.

Singer, T., Seymour, B., O'Doherty, J., Kaube, H., Dolan, R. J., & Frith, C. D. (2004). Empathy for pain involves the affective but not sensory components of pain. *Science, 303,* 1157–1162.

Singer, T., Seymour, B., O'Doherty, J. P., Stephan, K. E., Raymond , J. D., & Frith, C. D. (2006). Empathic neural responses are modulated by the perceived fairness of others. *Nature, 439,* 466–469.

Spence, S. A., & Frith, C. D. (1999). Towards a functional anatomy of volition. *Journal of Consciousness Studies, 6,* 11–29.

Tanner, C. (2009). To act or not to act: Nonconsequentialism in environmental decisionmaking. *Ethics & Behavior, 19,* 479–495.

Todd, R. M, & Lewis, M. D. (2008). Self-regulation in the developing brain. In J. Reed & J.Warner-Rogers (Eds.), *Child neuropsychology: Concepts, theory and practice* (pp. 285-315). London: Wiley-Blackwell.

Todd, R. M., Lewis, M. D., Meusel, L. A., & Zelazo, P. D. (2008). The time course of social-emotional processing in early childhood: ERP responses to facial affect and personal familiarity in a Go-Nogo task. *Neuropsychologia, 46,* 595–613.

Tucker, D. M., Derryberry, D., & Luu, P. (2000). Anatomy and physiology of human emotion: Vertical integration of brain stem, limbic, and cortical systems. In J. C. Borod (Ed.), *The Neuropsychology of Emotion* (pp. 56–79). New York: Oxford University Press.

Turiel, E. (1983). *The development of social knowledge: Morality and convention.* Cambridge, UK: Cambridge University Press.

United Nations Development Programme (2007). Human development report 2007/2008: *Fighting climate change: Human solidarity in a divided world.* Retrieved from http://hdr.undp.org/en/reports/global/hr2007-8/.

Van Veen, V., & Carter, C. S. (2002). The anterior cingulate as a conflict monitor: fMRI and ERP studies. *Physiology & Behavior, 77,* 477– 482.

Vignemont, F., & Singer, T. (2006). The empathic brain: How, when and why? *Trends in Cognitive Sciences, 10,* 435–441.

Wicker, B., Keysers, C., Plailly, J., Royet, J., Gallese, V., & Rizzolatti, G. (2003). Both of us disgusted in my insula: The common neural basis of seeing and feeling disgust. *Neuron, 40,* 655–664.

Wiener, N. (1948). *Cybernetics: Or control and communication in the animal and machine.* Cambridge, MA: MIT Press.

Wilson D. S., & Sober, E. (1999). Multilevel selection and the return of group-level functionalism. *Behavioral and Brain Sciences, 21,* 305–306.

Xu, X., Zuo, Z., Wang, W., & Han, S. (2009). Do you feel my pain? Racial group membership modulates empathic neural responses. *The Journal of Neuroscience, 29,* 8525–8529.

Zola-Morgan, S., & Squire, L. R. (1993). Neuroanatomy of memory. *Annual Review Neuroscience,* 547–563.

Section 5

Making Sustainability Personally Relevant

12

Acting on Emotion

MARCEL ZEELENBERG and JANNE VAN DOORN

O ur behavioral choices are only rarely the result of a conscious evaluation of all possible courses of action and their potential future consequences. Often we simply act as we feel and follow our gut reactions toward some object or action. If something does not feel right, it is likely that we refrain from doing it. The decision not to litter, for example, typically does not stem from calculations of the costs and benefits of this behavior, weighted by their importance and likelihood of occurrence and the persons incurring these costs and benefits, but more often simply follows from the fact that we feel bad about littering.

Of course, evaluations of the consequences of our choices may have been computed at some time earlier and our current feelings could be a reflection of those more elaborate evaluative processes, or alternatively, these evaluations may have been communicated to us by others, but the point here is that on a day-to-day basis we are more likely to act on how we feel about things than on explicit reasoning about the consequences. Moreover, it has long been known that we often lack the ability and the motivation for making all these calculations: we are only rational within the limits of our cognitive capacities (*bounded rationality*) and we often settle for outcomes that are good enough (*satisficing*), instead of aiming to maximize our outcomes (Simon, 1955, 1956). A recent review that centered on the question of whether conscious thoughts cause behavior concluded that its influence has often been overstated (Baumeister, Masicampo, & Vohs, 2011). Conscious deliberations do exist, but also often as a result of behavior, revealing the fact that rational choice is not very plausible if this refers to the process of making decisions. Importantly, the fact that we often turn to simpler choice strategies (such as relying on our feelings) has a big advantage. Especially under time pressure, these strategies may often outperform rational calculation because they are more efficient (Payne, Bettman, & Johnson, 1993). Thus, our bounded rationality may be helped by the fact that we have emotion. One of the things that emotion does is restrict the size of the consideration set (the alternatives that we inspect seriously) and focus the decision maker on certain relevant aspects of the alternative courses of action (Hanoch, 2001). Also, emotion helps in assigning value to objects and alternatives (they indicate what we find important) and may help us to obtain those by providing the motivation for doing so. Put differently, emotions often steer our choices and may do so more efficiently than rational evaluation of the options and their consequences.

It is important to stress that although behavioral choices do not stem from elaborate rational calculations, this does not make behavior less predictable and less understandable than when rational deliberation is driving our behavioral choices. We find this important because the dominant approach in most social and behavioral sciences for predicting behavioral choices is the theory of rational choice, or some variant of it. This theory, which is present in economics, sociology, psychology, and other social and behavioral sciences, assumes that we are aware of all possible courses of action, all consequences of each course of action and their likelihood of occurrence, and that we are able to integrate this information and use it to make a choice that maximizes our utility. Thus, more or less elaborate evaluations of outcomes are assumed to be made and the results of these are considered to be predictive of behavior. Moreover, many proponents of rational choice theory consider emotions as unpredictable, unstable, immeasurable, and thus unscientific.

But emotions are lawful phenomena (Frijda, 1988, 2006) and more often than not they appear, behave, and disappear in a unsurprising and consistent way. As part of this, emotions also reliably and predictably facilitate certain behaviors more than other behaviors. Thus, our argument is that we need a theory of emotion when we want to understand behavior—a theory about what emotion is about and how emotion influences action. That is what we present here, illustrating it with our own research. Let us first explain what emotions are and how they relate to action (presenting our feeling-is-for-doing approach), and next suggest how this knowledge may be valuable in facilitating sustainable behaviors.

EMOTION, APPRAISAL, AND EXPERIENTIAL CONTENT

Emotions are studied by psychologists, philosophers, and other researchers and there has always been dispute concerning the exact definition (Kleinginna & Kleinginna, 1981). Luckily, there is consensus on several important aspects of emotion, making the dispute about the exact definition more or less academic. Students of emotion agree that emotions are momentary experiences that we feel in the here and now. Emotions are about something or someone: you are angry with someone; you regret a choice, and so on. They arise when we evaluate events or outcomes as relevant for our concerns or preferences (i.e., they stem from appraisals) and therefore we do not become emotional over trivial things. Emotions are also to some extent *cognitively impenetrable*: one cannot simply choose to have or not have emotions, given certain events or outcomes that are relevant for one's concerns (Frijda, 1986, p. 468). Of course, this does not imply that we are slaves to our emotions, passively undergoing them. Quite the contrary. We try to regulate our emotions by acting in such a way that the emotion attenuates or prolongs. Indeed, much of the impact of emotion on behavior stems from regulative attempts (Baumeister, Vohs, DeWall, & Zhang, 2007; Zeelenberg & Pieters, 2007).

Emotions are nowadays often conceptualized as multicomponent experiences. They manifest themselves in different psychological subsystems, such as cognitive appraisals, hedonic experiences, bodily sensations, motivational goals, and action tendencies (e.g., Frijda, 1986; Lazarus, 1991). Componential theories of emotion emphasize that insight in patterns of changes across several components are necessary for a full understanding of emotions. Studies using a componential approach have distinguished many emotions at a high level of phenomenological detail (e.g., Breugelmans & Poortinga, 2006; Frijda, Kuipers, & Ter Schure, 1989; Roseman, Wiest, & Swartz, 1994).

The most studied component of emotion is the *appraisal* of the emotion-eliciting event with respect to one's goals (for a review of appraisal theories of emotion, see Scherer, Schorr, & Johnstone, 2001). Thus, we become emotional over things evaluated as relevant for these goals or concerns, and the emotions we feel are positive when the event is evaluated as conducive to our goals and negative when they are evaluated as hindering them. But the relation between appraisal and emotion goes beyond the induction of positive and negative emotions. Specific emotions are associated with specific patterns of appraisals of the emotion-eliciting event. If we hold someone responsible for a negative event that happens to us, we are likely to become angry. When we attribute it to uncontrollable circumstances, we are more likely to become sad. People may differ in the specific appraisals that are elicited by a particular event, but the same patterns of appraisals always give rise to the same emotions. An understanding of appraisals is important because it may help researchers to understand why specific emotions arise and hence provide a solid theoretical basis for emotion manipulation. Research on appraisal processes, however, remains relatively mute when it comes to predicting behavior (Frijda & Zeelenberg, 2001). The emotion–behavior link, which is central in this chapter, will be discussed later; first we address other components of emotional experiences.

We follow Roseman et al. (1994) in the description of the components that together comprise the *experiential content* of the emotion. Roseman et al. proposed that emotions could be differentiated in terms of the following five experiential categories: feelings, thoughts, action tendencies, actions, and emotivational goals. *Feelings* are perceived physical or mental sensations. *Thoughts* are ideas, plans, conceptions, or opinions produced by mental activity. *Action tendencies* are impulses or inclinations to respond with a particular action. *Actions* include behavior that may or may not be purposive. *Emotivational goals* describe the goals that accompany discrete emotions (wanting to avoid danger in case of fear, or wanting to recover from loss in case of sadness). Thus, emotivational goals refer to desired goal states ("I want to be environmentally conscious"), whereas action tendencies refer to specific behavioral responses ("I want to separate my garbage"). These emotivational goals (also referred to as *emotivations*) are similar to what Frijda refers to as "changes in patterns of action readiness" (Frijda, 1986, 2006). *Action readiness* refers to motivational states that may involve attentional focusing, arousal, muscular preparation or actual action, goal priority, or felt readiness. Action readiness is defined by having control precedence, which means that it may overrule other goals. Many emotions can be differentiated in terms of action readiness.

We have used Roseman et al.'s (1994) approach to compare the experiential content of a number of related emotions such as anger and dissatisfaction (Bougie, Pieters, & Zeelenberg, 2003), regret and disappointment (Zeelenberg, van Dijk, van der Pligt, & Manstead, 1998), regret and guilt (Zeelenberg & Breugelmans, 2008), different types of one emotion such as person-related disappointment and outcome-related disappointment (van Dijk & Zeelenberg, 2002), and malicious envy and benign envy (van de Ven, Zeelenberg, & Pieters, 2009). Knowing the experiential content of an emotion therefore implies knowledge of the motivations that arise during this experience. For example, when we realize that the experience of anger in consumers goes with feelings like exploding, thoughts of unfairness and violence, and tendencies to let go and behave aggressively, it simply follows that these consumers are motivated to retaliate (Bougie et al., 2003). The experiential content of an emotion thus reflects how emotions are felt and what emotions mean to the person experiencing them; it is the real emotional experience.

Specific appraisals elicit specific emotions, with specific experiential contents. In our feeling-is-for-doing approach (Zeelenberg & Pieters, 2006) we reserve a special role for the experiential content of emotions and for the motivational aspect that is part of it. We have proposed that this experiential content is the proximal cause of all that follows. Knowledge about the experiential content of an emotion (how it feels, how it is experienced by a person) allows us to make specific behavioral predictions about what people are likely to do when they feel the emotion. We have tested these predictions for, among others, regret and disappointment (Zeelenberg & Pieters, 1999, 2004; Martinez, Zeelenberg, & Rijsman, 2011a & b), malicious envy and benign envy (Van de Ven, Zeelenberg, & Pieters, 2009), guilt (De Hooge, Nelissen, Breugelmans, & Zeelenberg, in press; Nelissen & Zeelenberg, 2009), and shame (De Hooge, Breugelmans, & Zeelenberg, 2008). We come back to this research later in this chapter.

Taken together, we argue that when interested in how emotion impacts action, a focus on specific emotions is needed. In order to do that, we have to understand how emotions are experienced by the decision maker and what motivations are associated with the experience, to be able to predict the behavior that will follow. This is the core element of the approach to which we turn now.

FEELING IS FOR DOING

We first presented our approach in Zeelenberg and Pieters (2006), and refer the reader to that chapter for an elaborated exposition (see also Zeelenberg, Nelissen, & Pieters, 2007; Zeelenberg, Nelissen, Breugelmans, & Pieters, 2008). Our approach has its roots in the philosophy of pragmatism of William James (1907, 1909). The core element of our approach is that emotion has evolved for reasons of behavioral guidance (see also Hasselton & Ketelaar, 2006; Ketelaar, 2004). They may help us to overcome the cognitive limitations within ourselves and constraints placed upon us within the decision environment. We think that emotions serve this function because emotions prioritize certain goals and thereby mobilize energy and give direction to behavior (Bagozzi, Baumgartner, Pieters, & Zeelenberg, 2000; Frijda, 1986, 2006). Behavior, therefore, should be central in understanding emotion. Our ideas fit well with Averill's take on the emotion anger: "the desire to gain revenge on, or to get back at the instigator of anger can almost be taken as a definition of anger" (1982, p. 178). A summary of our approach in five broad propositions is presented in Table 12.1 and explained in the following text.

In our feeling-is-for-doing approach we conceptualize emotions as motivational (*proposition 1*). This is by itself not new, but in behavioral decision research it is often forgotten. We propose that emotions prioritize action, that is, commit decision makers to certain courses of action by providing control precedence (Frijda, 1986). The experience of an emotion brings forward an associated goal that may overrule other goals. For example, when one is fearful, running away from the fear-evoking stimulus (e.g., a big, scary, hairy spider) has priority. Different emotions are associated with different goals (e.g., Nelissen, Dijker, & De Vries, 2007a) and thus it follows that different emotions have their idiosyncratic impact on decision making (*proposition 2*). For example, anger motivates us to move against the source of our anger, whereas fear motivates us to move away. The feeling-is-for-doing approach thus puts emphasis on the forward-looking, motivational function of emotions (see also, Zeelenberg et al., 2007). It explains how emotions may be instrumental in achieving the goal one is striving for. That is, emotions provide information about how one is currently doing. This affective feedback informs about the extent of goal progress (e.g., *I am still not safe!*). But the impact of emotion goes further in that it provides the decision maker with clear guidelines for how to attain these goals (e.g., *I better climb up that tree!*). Further in this chapter, we explain this approach in more detail and review some of our own studies that have tested its predictions.

As stated in *proposition 3*, the motivational function of emotion cannot be reduced to the overall valence of the specific emotions. This is important because often emotion is equated with affect and only the affect dimension is taken into account. Such a hedonic approach was favored by Freud (1920/1952, p. 365, emphasis in the original) who argued: "our entire psychical activity is bent

TABLE 12.1   Propositions Summarizing the Feeling-Is-for-Doing Perspective

1.	The emotional system is the primary motivational system for goal-directed behavior.
2.	Each specific emotion serves distinct motivational functions in goal striving.
3.	These motivational functions cannot be reduced to the overall valence of the specific emotions.
4.	The distinct motivational functions are rooted in the experiential qualities of the specific emotions.
5.	Emotions can be either endogenous (an integral part) or exogenous (environmentally invoked) to the goal-striving process, their effect on behavior being contingent on their perceived relevance to the current goal.

Source: Zeelenberg, M., & Pieters, R. (2006). Feeling is for doing: A pragmatic approach to the study of emotions in economic behavior. In D. DeCremer, M. Zeelenberg, & J. K. Murnighan (Eds.), *Social psychology and economics* (pp. 117–137). Mahwah, NJ: Erlbaum.

upon *procuring pleasure* and *avoiding pain.*" However, research has now convincingly shown that different specific emotions are associated with different behaviors that cannot be reduced to the valance of the emotion (e.g., Lerner & Keltner, 2000; Zeelenberg & Pieters, 1999).

As explained earlier, the experiential content of emotion (cf. Roseman et al., 1994) is the source of the differential motivational functions (*proposition 4*). Specific relations among emotion, motivation, and behavior are slightly more complex as the same specific emotion in different situations may activate different behaviors, depending on the overarching goal toward which people strive. Put differently, emotions do not automatically call for a specific action, but rather they reflect a concern of the decision maker that is potentially threatened (in the case of negative emotions) or served (in the case of positive emotions). The emotion then facilitates behavior that is in line with our concerns and that is aimed at closing the gap between the current situation and the goal strived for (Frijda & Zeelenberg, 2001). Depending on the situation one is in, different behaviors can fulfill this role ("many roads lead to Rome"), but which action will be performed is based on their accessibility, acceptability, and their instrumentality to the current overarching goal. Thus, because of the specific meaning that they convey to the decision maker, specific emotions may help us to better understand the goals and motivations of the decision makers and hence better predict the specific behaviors the decision makers engage in or refrain from.

Our final *proposition 5* differentiates between endogenous and exogenous influences of emotion. Emotions are endogenous when the experience is relevant to the decision at hand, and they are thus an integral part of the goal-setting and goal-striving process. For example, the disgust experienced when thinking about dirty streets may impact littering behavior, and the guilt one feels toward one's children may cause one to use less energy. Likewise, the anger about goal frustration is endogenous, when it influences future behavior with respect to that goal. But disgust felt while watching a horror movie may perhaps spill over to behaviors later on, and may eventually cause one to get rid of garbage more quickly even when this means littering. Such an impact of emotion, which is not directly related to the inducing situation and the motivations that were relevant then, is referred to as *exogenous*. Exogenous emotions, or emotional influences, are those that are not related to the current decision, and are external to the actual goal-setting and goal-striving process, although they may—exogenously—influence this. The distinction is relevant as research has often studied the effects of emotions, feelings, or moods that should be irrelevant for the current decision. As a consequence, we know much about the failing motivational system, but too little about how and when the system works in the service of goal pursuit. In sum, an *endogenous emotion* is part of current goal pursuit, while an *exogenous emotion* comes from outside, and its effects may "steam through" current goal pursuit. Many effects of exogenous emotions that seem erratic at first sight can be understood if one is aware of the effects of endogenous emotions.

ILLUSTRATIONS OF HOW EMOTIONS
INFLUENCE BEHAVIOR

Here we describe examples of research projects that illustrate the insights of the feeling-is-for-doing approach in studying the effects of emotions on behavioral decisions. The first project shows differential effects of two very similar emotions that both follow negative decision outcomes. We compared the behavioral consequences of regret and disappointment (Zeelenberg & Pieters, 1999, 2004). In two surveys we examined the behavioral decisions of consumers who were dissatisfied with the delivery of a service and provided clear support for the feeling-is-for-doing approach. Consumers were questioned about regret and disappointment, consumer satisfaction, and about the behaviors they engaged in after the negative experience with the service provider. The surveys clearly showed that experiences of disappointment were associated with word-of-mouth communication (talking to others about the bad experience), whereas the experiences of regret were associated with switching to other service providers. What's more, these differential behavioral effects were found over and above the effects of general dissatisfaction, clearly revealing the usefulness of studying the effects of specific emotions. These results are consistent with what we expected on the basis of the experiential content of regret and disappointment (Zeelenberg et al., 1998). Regretful consumers are those who realize that there is a better option, and they switch to that alternative service provider. Disappointed customers are inclined to share the experience with others (perhaps as a means of obtaining sympathy or comfort from others). These differential findings concerning regret and disappointment are supported by recent neuroscientific studies using patients with damage to the orbitofrontal cortex (Camille et al., 2004) and studies using fMRI techniques (Coricelli et al., 2005).

A second project concerns the effects of shame on prosocial behavior (De Hooge, Breugelmans, & Zeelenberg, 2008). To my knowledge this was the first study to show that the same emotion can have different endogenous and exogenous influences. Shame is one of the moral emotions, which are linked to the interests of other people and that motivate prosocial behavior (Haidt, 2003). The prosocial effects of shame had hitherto not been experimentally demonstrated. One reason for this is that the effects of shame, and indeed of most emotions, have only been studied exogenously (e.g., De Hooge et al., 2007). When ashamed, people experience a threatened or damaged self, and they are motivated to cope with this threat (De Hooge et al., 2010, 2011; Tangney & Dearing, 2002). This may induce a tendency to hide or withdraw from the shame-eliciting event. But when shame is exogenous and thus not elicited by the present situation, the person has already achieved the motivation of hiding or withdrawing from the shame-inducing event. Consequently, the common situational carryover effects that are observed with other emotions are not easily found with exogenous shame. When the person is still in the shame-inducing situation, and the emotion is thus endogenous, the shame has to be acted upon (it is a painful emotion that reflects on the self and clearly calls for action). In that case people are motivated to restore the damaged self (De Hooge et al., 2009, 2010) and shame motivates prosocial behavior. This is what we found in four experiments using a variety of different inductions of shame and measures of prosocial behavior (Hooge et al., 2008). Endogenous shame motivated prosocial behavior but exogenous shame had no effect at all. This study clearly documented the necessity of studying endogenous effects of emotions if we are to truly understand their influence on decision making.

A third example is our recent research on malicious envy and benign envy (Van de Ven et al., 2009, 2010, 2011). A first set of studies showed that experiences of these two emotions could be distinguished not only in the Netherlands, where two separate words exist for them, but also in the United States and Spain, where the language does not make a difference and the word envy is used for both experiences. Both types of envy are felt when there is a social comparison other who is better off on a relevant dimension (which can be a personal characteristic but also a possession), and both envy types lead to a motivation to reduce the gap with the envied person. Benign envy was found to be associated with increased motivation to obtain the similar position (making the social comparison less painful), while malicious envy was associated with more hostile intentions and willingness to differentiate from the other (making the social comparison less relevant). In subsequent research it was found that benignly envious people are willing to pay a premium to obtain the product that elicited their envy (in these studies, an iPhone), while maliciously envious people do not show that behavior. Instead, they are willing to pay more for related items that allow them to differentiate themselves from the social comparison other (in this case a Blackberry phone). Interestingly, people are aware of this and try to prevent others from envying them, but also here they are sensitive to the differences in envy. When people fear being maliciously envied they become more prosocial, but not when the other will be benignly envious (Van de Ven et al., 2010).

EMOTION AND SUSTAINABLE BEHAVIOR

Our approach borrows many ideas from old and sometimes forgotten insights in the psychology of emotion, but nevertheless we believe that attempting to integrate these insights is valuable and insightful. We also believe that studying emotions by focusing on their motivational component is a fruitful way to come to a better understanding of both the role of emotion in behavioral decisions and more generally the function of emotions. This should ultimately enable us to understand a variety of human behaviors, including those related to sustainability issues.

Now how could these insights into the psychology of emotion be of help in understanding and promoting sustainable behavior? A simple way would be to associate certain negative emotions to harmful behaviors and positive emotions to sustainable behaviors. For example, associating regret with environmentally unfriendly behaviors could induce a reluctance to engage in those behaviors. We know that regret is aversive and can induce behaviors that prevent it from happening and that this works via its relation to responsibility for the actions (see, for a discussion of responsibility in regret, Zeelenberg & Pieters, 2007). Richard, van der Pligt, and De Vries (1996) showed that linking regret to unsafe sex led to an increase in reported condom use. It is likely that similar effects could be obtained with many sustainable behaviors that have consequences for the decision maker him- or herself, or for the people they care about.

One group of emotions that is also interesting in this context is moral emotions. Exploiting natural resources and polluting the environment can be seen as immoral, as the interest in the welfare of society or other persons is lost, and might induce an individual to feel *morally* responsible to take part in sustainable behavior. As argued by Minton and Rose (1997), a sense of personal moral obligation is more likely to lead to action in the form of environmentally friendly product choice, search, and recycling than general environmental attitudes. Besides, when people experience moral emotions, they might want to act sustainable as a way to repair the negative feelings these emotions generate.

There is, however, a caveat here. As is explained previously, emotions do not have a clear one-to-one relation with behavior. Rather, their impact on behavior occurs via a motivational process. Since goals can be achieved via multiple behaviors, it is important that the linkage between emotions and the desirable behavior is unambiguous. This is not always the case. Earlier we described our research that showed that shame (clearly a moral emotion) can induce prosocial behavior, and because sustainable behavior can be regarded as prosocial, it seems obvious that shame can also bring about sustainable behavior. Remember, however, that shame only results in prosocial behavior when it is endogenous to the situation. Thus, inducing shame in people does not necessarily lead to environmentally friendly behaviors. First of all, shame may have no effect at all when it is not perceived to be related to the decision to behave in an environmentally friendly manner. But, in addition, shame only elicits sustainable behavior when this is perceived as solving the problem of the threatened self that is central in shame. For example, if there is a common acceptance to use recycled products in one's group of friends, one might not want to purchase environmentally unfriendly products to avoid feeling ashamed when "getting caught" for not contributing. However, if other behaviors are more instrumental to that goal (e.g., withdrawal behaviors such as private consumption), it is likely that they may be chosen. Thus, if one is ashamed over the amount of energy one uses, or the bad mileage of one's car, one could simply not talk about it, or lie when people ask about it. Moreover, it has also been found that if one tries to make people ashamed and they feel too much pressure is placed upon them, they could be shamed into anger (Tangney, Wagner, Fletcher, & Gramzow, 1992) and show destructive behavior.

A similar line of reasoning applies to the other moral emotion: guilt. Guilt also induces prosocial behaviors, helping others around us (e.g., Nelissen et al., 2007b; De Hooge et al., 2007), similar to shame. This effect of guilt has been widely documented and is much more stable than that of shame. This effect of guilt has also proven its effectiveness in consumer research, with *guilt appeals* becoming more popular as a persuasion technique. In this technique consumers are motivated to buy a product or adopt certain behavior in order to reduce or avoid having guilt feelings (see Burnett & Lunsford 1994; Coulter & Pinto, 1995; Huhmann & Brotherton, 1997). For example, fund raisers use guilt appeals and offer guilt-reducing solutions to influence consumers: depicting a sick person in need of help in a charity fund-raising ad may stimulate people to donate money, as they want to reduce the guilt that is elicited by the image (Hibbert, Smith, Davies, & Ireland, 2007; Basil, Ridgway, & Basil, 2008). Another guilt appeal, as is often used with products, has a more future-oriented focus. Ads including such a guilt approach emphasize that *not* buying the product they advertise could elicit a bad outcome in the future (Coulter & Pinto, 1995; Huhmann & Brotherton, 1997). For example, not buying apple juice that has no preservatives and coloring might eventually harm your child's health. As parents feel responsible for their children's health, such guilt appeals increase the chance that the product is being purchased. Since guilt appeals are aimed to stimulate the public to think about their moral obligations toward other people, these appeals might be especially suitable in the sustainability context. Advertisers could use guilt appeals in motivating consumers to buy biological meat or fair trade products as well. Inducing guilt by, for example, showing poor, hardworking farmers who are clearly less fortunate than consumers themselves might then encourage voluntary compliance to purchase fair trade products as a way of "buying off" the guilt feelings elicited.

Guilt appeals could also be suitable in stressing the detrimental consequences of people's current environmentally unfriendly behavior for future generations. When people would feel guilty toward their children or more generally future generations, this might bring forward a motivation to act sustainable as a way of reducing this negative guilt feeling. It is important for the current generation to act sustainable, for future generations to have the same environmental benefits. However, emphasizing the fact that we are responsible for our children and their futures may result in taking action that is to their advantage, but at the same time could be to the disadvantage of others. As De Hooge et al. (in press) have shown, when the person to whom we feel guilty is present, we tend to show this prosocial behavior *only* toward that person, at the expense of the others around us (who will be relatively ignored). This could mean that we invest more in the health and education of our children and invest less in more global action that could be beneficial for many (on the societal level, such feelings of guilt could lead to moving polluting industries away from our country to distant countries).

What we mean with the caveats portrayed in this chapter is that research on the emotion behavior link could be very helpful in making people more environmental friendly, inducing all sorts of sustainable behaviors, but that one should be aware of the intricacies of this relation. Emotion does not simply result in behavior. Its influence occurs via the motivations that are associated with emotional experience. Insight in the experiential content of emotion, and thus in how emotion is felt and what goals are associated with it, should allow for insight into how to facilitate people acting in a way that is good for our environment and the future of it.

SUMMARY AND CONCLUSIONS

In this chapter we have reviewed our motivational account of the effects of emotion on decision making, which we refer to as the feeling-is-for-doing approach. This approach recognizes that the differential impact of specific emotions occurs via the association between emotion and motivation. Emotions arise when events or outcomes are relevant for one's concerns or preferences and they prioritize behavior that acts in service of these concerns. As such, emotions can be understood as functional programs for intuitive decision making, imposing upon the decision maker inclinations for action that, in a given situation, serve current strivings. Investigating these dynamics should further our understanding of both decision processes and the dynamics of emotional experiences. Put differently, when we realize that feeling is here for the sake of our doing, we also realize that progress in studying how to promote sustainable behavior cannot be done without scrutinizing the functional role of emotion.

REFERENCES

Averill, J. R. (1982). *Anger and aggression: An essay on emotion*. New York: Springer-Verlag.

Bagozzi, R. P., Baumgartner, H., Pieters, R., & Zeelenberg, M. (2000). The role of emotions in goal-directed behavior. In S. Ratneshwar, D. G. Mick, & C. Huffman (Eds.), *The why of consumption: Contemporary perspectives on consumer motives, goals, and desires* (pp. 36–58). New York: Routledge.

Basil, D. Z., Ridgway, N. M., & Basil, M. D. (2008). Guilt and giving: A process model of empathy and efficacy. *Psychology & Marketing, 25,* 1–23.

Baumeister, R. F., Masicampo, E. J., & Vohs, K. D. (2011). Do conscious thoughts cause behavior? *Annual Review of Psychology, 62,* 331–161.

Baumeister, R. F., Vohs, K. D., DeWall, C. N., & Zhang, L. Q. (2007). How emotion shapes behavior: Feedback, anticipation, and reflection, rather than direct causation. *Personality and Social Psychology Review, 11,* 167–203.

Bougie, R., Pieters, R., & Zeelenberg, M. (2003). Angry customers don't come back, they get back: The experience and behavioral implications of anger and dissatisfaction in services. *Journal of the Academy of Marketing Sciences, 31,* 377–391.

Breugelmans, S. M., & Poortinga, Y. H. (2006). Emotion without a word: Shame and guilt with Rarámuri Indians and rural Javanese. *Journal of Personality and Social Psychology, 91,* 1111–1122.

Burnett, M. S., & Lunsford, D. A. (1994). Conceptualizing guilt in the consumer decision making process. *Journal of Consumer Marketing, 11,* 33–43.

Camille, N., Coricelli, G., Sallet, J., Pradat-Diehl, P., Duhamel, J. R., & Sirigu, A. (2004). The involvement of the orbitofrontal cortex in the experience of regret. *Science, 304,* 1167–1170.

Coricelli, G., Critchley, H. D., Joffily, M., O'Doherty, J. P., Sirigu, A., & Dolan, R. J. (2005). Regret and its avoidance: A neuroimaging study of choice behavior. *Nature Neuroscience, 8,* 1255–1262.

Coulter, R. H., & Pinto, M. B. (1995). Guilt appeals in advertising: What are their effects? *Journal of Applied Psychology, 80,* 697–705.

De Hooge, I. E., Breugelmans, S. M., & Zeelenberg, M. (2008). Not so ugly after all: When shame acts as a commitment device. *Journal of Personality and Social Psychology, 95,* 933–943.

De Hooge, I. E., Nelissen, R. M. A., Breugelmans, S. M., & Zeelenberg, M. (2011). What is moral about guilt? Acting "prosocially" at the disadvantage of others. *Journal of Personality and Social Psychology, 100,* 462–473.

De Hooge, I. E., Zeelenberg, M., & Breugelmans, S. M. (2007). Moral sentiments and cooperation: Differential influences of shame and guilt. *Cognition and Emotion, 21,* 1025–1042.

De Hooge, I. E., Zeelenberg, M., & Breugelmans, S. M. (2010). Restore and protect motivations following shame. *Cognition and Emotion, 24*, 111–127.

De Hooge, I. E., Zeelenberg, M., & Breugelmans, S. M. (2011). A functionalist account of shame induced behavior. *Cognition and Emotion, 25*, 939–946. DOI: 10.1080/02699931.2010.516909.

Freud, S. (1920/1952). *A general introduction to psychoanalysis*. New York: Washington Square Press.

Frijda, N. H. (1986). *The emotions*. Cambridge: Cambridge University Press.

Frijda, N. H. (1988). The laws of emotion. *American Psychologist, 43*, 249–358.

Frijda, N. H. (2006). *The laws of emotion*. Mahwah, NJ: Erlbaum.

Frijda, N. H., Kuipers, P., & Ter Schure, E. (1989). Relations among emotion, appraisal and emotional action readiness. *Journal of Personality and Social Psychology, 57*, 212–228.

Frijda, N. H., & Zeelenberg, M. (2001). Appraisal: What is the dependent? In K. R. Scherer, A. Schorr, & T. Johnstone (Eds.), *Appraisal processes in emotion: Theory, methods, research* (pp. 141–155). New York: Oxford University Press.

Haidt, J. (2003). The moral emotions. In R. J. Davidson, K. R. Scherer, & H. H. Goldsmith (Eds.), *Handbook of affective sciences* (pp. 852–870). Oxford: Oxford University Press.

Hanoch, Y. (2001). "Neither an angel nor an ant": Emotion as an aid to bounded rationality. *Journal of Economic Psychology, 23*, 1–25.

Hasselton, M. G., & Ketelaar, T. (2006). Irrational emotions or emotional wisdom? The evolutionary psychology of emotions and behavior. In J. P. Forgas (Ed.), *Affect in social thinking and behavior* (pp. 21–39). New York: Psychology Press.

Hibbert, S., Smith, A., Davies, A., & Ireland, F. (2007). Guilt appeals: Persuasion knowledge and charitable giving. *Psychology & Marketing, 24*, 723–742.

Huhmann, B. A., & Brotherton, T. P. (1997). A content analysis of guilt appeals in popular magazine advertisements. *Journal of Advertising, 26*, 35–45.

James, W. (1907/1995). *Pragmatism*. New York: Dover Publications.

James, W. (1909/2002). *The meaning of truth*. New York: Dover Publications.

Ketelaar, T. (2004). Ancestral emotions, current decisions: Using evolutionary game theory to explore the role of emotions in decision-making. In C. Crawford & C. Salmon (Eds.), *Darwinism, public policy and private decisions* (pp. 145–168). Mahwah, NJ: Erlbaum.

Kleinginna, P. R., & Kleinginna, A. M. (1981). A categorized list of emotion definitions, with suggestions for a consensual definition. *Motivation and Emotion, 5*, 345–379.

Lazarus, R. S. (1991). *Emotion and adaptation*. New York: McGraw Hill.

Lerner, J. S., & Keltner, D. (2000). Beyond valence: Toward a model of emotion specific influences on judgment and choice. *Cognition and Emotion, 14*, 473–493.

Martinez, L. F., Zeelenberg, M., & Rijsman, J. B. (2011a). Regret, disappointment and the endowment effect. *Journal of Economic Psychology, 32*, 962–968.

Martinez, L. F., Zeelenberg, M., & Rijsman, J. B. (2011b). Behavioural consequences of regret and disappointment in social bargaining games. *Cognition and Emotion, 25*, 351–359.

Minton, A. P., & Rose, R. L. (1997). The effects of environmental concern on environmentally friendly consumer behavior: An exploratory study. *Journal of Business Research, 40*, 37–48.

Nelissen, R. M. A., Dijker, A. J. M., & Vries, N. K. de (2007a). Emotions and goals: Assessing relations between values and emotions. *Cognition and Emotion, 21*, 902–911.

Nelissen, R. M. A., Dijker, A. J., & De Vries, N. K. (2007b). How to turn a hawk into a dove and vice versa: Interactions between emotions and goals in a give-some dilemma game. *Journal of Experimental Social Psychology, 43*, 280–286.

Nelissen, R. M. A., & Zeelenberg, M. (2009). When guilt evokes self-punishment: Evidence for the existence of a Dobby effect. *Emotion, 9,* 118–122.

Payne, J. W., Bettman, J. R., & Johnson, E. J. (1993). *The adaptive decision maker.* Cambridge: Cambridge University Press.

Richard, R., Van der Pligt, J., & De Vries, N. K. (1996). Anticipated regret and time perspective: Changing sexual risk-taking behavior. *Journal of Behavioral Decision Making, 9,* 185–199.

Roseman, I. J., Wiest, C., & Swartz, T. S. (1994). Phenomenology, behaviors, and goals differentiate discrete emotions. *Journal of Personality and Social Psychology, 67,* 206–211.

Scherer, K. R., Schorr, A., & Johnstone, T. (Eds.). (2001). *Appraisal processes in emotion: Theory, methods, research.* New York: Oxford University Press.

Simon, H. A. (1955). A behavioral model of rational choice. *Quarterly Journal of Economics, 69,* 99–118.

Simon, H. A. (1956). Rational choice, and the structure of the environment. *Psychological Review, 63,* 129–138.

Tangney, J. P., & Dearing, R. L. (2002). *Shame and guilt.* New York: Guilford Press.

Tangney, J. P., Wagner, P. E., Fletcher, C., & Gramzow, R. (1992). Shamed into anger? The relation of shame and guilt to anger and self-reported aggression. *Journal of Personality and Social Psychology, 62,* 669–675.

Van Dijk, W. W., & Zeelenberg, M. (2002). What do we talk about when we talk about disappointment? Distinguishing outcome-related disappointment from person-related disappointment. *Cognition and Emotion, 16,* 787–807.

Van de Ven, N., Zeelenberg, M., & Pieters, R. (2009). Leveling up and down: The experience of malicious and benign envy. *Emotion, 9,* 419–429.

Van de Ven, N., Zeelenberg, M., & Pieters, R. (2010). Warding off the evil eye: When the fear of being envied increases prosocial behavior. *Psychological Science, 21,* 1671–1677.

Van de Ven, N., Zeelenberg, M., & Pieters, R. (2011). The envy premium: How envy increases product value. *Journal of Consumer Research, 37,* 984–998.

Zeelenberg, M., & Breugelmans, S. M. (2008). The role of interpersonal harm in distinguishing regret from guilt. *Emotion, 8,* 589–596.

Zeelenberg, M., Nelissen, R. M. A., & Pieters, R. (2007). Emotion, motivation and decision making: A feeling is for doing approach. In H. Plessner, C. Betsch, & T. Betsch (Eds.), *Intuition in judgment and decision making* (pp. 173–189). Mahwah, NJ: Erlbaum.

Zeelenberg, M., Nelissen, R. M. A., Breugelmans, S. M., & Pieters, R. (2008). On emotion specificity in decision making: Why feeling is for doing. *Judgment and Decision Making, 3,* 18–27.

Zeelenberg, M., & Pieters, R. (1999). Comparing service delivery to what might have been: Behavioral responses to disappointment and regret. *Journal of Service Research, 2,* 86–97.

Zeelenberg, M., & Pieters, R. (2004). Beyond valence in customer dissatisfaction: A review and new findings on behavioral responses to regret and disappointment in failed services. *Journal of Business Research, 57,* 445–455.

Zeelenberg, M., & Pieters, R. (2006). Feeling is for doing: A pragmatic approach to the study of emotions in economic behavior. In D. DeCremer, M. Zeelenberg, & J. K. Murnighan (Eds.), *Social psychology and economics* (pp. 117–137). Mahwah, NJ: Erlbaum.

Zeelenberg, M., & Pieters, R. (2007). A theory of regret regulation 1.0. *Journal of Consumer Psychology, 17,* 3–18.

Zeelenberg, M., Van Dijk, W. W., Van der Pligt, J., & Manstead, A. S. R., (1998). The experience of regret and disappointment. *Cognition and Emotion, 12,* 221–230.

13

The Psychology of Sustainability
Attitudes, Identities, Actions, and Engaging with the Welfare of Others

PAUL SPARKS

BACKGROUND

"[W]hat we face in the West today is not an ecological crisis, nor a crisis of economics, nor a crisis of structure. It is a crisis of the mind. A crisis of the stories we tell ourselves, of the position we wish to give ourselves in the creation, and of the purpose that we give to our existence" (Palmer, 1992, cited in Gladwin et al., 1997, p. 245).

Most people are aware of a growing concern about the state of the planet. Average global temperatures are increasing, various other climate changes are predicted, sea and population levels are rising, and many of the resources of which we make use are finite. The United Nations Copenhagen meeting designed to address climate change has just come and gone with no radical agreements. "We are all environmentalists now," it has been suggested (Glaeser, 2007), indicating that "we are all aware and committed to the environment." While this may be seen as a rash overstatement about people's identities and values, there does seem to be some apparent exasperation not only at individual and collective inertia but also that people's expressions of concern for the environment are not reflected in their behaviors. There are regular suggestions, albeit framed in slightly different ways, that people's attitudes do not match their actions (e.g., Gagnon Thompson,& Barton, 1994; Worldwide Fund for Nature (WWF), 2008). Is there a real attitude–behavior discrepancy here? If there is, can the discrepancy be resolved in such a way as to promote pro-environmental behaviors and further the cause of sustainability?

The aims of this chapter are to consider the links between the psychological literature on the attitude–behavior relationship in relation to the notion of *multiple selves* and to look for some points of congruence and divergence between the domains of health-related and environment-related action. Because of space constraints, I have ridden roughshod over the need for clear definitions of terms and have omitted a number of important caveats to some of the general assertions that are made. The result is a tad loose and polemical. To cut to the chase, the trail of thought to be outlined here is:

i.   significant attitude–behavior relationships have been demonstrated in the health and other domains;
ii. one can focus on both correspondence or mismatch (depending, I guess, on what one's goals are);
iii. measures of identity can predict people's intentions and behavior (independently of the effects of attitudes);
iv. the same general patterns can be seen in the environmental domain (and I suspect that most claims of attitude–behavior inconsistencies actually have to do with discrepancies between behavior and, for example, people's knowledge, awareness, beliefs, or environmental concern);
v.   why measures of identity have their effects is unclear; however,
vi. the utility of the metaphor of multiple selves requires critical examination;
vii. two aspects of motivation in the environment domain differ somewhat from those in the health domain: namely *morality* and *collective action*, both of which involve the relationships we have with others (other selves);
viii. the relationship between people (i.e., between different selves) is crucial here—this is the real issue in the domain of environmental sustainability when we talk about coordination between different identities (that is, coordination between people rather than within them); and
ix. this challenge of coordination may be assisted by a broader recognition of common humanity (rather than intergroup identity, for example).

While acknowledging that people need to manage their different motives (perhaps due to temporal discounting, impulsiveness, or whatever), the focus in the present chapter is on the idea that the environmental domain invites us to engage in a reexamination of our relationships to others who affect and are affected by our actions: it is in this sense that coordination between multiple selves (i.e., different people) becomes such a crucial issue in the challenges posed by sustainability.

Concern about a discrepancy between attitudes and actions (or behavior) strikes a social psychologist as rather odd. Such discrepancies were widely discussed many years ago and appeared to wither in light of Ajzen and Fishbein's claim that a bit of precision in formulation and measurement of attitudes and behavior would deal with the apparent discrepancy. Thus, the well-cited suggestion that "It is considerably more likely that attitudes will be unrelated or only slightly related to overt behaviors than that attitudes will be closely related to actions" (Wicker, 1969, p. 65) was countered with the response from Ajzen and Fishbein that "appropriate measures of attitude are strongly related to action" (1980, p. 27). This was seen as one of the major contributions of the theory of reasoned action (TRA). Other perspectives that could also explain apparent discrepancies between attitudes and behavior were also available, but much less widely cited. For example, Lord and colleagues proposed that representations of attitude objects that were at odds with the encountered attitude objects might lead to attenuated attitude–behavior relationships (Lord, Lepper, & Mackie, 1984). Thus, LaPiere's famous Chinese couple may not have fitted the prototype or stereotype of Chinese couples that were salient to people when they expressed their attitudes about whether or not such people would be accepted as guests at their hotels and restaurants. Certainly the environmental problems that we are facing are real, but to what extent are attitude–behavior discrepancies a part of those problems?

So, 30 years ago psychologists inherited the idea that "any behavioral criterion can be predicted from attitude—be it a single action or a pattern of behavior—provided that the measure of attitude corresponds to the measure of behavior" (Ajzen & Fishbein, 1980, p. 27). A recent meta-analysis of meta-analyses of the relationship between attitudes and behavior has reported a weighted mean correlation between attitudes and behavior of $r_+ = .34$ (Conner & Sparks, 2005). In fact, of course, a strong influence of subjective norms or (later, within the theory of planned behavior [TPB]) perceived behavioral control meant that one would never expect a close relationship between attitudes and behavior as a matter of necessity but this issue was largely ignored. Instead, following Ajzen (1991), a great deal of attention was paid to the addition to the TPB of further predictor variables, to the interactions between different variables (in order to identify moderation effects), and to a limited extent, some conceptual issues relating to key constructs, such as attitudes. Among the additional variables that have attracted a good deal of attention are, for example, moral norms/injunctive norms (Beck & Ajzen, 1991; Manstead, 2000), descriptive norms (White, Terry & Hogg, 1994), self-identity (Sparks, 2000), and anticipated regret (Richard, van der Pligt, & de Vries, 1996).

This leaves us with a situation in which measurement precision and additional explanatory variables might help explain why attitudes do not map entirely exactly onto behavior (although there are also technical reasons why measured attitudes do not predict behavior better than they do [Sutton, 1998]). Other factors, such as the existence of multiple attitudes—some implicit, some explicit (Wilson, Lindsey, & Schooler, 2000), nonattitudes (Converse, 1970), and ambivalent attitudes (Thompson, Zanna, & Griffin, 1995) may also affect the strength of the relationship between measured attitudes and behavior.

Furthermore, if people claim to value their health and still engage in an unhealthy behavior (e.g., drinking to excess on an infrequent but regular basis), we don't usually rush to claims of inconsistency. We acknowledge they may value other things also, such as the pleasures of indulgence or freedom from the influence of others who would seek to dictate or otherwise influence how they should behave. Their attitudes may be prima facie attitudes: initial judgments that are open to subsequent modification. Or those people may carry out other behaviors that indicate to them that they are promoting their own health: that is, they may believe that they can achieve the goal of health through other means.

Empirically, we might expect that composite measures of healthy behavior might be better predicted by these people's attitudes (toward health in general) than are measures of single healthy behaviors. Here again lurks the importance not only of correspondence between the variables that we are measuring but also a reminder that models such as the TRA and TPB are designed to assess goals in the form of *behaviors* rather than goals that are in the form of *outcomes*. Thus, attitudes toward the broad and abstract notion of "my health" may have no obvious corresponding behaviors—especially perhaps if one subscribes to Benjamin Franklin's dictum that "Nothing is more fatal to health than an overcare of it" (cf. Crawford, 1984)!

IDENTITY

"People behave sometimes as if they had two selves, one who ... wants a lean body and another who wants dessert. ... The two are in continual contest for control" (Schelling, 1980, pp. 95–96).

Measures of people's identity have also been shown to be of some predictive use in the TRA/TPB framework (e.g., Sparks & Shepherd, 1992; Theodorakis, 1994; Terry, White & Hogg, 1999), although there have been some suggestions that such measures may sometimes serve as a proxy for past behavior (Sparks, 2000) or that they are effectively a measure of people's intentions (Fishbein, 1997). Furthermore, the contribution that measures of identity make to the prediction of intentions or behavior over and above the standard TPB predictors seems to be very modest (Conner and Armitage, 1998).

One of the more significant novel developments in this area, and one that shows a very useful synthesis between research perspectives, is the integration of social identity theory and the TPB (e.g., Terry, Hogg, & White, 1999; White, Terry, & Hogg, 1994). As well as emphasizing the usefulness of more complete measures of social influence processes than is afforded by standard subjective norm measures, this research has inspired a body of research that shows that group identification can moderate the effect of those social influence variables (that is, and to keep everything at a very simple level, greater group identification leads to stronger relationships between social influence variables and measures of intention and behavior). It is also of interest to note here—with a view to the sustainability themes that will be addressed later—that subjective norm measures have been reported to be more useful (in terms of prediction) for cooperative behaviors than for competitive behaviors (Ajzen & Fishbein, 1980).

So, measures of identity have proved to be valuable predictors within the structure of the TPB, albeit in a very modest way. Measures of identity may also serve, under some conditions, as useful moderators of other relationships within the TPB, and it may be that their relationship with other model variables requires some reexamination (see, e.g., Eagly and Chaiken's 1993 chapter "Composite Model of Attitude–Behavior Relations").

As the previous quote from Shelling indicates, however, there is perhaps the idea of multiple selves or multiple identities that merits attention. The notion of a plurality of selves has a long history within social psychology. James (1890) spoke of the "rivalry and conflict of the different selves," for example, and his notion of the plurality of social selves was developed famously in Goffman's ideas about self-presentation (Goffman, 1959). The issue of multiple (and possibly conflicting) identities has not to date been addressed within applications of the TPB.

SUSTAINABILITY

"As a *citizen*, I am concerned with the public interest, rather than my own interest; with the good of the community, rather than simply the well-being of my family... as a *consumer* ... I concern myself with personal or self-regarding wants and interests; I pursue the goals I have as an individual. I put aside the community-regarding values I take seriously as a citizen, and I look out for Number One instead" (Sagoff, 1988, p. 8).

The framework and issues outlined previously apply quite readily to any domain of action, including pro-environmental actions. Indeed, numerous studies attest to the usefulness of the TPB in the prediction of intentions and/or behavior in the environmental domain (e.g., Fielding, MacDonald, & Louis, 2008; Heath & Gifford, 2002; Mannetti, Pierro, & Livi, 2004). And, as might be expected, general measures of attitude correspond better with general, rather than specific, measures of behavior (Weigel & Newman, 1976). However, in distinction to attitudes toward behaviors, attitudes toward targets (such as the environment or sustainability, for example) would be seen as external variables from a TRA/TPB perspective and thus be expected to have only a tenuous link to behavior. Moreover, one might expect a stronger relationship between attitudes toward "*my* health" and attitudes toward "me carrying out health-related behavior X" than between attitudes toward "the environment" and attitudes toward "me carrying out environment-related behavior Y," both because of the more obvious involvement of personal outcomes and because of the higher subjective probability of tangible impact in the former case.

Measures of identity within TPB studies help predict intentions to engage in pro-environmental behaviors; for example, to purchase organic food produce (Sparks & Shepherd, 1992), to recycle (Nigbur, Lyons, & Uzzell, in press; Terry, Hogg, & White, 1999), and to engage in environmental activism (Fielding, MacDonald, & Louis, 2008). Different kinds of identity (e.g., in terms of dispositions or group membership) have been employed in these studies and have been measured in somewhat varying ways.

However, how is it that measures of identity exert the effects they do? These processes have not been well articulated or experimentally tested in the literature. Putting aside for now the possibility that identity merely serves as a proxy for past behavior or behavioral intentions, let us consider some (interrelated) potential candidates.

Identity and morality. The potentially close relationship between a person's identity and their moral judgments (or commitments or convictions) needs to be borne in mind in relation to this issue (Sparks & Shepherd, 1992) since moral judgments and attitudes can be expected to sometimes exert independent effects on people's intentions and behavior (Manstead, 2000). For example, people's moral judgments may relate to things that they care about (and/or, of course, they may care about *having those judgments*) and these judgments (views/opinions) may become an important part of a person's identity. That is, the idea is that people's core commitments are often central to their sense of their own identity (Calhoun, 1995; Frankfurt, 1988). Alternatively expressed, identities may become *assertions of morality* (March, 1994, p. 65). Importantly, these commitments may reflect concerns that are not captured within people's attitudes (but see, e.g., Skitka, Bauman, & Sargis, 2005).

Identity and affect. Second, and despite the current cognitive emphasis of much identity-related research, expressions of self-identity may capture an affective response to the issue at hand. Measures of identity and affect are often closely related (Hinds & Sparks, 2008) and ideas about the role of affect in influencing behavior have a meritorious history. People may identify with what they care about (Frankfurt, 1988), and what they care about can have a significant impact on their behavior: "If a mother who is tempted to abandon her child finds that she simply cannot do that, it is probably not because she knows (or even because she cares about) her duty. It is more likely because of how she cares about the child, and about herself as its mother, than because of any recognition on her part that abandoning the child would be morally wrong" (p. 90). To the extent that people's expressions of identity capture some experiential factors that are not well represented in people's expressions of attitude, one might expect self-identity to operate independently of attitudes in predicting people's intentions and behavior. The view that affective factors are neglected, or underrepresented, within the TPB is widespread (e.g., Conner & Sparks, 2005).

Identity as a decision heuristic. At a more cognitive level, expressions of identity may act as simple (but effective) decision heuristics: they may give a clear indication of what a person should do in given situations (March, 1994). They are thus part of a rule-following approach to decision making that may be contrasted with a more rational approach based on a consideration of the consequences of choice options (conforming, in March's terms, to a *logic of appropriateness* rather than to a *logic of consequences*). That is, identities form part of the rules for appropriate behavior in particular situations. Such expressions of identity may or may not be congruent with people's expressed attitudes but the existence of ambivalence about decision options and of clashes between people's first-order and second-order desires (people may have a first-order desire to do X but a second-order desire that they would prefer not to have the desire to do X [Frankfurt, 1988]) would suggest that some evaluative component other than what is captured in expressions of attitude might be expected to play a useful role in influencing attitudes and behavior. To the extent that some forms of identity serve as behavioral rules, they may disengage the cost–benefit calculus (Prelec & Herrnstein, 1991, p. 323). Moreover, the TPB is very much tied to a logic of consequences (at least, in the formation of attitudes): to the extent that a different form of decision making is represented in measures of identity, one might expect predictive effects of identity independent from those of attitudes.

Identity and possible selves. Expressions of self-identity may encapsulate what sort of person someone would like to become. To the extent that possible selves (Markus & Nurius, 1986), potential selves (James, 1890), or ideal and ought selves (Higgins, 1996) act as motives for action, these effects also might act independently of attitudes (if, for example, expressions of attitude capture shorter-term concerns or outcomes). In this sense, identities would become what Markus and Nurius have called "the cognitive components of hopes, fears, goals, and threats" (1986, p. 954).

MULTIPLE SELVES?

People may thus access identities as guides to appropriate action (March, 1994) but is ascribing identity work to every motive that people experience a coherent strategy? That a person can have different motives and conflicting goals is clear. What is less obvious is the extent to which we might usefully impute *identity* processes of some sort within what is going on here. Different identities may serve to frame action in different ways or may give different indications of what is appropriate behavior, but (a) not all motives will be attached to particular identities (at least not in a way that is psychologically meaningful), and (b) not all identities will be associated with unambiguous directions for action. So, I suspect that the metaphor of multiple selves has limited applicability, especially *if* the metaphor is likely to be treated literally. The relationship between intrapersonal conflict and interpersonal cooperation has been addressed elsewhere (e.g., Elster, 1985) and I am inclined to the view that this *multiple selves* metaphor does not serve an obviously useful function (cf. Elster, 1986). Of course, to the extent, for example, that attribution of one's actions to *a different self* serves as a justification device that a person may use to deflect responsibility away from themselves, the notion is of considerable psychological interest.

The problem of inconsistent preferences arising from temporal discounting of future outcomes is one of the reasons why the notion of multiple selves has become popular. Self-management is important: "There are things we hope to do that we are not sure we shall do and things we hope not to do that we are fearful we may do, and we seek ways to make our future behavior conform with what we now perceive to be our true or genuine or legitimate or long-range interest" (Shelling, 1992, p. 168). This certainly rings true at one level: we are aware of different preferences that we experience, partly as a function of framing (as perhaps a result of temporal construal) and partly as a function of incompatible goals. And our choices can be changed by the ways in which choices are framed for us (e.g., LeBoeuf, Shafir, & Belyavsky Bayuk, 2010) or in the way that the *choice architecture* is arranged (Thaler & Sunstein, 2008). So the notion of inconsistent preferences is not really contested. But where do multiple selves fit in here exactly? The notions of multiple identities and multiple motives do not seem to be conceptually problematic and can be seen to be psychologically important, but why entertain the notion of multiple selves over and above this?

THE PSYCHOLOGY OF SUSTAINABILITY: TWO THEMES

"Until this century, most of mankind lived in small communities. What each did could only affect a few others. But conditions have now changed. Each of us can now, in countless ways, affect countless other people. We can have real though small effects on thousands or millions of people" (Parfit, 1986, p. 86).

Where people's actions in the domain of environmental sustainability can be seen to differ somewhat from their actions in the domain of health is in relation to two interrelated themes that draw on the notion of identity: (i) morality and (ii) collective action. Morality is closely involved in environmental issues since the welfare of others is at stake (and dominates) in concerns about sustainability (Dresner, 2008). Collective action is implicated because many of the environmental problems we face are social dilemmas that need to be solved by collective cooperation. Both of these themes involve our relationships to others.

These themes are not the prerogative of the environmental domain of course, but they feature within that domain more frequently and more centrally than they do within many other domains (such as health) in which personal outcomes are more salient. Admittedly, the extent to which people's actions in the environmental domain are, or need to be, motivated by a concern with others' welfare is a moot point. Some have argued that the morality of a motive should not be confused with the morality of action (Kaplan, 2000); that is, good motives can lead to poor outcomes and bad motives can lead to desirable outcomes. It has even been suggested that the way to promote pro-environmental actions is to recognize a basic human orientation toward self-interest: "the cynicism of the economist and the biologist about man's selfish, shortsighted nature seems justified. The optimism of the environmental movement about changing that nature does not" (Ridley & Low, 1994, p. 12). For Ridley and Low, a system of rewards and incentives geared toward self-interest motives can best serve the interests of the environment. Notwithstanding these issues, and the various counterarguments to them, there does seem to be a level of complexity and urgency to pro-environment-related actions: motives that relate to the welfare of others might be expected to be more dominant and those that relate to self-interest to be less dominant in this domain. Certainly, measures of moral norms are often independent predictors of people's behavioral intentions in applications of the TPB to environmental issues (Harland, Staats, & Wilke, 1999; Sparks, Hinds, Curnock, & Pavey, in press; Sparks & Shepherd, 2002).

In the environmental domain, others' welfare is more implicated than it is in the domain of health-related behaviors. Even though personal risks do not *come alone* and one's own health-related actions impact on others' health and well-being (such that responsibility for others is involved), it is in the environmental domain that the welfare of others (including future generations) is a more prominent theme. The environmental domain is thus more often associated with outcomes of actions that affect others. Of course, environmental actions may be carried out for outcomes that serve self-interest (e.g., saving money, self-presentation, the beneficial effects of less materialistic lifestyles on well-being), but moral demands will also be present to a degree that is not present for actions in the domain of personal health, such that moral considerations are likely to be a more influential motivational factor in the former.

Our relationships to others are what marks out the sustainability domain from many others. The nature of globalization means that we impact on the lives of others in a way that was not true for generations past. Parfit (1986) suggests that we should accept a moral view in which acts that are "one of a set of acts that will together harm other people" (p. 86) are wrong, even if a single act causes no harm in itself. Others have claimed that we should adopt a notion of global citizenship (Attfield, 1999) or environmental citizenship (Dobson, 2007), that we subscribe to a form of cosmopolitanism that takes into account the welfare of people who are strangers to us. Many of these discussions appeal to a common humanity: "The challenge, then, is to take minds and hearts formed over the long millennia of living in local troops and equip them with ideas and institutions that will allow us to live together as the global tribe we have become" (Appiah, 2006, p. xiii).

The domain of sustainability is also characterized by familiar problems that affect collective action and cooperation: "Once one starts thinking about human behavior in terms of social dilemmas, they begin to appear everywhere" (Osbaldiston & Sheldon, 2002, p. 38). This is perhaps the most pressing multiple-selves or multiple-identities issue in the domain of sustainability. The big challenge is the coordination between individuals to achieve outcomes that individuals cannot achieve on their own while at the same time mitigating the impact of free riders who threaten to undermine cooperative motives.

Many of the outcomes that we are concerned about are collective action problems: they involve the cooperation between individuals for their solution but where the tangible benefits to, or contribution of, any one individual are relatively insignificant. Again, this may be true for some actions (e.g., taking the bus rather than driving your car) but not for others where individual actions may bring significant tangible benefits (e.g., writing to one's Member of Parliament (MP) to persuade them to vote for pro-environmental legislation). This raises different psychological issues than in the case of actions in the health domain, since the cooperation of others (rather than cooperation with oneself over time) is often a requirement for effective action.

POLICY IMPLICATIONS

"Man is a double being and can take, now the god's-eye view of things, now the brute's-eye view" (Huxley, cited in Appiah, 2008, p. 150).

Some tentative policy recommendations (for individuals and organizations) can be derived from some of the issues raised.

Be aware of the broader influences on value salience. People in the West grow up within a culture of consumerism. People are exposed to hundreds of brand messages every day (Lawson, 2009) and it has been suggested that "Advertising serves not so much to advertise products as to promote consumption as a way of life" (Lasch, 1979, p. 72). This is just one example of how particular values are made salient to people and can be expected to influence them in their day-to-day actions. Is it any surprise that consumerist values get internalized or made salient to people for so many of their waking hours? Are there similar processes by which the values of sustainability might be made more prominent? These would of course need to avoid large-scale reactance effects, although accusations of indoctrination might be difficult to avoid.

Be aware of the influence of the actions of other people. Related to the previous point, behavioral norms can be expected to exert a significant effect. What other *selves* are doing has a huge influence on what people do (Cialdini, 2005; Hirshleifer, 1995) and in ways that people often may not realize (e.g., Chartrand & Bargh, 2000). People may be unaware of some of these influences and aware of others. Within this latter grouping might fall people's reluctance to engage in cooperative actions if others are seen to be free riding the system with impunity.

Those who benefit from others' input but who don't contribute may often have the effect of reducing general levels of cooperation (Fehr & Gintis, 2007). Making judicious use of normative information (e.g., the number of people who contribute to positive actions of one sort or other) where appropriate may often be a positive move, for example.

Be aware of the potential pitfalls of a *multiple selves* rhetoric! Consider ditching all talk of multiple selves. I know of no empirical work that has addressed this issue, but there may be conditions under which attribution of negative actions to *different selves* serves to rationalize (and thereby maintain) that behavior. This connection between identity and responsibility is also apparent in the concern that people view their social identities as somehow impelling them to act in particular ways such that their own behavioral choices are limited (Sen, 2006). Do multiple selves provide us with anything substantial over and above multiple identities and multiple motives? We already have selves that are Protean (Lifton, 1993): are there compelling reasons to risk encroaching on philosophical concerns with the question of personal identity by entertaining the additional baggage of multiple selves?

Be aware of the potential benefits of the rhetoric of sustainability. Psychology has not engaged much to date with the language of sustainability; doing so might bring benefits that exceed those of focusing on *the environment* (cf. Dresner, 2008). There may also be greater opportunities for interdisciplinary dialogue and developments were it to do so. Crossing those disciplinary boundaries may be important and allow for some synthesis of theoretical and practical ideas.

CONCLUDING COMMENTS

"Poverty makes growth necessary for much of the world. ... By contrast, we who live in rich countries, awash in goods and services, have no such compelling argument. Indeed, we may have good reason to dismantle the engine of growth—not because growth is a threat to our relationship with nature, but because it is a threat to our relationships with one another" (Marglin, 2008, p. 4).

Two concluding points draw this short chapter to a close: the first marks certain misgivings about the multiple-selves metaphor; the second is more upbeat in discussing a reorientation of values that sustainability invites.

The claim of an apparent discrepancy between attitudes and behavior in the domain of sustainability needs to be dealt with through a detailed examination of the precise nature of that *gap*. For example, people may not know how to express or instantiate their environmental values in action, or they may be persuaded that their (small) actions are making a (significant) difference, that they are already doing their bit to save the planet and that they can rest on their green laurels (cf. Marshall, 2007; Monin & Miller, 2001). Some people, some of the time, may be more concerned with self-presentation than with actual actions. All these issues can be grasped and perhaps dealt with without recourse to the rhetoric of different selves. Sure, people will choose the nonorganic option over the more expensive organic alternative, or take that flight to exotic sunnier climes rather than holidaying in more familiar chilly zones. Such choices can be interpreted in terms of the different motives that people have and it may be that contextual factors can influence which motives are dominant at points of decision.

It may be that the different identities that we have (whether they relate, for example, to dispositions, social roles, or group memberships) indicate what actions are appropriate for us to follow in particular contexts. However, the behaviors prescribed by those identities are rarely narrowly defined (identities are perhaps often more like principles than clear behavioral rules) and we retain some freedom of choice within our identities about what actions we should take (Sen, 2006). Multiple selves are relevant here insofar as they are used as a metaphor to reflect different goals or where identity (as some psychological reality) really serves as an instigator of action (rather than merely as a turn of phrase to describe that action). But it would be useful to ascertain *when, why,* and *how* different identities influence decision processes here, rather than simply conjoining an identity (or *self*) to whatever motive dominates the selection of choice options. The psychology of sustainability involves complicated issues that certainly don't require unnecessarily complex conceptual baggage. The notion of multiple selves perhaps helps to highlight multiple goals, motives, or tendencies, but we should perhaps be aware of obfuscating important issues.

On the other hand, the challenge of sustainability perhaps induces us to a reorientation of values, even a reexamination of our own identities, a consideration at least of the cosmopolitan position "we have obligations to others, obligations that stretch beyond those to whom we are related by the ties of kith and kin, or even the more formal ties of shared citizenship" (Appiah, 2006, p. xv). Such a position includes "connection not *through* identity but *despite* difference" (p. 135) or "connection through humanity' (p. 153). For Sen (2006), the very "plurality of our identities" (p. 16) is a cause for hope that that shared humanity can be recognized.

Social psychology as a discipline is largely predicated on social influence processes but has perhaps neglected research into the psychological benefits that accrue from broader social relationships, of personal engagement with others in local and global communities. However, the importance of relatedness is acknowledged in some perspectives (e.g., Deci & Ryan, 2000), a sense of connectedness is central to some interpretations of identity (Stets & Biga, 2003), and our engagement with others is central to recent discussions about social capital (e.g., Putnam, 2000). An acknowledgment of the importance (in many ways) of, and reorientation toward, other selves requires a focus on different values to those of materialism, consumerism, and the marketplace. However, it perhaps requires less a rejection of self-interest than a different interpretation of what self-interest involves (Singer, 1997).

Part of this reorientation might include a serious reconsideration of the broader social influence processes that shape our values and preferences. Addressing some of the problems of consumer society, Scitovsky (1976) raised the question, "Could it not be that we seek our satisfaction in the wrong things, or in the wrong way, and are then dissatisfied with the outcome?" (p. 4), and more recent work has noted the difference between *expected* utility and *experienced* utility (Kahneman, 2003), which may provide a partial explanation of this phenomenon. Important here is not to understate the pleasures of consumption, or to simplify the psychological consequences of a lifestyle high in materialism, or to underestimate the difficulty of engaging at an emotional level with large numbers of people on different parts of the planet (cf. Slovic, 2007). At the same time, however, it may be worth considering the point made recently by the Archbishop of Canterbury in the context of people's wishes for ever-increasing material prosperity: "Many of the things which have moved us towards ecological disaster have been distortions of who and what we are and their overall effect has been to isolate us from the reality we are part of" ("Climate crisis," 2009) and the idea that "Seldom in our history have our moral imperatives and our naked self-interest been so closely aligned" (Frank, 1999, p. 13). It is to be hoped that the choice architecture (Thaler & Sunstein, 2008) that frames important decisions affecting our future will nudge us toward a full and proper reconsideration of these issues in a way that is conducive to taking sustainability, well-being, and our collective aspirations seriously.

REFERENCES

Ajzen, I. (1991). The theory of planned behavior. *Organizational Behavior and Human Decision Processes*, 50(2), 179–211.

Ajzen, I., & Fishbein, M. (1980). *Understanding attitudes and predicting social behavior*. Upper Saddle River, NJ: Prentice-Hall.

Appiah, K. A. (2006). *Cosmopolitanism: Ethics in a world of strangers*. London: Allen Lane.

Appiah, K. A. (2008). *Experiments in ethics*. Cambridge, MA: Harvard University Press.

Attfield, R. (1999). *The ethics of the global environment*. Edinburgh: Edinburgh University Press.

Beck, L., & Ajzen, I. (1991). Predicting dishonest actions using the Theory of Planned Behavior. *Journal of Research in Personality*, 25, 285–301.

Calhoun, C. (1995). Standing for something. *The Journal of Philosophy*, 92(5), 235–260.

Chartrand, T. L., & Bargh, J. A. (1999). The chameleon effect: The perception-behavior link and social interaction. *Journal of Personality and Social Psychology*, 76(6), 893–910.

Cialdini, R. B. (2005). Basic social influence is underestimated. *Psychological Inquiry*, 16(4), 158–161.

Climate crisis a chance to become human again, archbishop says. (2009, October 13). *Guardian*, p. 8.

Conner, M., and Armitage, C. J. (1998). Extending the theory of planned behavior: A review and avenues for further research. *Journal of Applied Social Psychology*, 28(5), 1430–1464.

Conner, M. T., and Sparks, P. (2005). Theory of planned behaviour and health behaviour. In M. T. Conner and P. Norman (Eds.), *Predicting health behaviour*. Berkshire, UK: Open University Press (pp. 170–222).

Converse, P. E. (1970). Attitudes and non-attitudes: Continuation of a dialogue. In E. R. Tufte (Ed.), *The quantitative analysis of social problems*. Reading, MA: Addison Wesley.

Crawford, R. (1984). A cultural account of "health": Control, release, and the social body. In J. B. McKinlay, (Ed.), *Issues in the political economy of health care (pp. 60–103*. New York: Tavistock.

Deci, E. L., & Ryan, R. M. (2000). The "what" and "why" of goal pursuits: Human needs and the self-determination of behavior. *Psychological Inquiry*, 11, 227–268.

Dobson, A. (2007). Environmental citizenship: Towards sustainable development. *Sustainable Development*, 15(5), 276–285.

Dresner, S. (2008). *The principles of sustainability*. London: Earthscan.

Eagly, A. H., & Chaiken, S. (1993). *The psychology of attitudes*. Fort Worth, TX: Harcourt Brace Jovanovich.

Elster, J. (1985). Weakness of will and the free-rider problem. *Economics and Philosophy*, *1*(2), 231–265.

Elster, J. (1986). Introduction. *The multiple self*. Cambridge: Cambridge University Press.

Fehr, E., and Gintis, H. (2007). Human motivation and social cooperation: Experimental and analytical foundations. *Annual Review of Sociology*, *33*(1), 43–64.

Fielding, K. S., MacDonald, R., & Louis, W. R. (2008). Theory of planned behaviour, identity and intentions to engage in environmental activism. *Journal of Environmental Psychology*, *28*, 318–326.

Fishbein, M. (1997). Predicting, understanding, and changing socially relevant behaviors: Lessons learned. In C. McGarty and S. A. Haslam (Eds.), *The message of social psychology*. Oxford: Blackwell, (pp. 77–91).

Frank, R. H. (1999). *Luxury fever: Money and happiness in an era of excess*. Princeton, NJ: Princeton University Press.

Frankfurt, H. (1988). *The importance of what we care about: Philosophical essays*. Cambridge: Cambridge University Press.

Gagnon Thompson, S. C., & Barton, M. A. (1994). Ecocentric and anthropocentric attitudes toward the environment. *Journal of Environmental Psychology*, *14*(2), 149–157.

Gladwin, T. N., Newbury, W. E., & Reiskin, E. D. (1997). Why is the northern elite mind biased against community, the environment, and a sustainable future? In M. H. Bazerman, D. M. Messick, A. E. Tenbrunsel, & K. A. Wade-Benzioni (Eds.), *Environment, ethics, and behavior* (pp. 234–274). San Francisco, CA: The New Lexington Press.

Glaeser, E. L. (2007). A road map for environmentalism. Harvard Kennedy School. Retrieved on August 6, 2011, from http://www.boston.com/news/globe/editorial_opinion/oped/articles/2007/05/21/a_road_map_for_environmentalism/.

Goffman, E. (1959). *The Presentation of Self in Everyday Life*. New York: Doubleday Anchor.

Harland, P., Staats, H., and Wilke, H. A. M. (1999). Explaining proenvironmental intention and behavior by personal norms and the theory of planned behavior. *Journal of Applied Social Psychology*, *29*(12), 2505–2528.

Heath, Y., & Gifford, R. (2002). Extending the theory of planned behavior: Predicting the use of public transportation. *Journal of Applied Social Psychology*, *32*(10), 2154–2189.

Higgins, E. T. (1996). Ideals, Oughts, and Regulatory Focus: Affect and motivation from distinct pains and pleasures. In P. M. Gollwitzer and J. A. Bargh (Eds.), *The Psychology of Action*. New York: The Guilford Press (pp. 91–114).

Hinds, J., & Sparks, P. (2008). Engaging with the natural environment: The role of affective connection and identity. *Journal of Environmental Psychology*, *28*(2), 109–120.

Hirshleifer, D. (1995). The blind leading the blind: Social influence, fads, and informational cascades. In M. Tommasi & K. Ierulli (Eds.), *The new economics of human behavior* (pp. 188–215). Cambridge: Cambridge University Press.

James, W. (1980). *The principles of psychology*. Cambridge, MA: Harvard University Press.

Kahneman, D. (2003). A perspective on judgement and choice: Mapping bounded rationality. *American Psychologist*, *58*(9), 697–720.

Kaplan, S. (2000). Human nature and environmentally responsible behavior. *Journal of Social Issues*, *56*(3), 491–508.

Lasch, C. (1979). *The culture of narcissism: American life in an age of diminishing expectations*. New York: Norton.

Lawson, N. (2009). *All consuming*. London: Penguin.

LeBoeuf, R. A., Shafir, E., & Belyavsky Bayuk, J. (2010). The conflicting choices of alternating selves. *Organizational Behavior and Human Decision Processes*, *111*(1), 48–61.

Lifton, R. J. (1993). *The protean self: Human resilience in an age of fragmentation*. New York: Basic Books.

Lord, C. G., Lepper, M. R., & Mackie, D. (1984). Attitude prototypes as determinants of attitude–behavior consistency. *Journal of Personality and Social Psychology*, 46(6), 1254–1266.

Mannetti, L., Pierro, A., & Livi, S. (2004). Recycling: Planned and expressive behaviour. *Journal of Environmental Psychology*, 24(2), 227–236.

Manstead, A. S. R. (2000). The role of moral norm in the attitude–behavior relationship. In D. J. Terry and M. A. Hogg (Eds.), *Attitudes, behavior and social context: The role of norms and group membership* (pp. 11–30). Mahwah, NJ: Erlbaum.

March, J. G. (1994). *A primer on decision-making: How decisions happen*. New York: The Free Press.

Marglin, S. A. (2008). *The dismal science: How thinking like an economist undermines community*. Cambridge, MA: Harvard University Press.

Markus, H., & Nurius, P. (1986). Possible selves. *American Psychologist*, 41(9), 954–969.

Marshall, G. (2007). *Carbon detox*. London: Gaia.

Monin, B., & Miller, D. T. (2001). Moral credentials and the expression of prejudice. *Journal of Personality and Social Psychology*, 81(1), 33–43.

Nigbur, D, Lyons, E., and Uzzell, D. (2010). Attitudes, norms, identity and environmental behaviour: Using an expanded theory of planned behaviour to predict participation in a kerbside recycling programme. *British Journal of Social Psychology*, 49(2), 259–284.

Osbaldiston, R., & Sheldon, K. M. (2002). Social dilemmas and sustainability: Promoting people's motivation to "cooperate with the future." In P. Schmuck & P. W. Schultz (Eds.), *The psychology of sustainable development* (pp. 37–58). New York: Kluwer.

Parfit, D. (1986). *Reasons and persons*. Oxford: Oxford University Press.

Prelec, D., & Herrnstein, R. J. (1991). Preferences or principles: Alternative guidelines for choice. In R. J. Zeckhauser (Ed.), *Strategy and choice* (pp. 319–340). Cambridge, MA: MIT Press.

Putnam, R. D. (2000). *Bowling alone: The collapse and revival of American community*. New York: Simon & Schuster.

Richard, R., van der Pligt, J., & de Vries, N. (1996). Anticipated affective reactions and prevention of AIDS. *British Journal of Social Psychology*, 34(1), 9–21.

Ridley, M., & Low, B. S. (1994). Can selfishness save the environment? *Human Ecology Review*, 1, 1–13.

Sagoff, M. (1988). *The economy of the Earth: Philosophy, law and the environment*. Cambridge: Cambridge University Press.

Scitovsky, T. (1992). *The joyless economy: The psychology of human satisfaction*. Oxford: Oxford University Press.

Schelling, T. C. (1980). The intimate contest for self-command. *The Public Interest*, 60, 94–118.

Schelling, T. C. (1992). Self-command: a new discipline. In G. Loewenstein and J. Elster (Eds.), *Choice over time* (pp.167–209). New York: Russell Sage Foundation.

Sen, A. (2006). *Identity and violence: The illusion of destiny*. London: Allen Lane.

Singer, P. (1997). *How are we to live? Ethics in an age of self-interest*. Oxford: Oxford University Press.

Skitka, L. J., Bauman, C. W., & Sargis, E. G. (2005). Moral conviction: Another contributor to attitude strength or something more. *Journal of Personality and Social Psychology*, 88(6), 895–917.

Slovic, P. (2007). "If I look at the mass I will never act": Psychic numbing and genocide. *Judgment and Decision Making*, 2(2), 79–95.

Sparks, P. (2000). Subjective expected utility-based attitude-behavior models: The utility of self-identity. In D. J. Terry and M. A. Hogg (Eds.), *Attitudes, behavior and social context: The role of norms and group membership* (pp. 31–46). Mahwah, NJ: Erlbaum.

Sparks, P., Hinds, J., Curnock, S., & Pavey, L. J. (in press). Connectedness and its consequences: A study of relationships with the natural environment. *Journal of Applied Social Psychology.*

Sparks, P., & Shepherd, R. (1992). Self-identity and the theory of planned behavior: Assessing the role of identification with "green consumerism." *Social Psychology Quarterly, 55*(4), 388–399.

Sparks, P., & Shepherd, R. (2002). The role of moral judgments within expectancy-value based attitude–behavior models. *Ethics & Behavior, 12*(4), 299–321.

Stets, J. E., & Biga, C. F. (2003). Bringing identity theory into environmental sociology. *Sociological Theory, 21*(4), 398–423.

Sutton, S. (1998). Explaining and predicting intentions and behavior: How well are we doing? *Journal of Applied Social Psychology, 28*(15), 1318–1339.

Terry, D. J., Hogg, M. A., & White, K. M. (1999). The theory of planned behavior: Self-identity, social identity, and group norms. *British Journal of Social Psychology, 38*(1), 225–244.

Thaler, R. H., & Sunnstein, C. R. (2008). *Nudge: Improving decisions about health, wealth and happiness.* London: Penguin Books.

Theodorakis, Y. (1994). Planned behavior, attitude strength, role identity, and the prediction of exercise behavior. *The Sport Psychologist, 8*(2), 149–165.

Thompson, M., Zanna, M., & Griffin, D. (1995). Let's not be indifferent about (attitudinal) ambivalence. In R. E. Petty & J. A. Krosnick (Eds.), *Attitude strength: Antecedents and consequences* (pp. 361–386). Mahwah, NJ: Lawrence Erlbaum.

Weigel, R. H., & Newman, L. S. (1976). Increasing attitude–behavior correspondence by broadening the scope of the behavioral measure. *Journal of Personality and Social Psychology, 33*(6), 793–802.

White, K. M., Terry, D. J., & Hogg, M. A. (1994). Safer sex behavior: The role of attitudes, norms, and control factors. *Journal of Applied Social Psychology, 24*(24), 2164–2192.

Wicker, A. W. (1969). Attitudes versus actions: The relationship of verbal and overt behavioral responses to attitude objects. *Journal of Social Issues, 25*(4), 41–78.

Wilson, T. D., Lindsey, S., & Schooler, T. Y. (2000). A model of dual attitudes. *Psychological Review, 107*(1), 101–126.

WWF (2008). *Weathercocks and signposts: The environmental movement at the crossroads.* Available at http://assets.wwf.org.uk/downloads/weathercocks_report2.pdf.

14

Toward Sustainable Social Identities
Including Our Collective Future Into the Self-Concept

TOM POSTMES, ANNA RABINOVICH, THOMAS
MORTON, and MARTIJN VAN ZOMEREN

D espite the doom and gloom about climate change, the last decades have
seen dramatic improvements in the climate of public opinion about this
issue. Today, a large majority of the public in Western countries accepts
the idea that we are changing the climate, is moderately willing to endorse the need
for making personal changes, and is generally supportive of governments making changes (Lorenzoni & Pidgeon, 2006). Nevertheless, it is also widely reported
that behavioral change is lagging behind these positive sentiments. Despite the
fact that the common good is evident and widely accepted, individuals remain
reluctant to acknowledge the personal relevance of these risks, or to make drastic
changes to their own behavior (e.g., Lorenzoni, Leiserowitz, Doria, Poortinga, &
Pidgeon, 2006). This is a classic commons dilemma-type situation, it would seem,
and as with all such dilemmas we may be tempted to think that humans are simply
too selfish and/or shortsighted to change their behavior. But given the right mindset, commons dilemma-type situations can actually produce remarkable amounts
of collaboration and prosocial behavior (Ostrom, 2000). This chapter will discuss
three related aspects of such mindsets: time perspective, social identity, and what
this is bound up with (stereotypes, norms, and values), and psychological predictors of collective action.

THE PROBLEM MATRIX

From a psychological perspective, global warming and the behavioral changes
required to stop it present a complex puzzle. A matrix of factors conspires to

disconnect *the individual* at this specific moment in time from *the problem* as it has emerged, and will develop. The three dimensions of this matrix are time, level of social abstraction, and level of problem abstraction. It is worth pausing to think about these issues, not just because they are the academic backgrounds to the current problem of climate change (and therefore worthwhile abstractions to ponder), but also because they may be the building blocks for a practical solution to the problems we face today.

One of the axes of this matrix is time (cf. Swim et al., 2009). Our unsustainable lifestyles have roots in the past, and the pressing demands for behavioral change are motivated by outcomes in the future. Psychologically, these large time differences need to be traversed, somehow. The scale of this mental time travel is unusually large: today's behavior toward nature is grounded in cultural orientations whose origin is as ancient as it is integral to the fabric of contemporary society. The Bible sanctions uses of nature thus: "God blessed them and said to them, 'Rule over the fish of the sea and the birds of the air and over every living creature that moves on the ground'" (Genesis, 1:28, new international translation). Although such cultural orientations are not the only source of today's problems, they exemplify a deep-seated assumption that humans are masters of nature. In this mentality, it is entirely justified to let natural resources pay the price for accelerating industrialization, the growth of wealth, and of populations. Today's problems are therefore the logical consequence of centuries of human activity, and it is unsurprising that psychologically, many people (even in the West) have difficulty personally relating to the problem of climate change as one that *we*, the present-day inhabitants of the Earth, are causing.

When looking toward the future, other psychological problems of time scale present themselves. Thinking about *the future* presents humans with several challenges. One of these is that the determinants of our behavior tend to be situational and the horizons of our actions short term. Most of our behavior conforms to situational norms or reacts to opportunities and problems that present themselves within specific social or physical situations. Even when our actions are not evoked by the situation or local context, they tend to be dominated by short-term needs, motives, and emotions that are less oriented toward the future than to current gratifications. Nonetheless, we frequently think about the future, and these thoughts about the future can, at certain times, exert considerable influence on our behavior. But our thinking about such long-term futures is curtailed by a tendency to project those same present-day hopes and fears onto it. For various reasons, then, human behavior tends to be geared toward the here and now, and perhaps for good reason: only rarely can humans accurately predict what the consequences of today's actions will be more than a season from now. Perhaps the biggest exceptions to this mindset can be found in the way humans provide for their children and in the accumulation of capital. Both of these are relevant to the issue at hand: future generations will suffer the worst of the consequences of climate change. Thus, the fact that the consequences of environmentally unsustainable practices are delayed in time presents a considerable challenge for behavioral change attempts: the self is psychologically distant to past sources of the problem, as well as its future solutions.

The second axis of the matrix is the level of *social abstraction* at which environmental issues play out. Here there is considerable scope for disagreement and conflict, but also for change. Although the problem is often presented and experienced as being a *human* problem, that is hardly a fair assessment. Within the human category, one can make distinctions among a number of subgroupings that are strikingly different in their relation to all aspects of the problem: its making, its consequences, and its solutions. One key distinction is between developed and developing parts of the world—an issue that has paralyzed progress in international climate treaty negotiations because the developed countries' past and current behaviors are threatening the developing countries' understandable desire for equality. Another key entity that has to be considered is the *nation*. Nations are particularly important social groupings for environmental issues because they provide the regulations within which its citizens and corporations seek to operate. Nations are also sources of national identity, and these national identities (as we shall see) may be characterized by sharply different attitudes toward environmental issues. And finally, it is worthwhile to distinguish among many cross-sections of societies as well. The same heterogeneity of international attitudes toward sustainability may also be found within nations, with differences between the political left and right, differences between rich and poor, differences between ethnic groups and regions, and differences between those who consider themselves "green" or otherwise environmentally active and the rest of the population.

All these categorizations are influential, because they are used to define and make sense of the problem in particular ways. To illustrate this, a categorization at the human level implies a distinction between humans and the rest of nature (as in the book of Genesis). This highlights the issues of power/exploitation and responsibility/sustainability, and fosters a perspective on climate change as a problem between *us* and nature. But solutions are typically not sought at this inclusive level of categorization. Rather, practical solutions introduce different levels of categorization, all of which introduce particular perspectives and political issues. For example, climate change treaties are negotiated between nations that are painfully different in levels of wealth. This raises issues of growth and its sustainability, and the equitable division of resources. In contrast, when environmental issues are seen as *individual* concerns, we tend to focus on lifestyles, consumption patterns, and self-interest. Thus, social categorization may play an important role in framing the problem of environmental change, and may affect the process of searching relevant solutions.

The third axis of the problem is the level of *problem abstraction*. This axis is not entirely independent of the former two, as it is related to levels of social categorization as well as issues of time. The scale of the problem of climate change is one that dwarfs the individual; it is both a global issue and one with a very long time span. Psychologically, this separates the individual from the issues at stake because humans are by definition limited in the scope in which their thoughts and actions can extend beyond their immediate environment. Thus, the individual needs to find a way of reconciling capabilities for local action with a global mindset (Rabinovich, Morton, Postmes, & Verplanken, 2009).

RECONNECTING THE SELF

The psychological matrix of the climate change issue outlines the dimensions along which the individual has to reach outside the boundaries of the physical self. Ostensibly the challenges set by each dimension are of very different kinds. The problem with levels of categorization is that, whichever way of framing the problem is chosen, the individual cannot easily connect to it in a personal and consequential way. It is, therefore, important to find ways of relating the self to higher levels of social categorization. A similar issue arises when the self needs to connect to very abstract social concerns. Here again the challenge is to recognize parallels between one's personal behavior and the worldwide issues in which these play a role. Finally, the issue of time also requires that the individual connect their present self to a long history and distant future. Although each of these issues represents unique challenges, in some sense they are also intimately related: the self needs to be reconnected to concerns that are far removed from the here and now, caused by and affecting humans in some generic way. Given this, part of the solution to each of these unique challenges may be found in the same principle: the self-concept and how it is conceived, in very narrow or more expanded terms.

Thinking about the self in more expanded ways is not the same as thinking abstractly (e.g., in terms of general principles and ideals). One can just as easily consider the holistic relationship between the self and generalized others in some abstract fashion, as the irreconcilable discrepancies between them. The issue is reconnecting the self. We deliberately use the word *re*connecting here, because both historically and culturally there is considerable evidence that the self-concept has, in all but the most recent history in the West, been a structure that was highly permeable to influences from outside, such as natural and spiritual forces, and a structure derived from a tight network of relationships (e.g., Henrich, Heine, & Norenzayan, 2010; Morris, 1973). In such situations, the self is intimately connected with the immediate environment in a stable network of relationships that influence and shape the individual. In modern life, the development of an autonomous sense of self makes it possible to act more independently, but it also gives people the possibility to nurture a range of different social identities (cf. Yuki, 2003). Thus, modern individuals have considerably more leeway to choose between acting independently or nurturing particular social relationships, or even one's relationship to nature. The individual thus acquires a certain degree of autonomous control over the ability to (re)connect with others, social identities and nature, by extending the self outward so that it includes those others (e.g., Taylor, 2007).

Through social identification, the self-concept can include various significant others (children, lovers, parents, pets) to the extent that individuals will act on behalf of those others as they would act on their own behalf. But, importantly, this capacity for the self-concept to include others is not limited to those individuals with whom the individual feels a special bond. Much of our self-concept (as well as our social behavior) is informed by our position in and relationship to social structures. Thus, we may identify with concrete social groups such as the family or with work groups. Within these groups, we may have roles and a particular position. But the self-concept is also equipped to be identified with more abstract social categories which do not *exist* as entities in any *real* sense, but only as social constructs: class, ethnicity, political orientation, religion, or nationhood (Postmes & Branscombe, 2010; Tajfel, 1974). Even at the level of identifications with such abstract groups, we may witness extraordinary levels of prosocial behavior or selflessness in certain communities and at certain moments in time. Ironically, these apparently selfless acts are enabled by a self-concept that is so plastic that it may define itself, across situations, in multiple very different ways, depending on which aspect of self is made salient: individual, professional, or national identity, for example.

When social groups are internalized as important aspects of the self-concept, they become *social identities* (Tajfel, 1978). Each of the various social identities to which one may have access constitutes an important resource for the individual, because they serve as a psychological bridge between the individual and the group (Turner & Oakes, 1986). Social identities are at the same time *shared* with others (e.g., they exist as intersubjective entities): they encompass a set of norms, stereotypes, values, and knowledge about the group and its relationship to other groups, nature, and so forth. This social sharedness among in-group members necessarily means that there is some degree of consensus about the social identity's content. This content is crucially important, for it provides a common frame of reference (of language, norms, etc.) within which individuals can cooperate, trade, build communities, assign meanings and values, and wage war (Turner, 1991). But they are also internalized: they become the *personal* norms of the individuals identified with the group. This process of internalization (originally referred to as depersonalization in self-categorization theory) blurs the distinction between public compliance and private acceptance, between normative and informational influence (Turner, 1987).

Research confirms that the salience of a shared social identity affects behavior in social dilemma-type situations. Whether people behave selfishly or not depends very much on how the boundaries of the self are defined (Kramer & Brewer, 1984). When the self can be stretched to include others involved in the dilemma, finding a solution becomes much easier (De Cremer & Van Vugt, 1999). Social identities can also be stretched in other ways. For example, they can be oriented toward the past, the present, and the future; they are about *being* and *becoming* (see also Postmes, Haslam, & Swaab, 2005; Reicher, 2000), something that also has consequences for cooperative, future-oriented actions. Using these theoretical advances in social identity as starting points, we can now begin to explore how processes of social identification play a role in environmental behavior. The discussion will first focus on the issue of how social identities are tied to the past, and how we may focus people on the future, collective action, and then move to consider how we can change the content of social identities by making intergroup comparisons, and conclude with organic methods for the formation of sustainable social identities.

USING SALIENCE TO MANIPULATE TIME PERSPECTIVE

In terms of connecting the self to the past, histories can be important building blocks for the current sense of identity, and many people experience social identities as a sense of historical continuity (Sani et al., 2007). Although systematic empirical research into the relationship between histories and social identity is a comparatively novel enterprise, there are now quite a few studies that show that invoking ideas of heritage and tradition is a powerful way to activate particular social identities and associated contents (e.g., Doosje, Branscombe, Spears, & Manstead, 1998; Liu & Hilton, 2005; Morton & Sonnenberg, 2011; Sindic & Reicher, 2008). Unfortunately however, as described in the introduction, the past is not really a very positive resource (at least in most Western countries) when it comes to sustainable behaviors: the historical lack of concern for the environment is part of the source of the problem, and thus it is unlikely to offer a resolution. Rather than invoking *old* and existing identities, one would have to be able to *create* new ones. The last two sections of this chapter deal with this issue in some detail.

Perhaps the issue of time offers more possibilities when looking toward the future. As noted above, the connection of the self-concept to future outcomes may play a crucial role in encouraging sustainable behavior. It has been argued that time perspective can have a profound impact on decision making and behavior. Specifically, a future time perspective is thought to help a person to "transcend [immediate] stimulus forces" (Zimbardo & Boyd, 1999, p. 1272), and delay gratification (see also Strathman et al., 1994). In a recent series of studies, we found some encouraging initial evidence for this idea (Rabinovich, Morton, Postmes, & Verplanken, 2012). In these studies, we manipulated time perspective by making a long-term time perspective salient (asking people to think about their circumstances in 5 or 10 years' time) or a short-term time perspective (circumstances next month). The results showed that people with a supportive attitude toward some issue (e.g., saving) were indeed more willing to forgo current gratification to maximize long-term gain when they adopted a long-term time perspective. Thus, a longer-term time perspective considerably strengthens the attitude–behavior relationship. Connecting the self to future outcomes should have similar outcomes for sustainable behaviors. Indeed, one study confirmed that the effects of time perspective on economic attitude–behavior consistency were also present in the environmental domain. When a short time perspective was made salient, the relationship between environmental attitudes measured one week previously and environmental intentions was only moderately strong ($\beta = .26$). However, when people's time perspective was extended (i.e., long term), the same relationship became very strong ($\beta = .62$).

While these patterns demonstrate the role of future thinking in fostering more positive intentions, in order to effect large-scale social change we clearly need to do more than focus individual minds on the future. Indeed, we also need large sections of the public to embrace sustainable solutions collectively. To promote collective action of this kind, we need to fuse individual orientations toward the future with social identities that have the capacity to engender and sustain positive action. Social identities are pivotal to collective action: they are the instruments by which people seek to transform existing social realities, and create new ones to realize their collective ideals (Van Zomeren, Postmes, & Spears, 2008). Indeed, research shows that social identification is a key predictor of collective action. However, identification with social groups alone will not always foster positive action—many social identities are bulwarks of conservatism and are thus unlikely vehicles for progressive reform toward sustainability. The content of social identities can drive behavior in very different directions. It is when social identities are also associated with positive ideals that they are able to support positive behavior. Particularly social identities that revolve around a desire for change are predictive of collective action: they are politicized, in the sense that group members have come to identify with the objectives for change to such an extent that this motivation is central to the shared identity of the group (Simon & Klandermans, 2001; Thomas, McGarty, & Mavor, 2009). Social identities of this kind are vehicles of transformation; unlike the norms and values of firmly established groups, they can be actively geared toward change.In sum, perspectives on collective action offer clear guidelines for how to promote self-reinforcing sustainable behavior in large segments of the population. If we can construct social identities that have ideals of sustainability at their core and that are shared by large segments of the population, behavior should follow suit quite effortlessly. Such a method would be cheap and effective. Just *how* to construct sustainable social identities will be the focus of the remainder of this chapter.

USING INTERGROUP SOCIAL COMPARISONS TO CHANGE NORMS

Social identity contents are produced in part by intergroup comparisons (Tajfel, 1978). Framed by historical and ideological understandings, group members can infer the norms and stereotypes of their in-groups from intergroup comparisons: what it means to be a member of a group is informed, in part, by the out-group. As an example, within a European context, certain countries may define themselves as green (e.g., Sweden and Switzerland), but they may only achieve this if they compare themselves to worse offenders than themselves such as the United States and the United Kingdom, rather than to developing countries, which have far better green credentials (Ethiopia and Nepal). It follows that one can promote the formation of particular social identity contents by encouraging specific social comparisons. Moreover, once those social identity contents have been defined, they should affect behavior. In one series of studies, we tested this hypothesis (Rabinovich et al., 2012). Specifically, and fully in line with self-categorization theory (Turner, Hogg, Oakes, Reicher, & Wetherell, 1987), we predicted that intergroup comparisons would affect self-stereotypes of the in-group in conjunction with personal values toward sustainability. These self-stereotypes and values would, in turn, affect environmental intentions and behaviors.

In three studies we varied intergroup comparison context, and then asked British members of the public a series of questions about their individual environmental values and intentions. Participants were randomly allocated to one of the three experimental groups. To manipulate intergroup comparison context, we asked participants in one group to write about differences between the British and a nation that was perceived to be doing worse on the environmental domain (i.e., the United States). Another group was asked to write about the differences between British people in general and a nation that was perceived to be doing better in terms of sustainability (i.e., Sweden). Thus, participants who compared their national group to the United States were involved in a positive intergroup comparison, whereas those who compared their national group to Sweden were involved in a negative intergroup comparison. A control group was not asked to compare their nation to any other group (participants in this group simply described British people in general). Importantly, the dimension of environmental behavior was not explicitly mentioned in this comparison task, and very few participants spontaneously referred to environmental issues in their lists of differences. Thus, out-group environmental stereotypes (perceptions of an out-group as either pro- or un-environmental) were activated implicitly.

After the comparison task we asked participants how environmentally friendly they thought British people were in general (i.e., the perceived in-group norm). We also asked them about the subjective importance of environmental values to their individual self, and their own intentions to perform a range of environmentally friendly behaviors (such as reducing one's electricity/gas consumption, buying mostly organic products, etc.). In the third study, we also included a measure of actual behavior (signing a petition, taking leaflets). In line with self-categorization theory, the results of the studies demonstrated that participants shifted their in-group perception away from the salient out-group comparison standard. Those who compared their national group to Sweden (engaged in a negative comparison with the group that was performing better) perceived their own group as being less environmentally friendly than participants in the control group (who did not engage in intergroup comparisons). Conversely, participants who compared themselves to the United States (engaged in a positive comparison with the group that was performing worse) perceived their own national group as being more environmentally friendly than participants in the control group. In other words, a negative comparison reduced the degree to which the in-group norm was perceived as "green", while positive comparison encouraged thinking about one's own group as strongly environmental.

Moreover, these shifts in perceived in-group norm translated into concordant shifts in individual environmental values and intentions to behave in a sustainable way. Participants who engaged in negative comparison reported that green values were less central to their self than participants in the control group. Conversely, participants who engaged in positive comparisons reported that environmental values were more central to who they were as an individual. These effects on environmental values were paralleled by significant shifts in behavioral intentions: after comparing their national group to Sweden, British participants reported reduced environmental intentions, but after comparing their group to the United States, British participants increased their reported intentions. Finally, the last study confirmed that these effects on norms, values, and intentions translated into actual behavioral differences between conditions. Thus, overall participants were acting in line with the in-group–out-group differentiation principle (we are different from them) by shifting their group evaluations and self-evaluations away from the comparison standard. Subsequent studies (Rabinovich & Morton, 2010a) confirmed and extended these results by showing that in contexts in which people take their own group as the referent (i.e., if their own group's perspective dominates how they look on other countries' behavior) then these distinctiveness-seeking effects are particularly likely to occur.

Together, this line of research confirms that social identity content is shaped by intergroup comparisons, in the manner predicted by self-categorization theory. As powerful as these techniques are, it is worth pausing at their long-term use for sustainable social identities. A clear limitation of these intergroup dynamics is that they rely on the existence of some out-group that can serve as a contrast—we would need the big polluters like the United States to keep up their bad work in order for other groups to feel green and good about themselves, and thereby encourage change. It follows from this that such social comparisons may produce sustainable social identities at certain junctures, but it is highly unlikely that they will be sustainable solutions themselves. There is an associated problem of the fluidity and flexibility of social comparisons: while intergroup comparisons may change how an individual conceives of their group and their self in a given moment, people engage in comparisons constantly and the targets for this change from moment to moment. As such, it is a moot point whether intergroup comparisons alone can sustain long-term behavior change. Overall, the value of this research is that it demonstrates that the dynamics of social identities *can* have marked effects on intentions and behaviors, and that they do so by changing the values individuals see as central to their self. However, in order to produce long-term and sustainable social change, we may have to think about ways of creating sustainable social identity content in a way that is more enduring and less dependent on the contextual fluctuations of the self.

THE ORGANIC CONSTRUCTION OF "GREEN" IDENTITIES

In the last section of this chapter we discuss new developments in research on social identity formation. As mentioned, the key question for years to come is how we can transform social identities so that they enable as many individuals as possible to act for the common good of the entire planet, and reorient people away from short-term goals and toward longer-term outcomes. It would appear that intergroup comparisons have a limited ability to achieve this ideal. But new research points to different and potentially better ways of changing existing identities, or even to define new social identities at a higher level of abstraction.

Recent research on social identity formation has distinguished two pathways to constructing social identities (Postmes, Baray, Haslam, Morton, & Swaab, 2006; Postmes et al., 2005; Postmes, Spears, Lee, & Novak, 2005; Swaab, Postmes, & Spears, 2008). One is the top-down process by which inferences about social identity are internalized as personal values; this is essentially the process described in the work on intergroup comparisons and personal value change (Rabinovich et al., 2012). But the social identity of a group is not merely mechanically deduced from intergroup comparisons and history. It can also be inferred from observations of the behavior of ordinary group members and leaders—a bottom-up process whereby shared norms and values are induced from the observations of the actions of individuals. In this process of induction, one may also find there is considerable debate within the in-group about the future course of action for the group—change becomes a focal point for group activities. For example, people may take note of individual actions by leaders who address the issue of climate change in ways suggesting change is required (Al Gore, Barack Obama) and they are in constant dialogue and debate with "ordinary" in-group members in order to induce how group membership is to be interpreted and enacted. As a result, existing identities are in a constant state of flux, and new identities can emerge.

Research from various quarters has now shed light on these processes. In many of the studies to date, intragroup discussions have been shown to be at the heart of the formation of new social identities, with a considerable capacity for changing individual group members' behavior. For example, Swaab et al. (2007) showed that a simple manipulation of the sharing of certain cognitions of individual group members was sufficient to prompt the emergence of a shared sense of identity in a subsequent phase of group negotiations. Importantly, this shared cognition not merely predicts the emergence of a shared identity; it also fosters the ability of the group for effective collective action.

Research in this vein that is directly relevant to the issue of climate change relies on the formation of (new) opinion-based groups (Bliuc, McGarty, Reynolds, & Muntele, 2007; McGarty, Bliuc, Thomas, & Bongiorno, 2009; Thomas et al., 2009; Thomas & McGarty, 2009). This research has shown that group discussion can lead its members to induce a shared identity revolving around a common opinion (Bliuc et al., 2007; Thomas & McGarty, 2009, for a review). Importantly, this shared identity then channels the group's actions toward changes in line with those opinions, in a manner not dissimilar to Lewin's (1947) classic action research in which he convinced American housewives to serve offal by having them reach a group decision. One series of studies by McGarty, Bongiorno, and Kurz (cited in Thomas & McGarty, 2009) is particularly relevant to climate change. The procedure used in this study was simple: they asked members to sign up for a new group whose goal was to agree on ways to reduce greenhouse gas emissions. They then measured their attitudes and behavioral intentions (e.g., for sociopolitical action such as signing petitions, attending meetings, voting). Compared with a control condition, the discussion groups showed significantly higher levels of solidarity and group identification. What is more, they saw a strong increase in pro-environmental action intentions, thus providing direct support for the idea that it would be possible to induce a shared identity based on a cluster of actions (or goals), and that this identity subsequently would promote collective action.

The implications of this line of research are interesting. In particular, it follows that small group dynamics can, in their own right, give rise to the induction of group norms and other aspects of identity. This means that social identity processes are not restricted to categorical groups, and hence an active intergroup context is not required in order to witness these social identity effects and harness them to drive social change. That is a significant advance, because these intergroup comparisons, so characteristic of international climate change conferences' political wrangling, can often be distractions from the real underlying issue of changing people's behavior fast. Moreover, inductive processes are likely to foster greater permanent loyalty and commitment from group members, whereas intergroup comparisons are shifting and therefore produce more transient states of intention.

Induction has the power to create social norms and values, which are likely to be more permanent features of the individual's life (Postmes et al., 2005). It would be important for future research to corroborate this prediction.

Finally, it would be important to point out that these inductive processes are not merely restricted to small groups and interpersonal settings. For example, through the systematic highlighting of threats of climate change, political leaders and mass media are in a position to change perceptions of the problem. But note that the perception of the problem (which currently attracts most media attention) is not really the relevant outcome variable. From this perspective it would be much more effective and important to systematically highlight *good* behaviors and note their rising popularity (and hence descriptively normative), as well as those *bad* behaviors that are in decline (and hence descriptively antinormative). In this respect, the induction of a shared social identity has many things in common with recent advances in understanding of the implicit formation of group norms (Cialdini & Goldstein, 2004; Keizer, Lindenberg, & Steg, 2008). The fact that leaders and the media are instrumental to achieving these changes in norms in an apparently top-down fashion should not disguise the fact that the processes involved in this can essentially be ones of bottom-up social identity construction. It is a well-known phenomenon in media studies that mass communications are effective to the extent they become conversation pieces (e.g., Morton & Duck, 2001, 2006), and in that sense, mass media messages are very much part of the discourse that produces social norms and identities.

DEVELOPING A MORAL FRAMEWORK FOR ACTION

From this vantage point, it becomes possible to identify the contours of a psychological and social program of behavioral change. In this vision, one should strive to induce social norms, values, and self-stereotypes that define groups or *cultures* at a level of social categorization that is as abstract and inclusive as possible, thereby expanding the self, and the circle of regard, as widely as possible. Importantly, the content of this inclusive social identity should be future oriented (motives, goals, etc.). The object would be to redefine and reinvent what humans *are*, by redefining a common consensual understanding of what we want humans to *become*, namely a species that can live sustainably, preserving available resources for future generations. Finally, the social norms attached to this social identity should be geared toward the behaviors that are deemed desirable or *optimal*—sustainable and sustained solutions, therefore.

As clear-cut as this objective might be, there are serious obstacles to its implementation. Ironically, the lack of public support or will is not among them. To the contrary, as noted in the introduction to the chapter, the public awareness of climate dangers in the Western world tends to be huge, and the desire for change is commensurate. This is a solid foundation and genuine opportunity for a sustained program of change. But despite this positive foundation, there is a pervasive lack of confidence in the ability to find practicable solutions, which is not unrelated to the pervasive disjuncture between individual actions and their global consequences. One specific aspect of this we should consider in greater detail, for it falls within the scope of social psychology to find some remedies for it.

One specific obstacle is that a sustainable program for change clashes with prevalent individualist tendencies. The organization of such a program is hard to imagine when people feel it is their inalienable right to make their own choices of consumption and lifestyle. Of course, decades of research in social psychology have shown that these authentically experienced feelings of autonomy and independence are somewhat self-delusional—the celebrated Western ideal of independence is expressed through the collective purchasing of jeans and iPods (Jetten, Postmes, & McAuliffe, 2002; Pronin, Berger, & Molouki, 2007). But delusional or not, this individual freedom of choice is also a deeply cherished value and universal right, which may stand in the way of support for sustainable collective action.

One pathway to overcoming these obstacles, we would argue, would be to rely on the power that moral convictions have for overcoming boundaries of the self and the collective at *any* level of social inclusion. Moral convictions develop in the same way as group norms, that is to say they are socially shared conventions that prescribe what is appropriate, and therefore right and wrong. But in the process of becoming *moral* beliefs, they transcend group boundaries and become applied as general principles of right and wrong (van Zomeren, Postmes, & Spears, 2012). Thereby, moral judgments tend to be universal judgments that delineate what one should aspire to do; they define ideals that apply to each and every person, and within each and every subgroup, organization, and society. In the case of environmental attitudes, we are already seeing a strong shift toward moralization of specific issues (the idea that particular treatment of animals is unacceptable, for example). But despite the broad public support for the issues involved, we have not quite reached the "natural" conclusion that it is universally accepted that certain rights extend to nature. Nevertheless, it would be fruitful to consider if something like a "universal declaration of natural rights" could remove the obstacles to environmentally sustainable action identified above.

The advantage of a hypothetical universal declaration of natural rights is that it simply extends the moral framework we already apply to humans, and makes it more inclusive. A conviction that animals, plants, and habitats have rights, too is therefore consistent with this somewhat individualist moral framework. It is entirely proper that one's own rights and freedoms do not infringe on the same rights of others. Of course, there will be moral dilemmas where particular rights conflict with each other, but these would not appear to be qualitatively different from the moral dilemmas we face today in other domains. In addition, there are practical benefits to such an approach: moral values tend to be internalized easily, and once internalized they appear to each and every individual who subscribes to them as perfectly natural *personal* beliefs. In sum, the firm establishment of these sustainable moral convictions may well provide a stable basis for a program of social change.

INTEGRATION: MORAL CONVICTIONS, SOCIAL IDENTITY FORMATION, AND SUSTAINABLE BEHAVIOR

In the last section of this chapter, we put the ingredients discussed so far together (see Figure 14.1) and evaluate whether the ingredients we have identified have

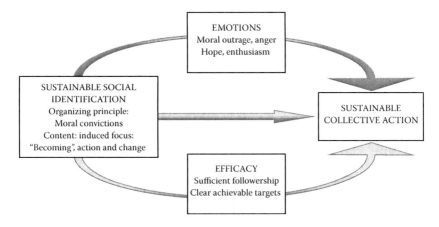

Figure 14.1   A social identity model of collective action, applied to sustainability.

the capacity to address the three dimensions of the problem matrix: extending the self across time, levels of social abstraction, and levels of problem abstraction. We have seen that social identities could become the key predictors of the sustainable collective actions that we would like to see people practice. Social identities have the capacity to extend the self across levels of social abstraction. We have also shown that social identities can be future oriented (focused on becoming, not on being) and thus connect the self to distant future goals. An additional benefit of orienting social identities toward the future, suggested by research, is that identities revolving around change are particularly strong predictors of collective action.

We also suggest that there may be a special role for moral convictions (Skitka, Bauman, & Sargis, 2005) in this process. These would be a way of organizing social identities around a common goal that extends beyond any single individual. In this sense, moral convictions can be a vehicle for rallying all of humankind. Importantly, the activation of these moral convictions means that the system would become self-organizing to a large extent: one can rely on the powers of induction for specific behavioral norms to emerge across societies and cultures. Because of their properties, moral convictions can be powerful motivators of collective action. Moral convictions connect individual believers to higher-order shared belief systems, and thereby they lead both to the formation of shared social identities (e.g., a community sharing the same moral convictions: see Van Zomeren et al., 2011, in press) and to the particular emotional responses, such as hope or moral outrage, which may propel collective action. Emphasizing the moral dimension of sustainability, therefore, should be a particularly powerful way of reconnecting self to abstract issues and ideals.

Social identities may channel individuals toward change, but they do so in conjunction with two other variables: efficacy and action-oriented emotions. Efficacy is of particular importance for climate change. The sense that change is achievable is a genuine prerequisite for people to be motivated into action. From this perspective, the attempt by the climate change lobby to present the problem of climate change as a huge and looming disaster is a double-edged sword. On the one hand, it increases the likelihood that people will realize that change is required. On the other hand, it may well decrease people's sense that change is achievable. This boils down to the fact that the success of collective action may depend on having clear and achievable targets for action that are perceived as viable and efficacious (as well as higher-order justification for these targets: Rabinovich et al., 2009). But importantly, according to the social identity model of collective action (Van Zomeren et al., 2008, 2011, 2012), the social support and solidarity provided by a shared social identity are themselves key prerequisites to tackling any issue efficaciously. The anticipation of mass followership thus precedes collective action: a lot can be achieved, provided a large majority is perceived as having the will to join in.

Emotions are no less relevant, because they provide the motivational bridge between social perceptions and actions. Although collective action research has most often concerned itself with injustice-related emotions such as anger (Van Zomeren, Spears, Fischer, & Leach, 2004; Van Zomeren, Leach, & Spears, 2010; Walker & Smith, 2002), other emotions are also likely to be relevant to environmental behavior. One of these is moral outrage (Thomas & McGarty, 2009), which is subtly different from anger because it is an emotional response that focuses on the restoration of what is just or moral, rather than the punishment of those who are immoral. Other important emotions could be hope and enthusiasm. These emotions release energy to act toward the realization of distant goals and ideals, and are thus particularly relevant to extending the self along the dimensions of the problem matrix, in the sense that hope and enthusiasm connect one to future ideals, as well as to the greater good and greater community. As with efficacy, these emotions can be sustained by shared social identities (Smith, Seger, & Mackie, 2007).

CONCLUSION

This chapter has argued that shared moral convictions can be the foundation for a bottom-up construction of sustainable social identities. These social identities and what is bound up with them (stereotypes, norms and values; emotions and a sense of efficacy) are strong predictors of collective action. Humans have the capacity for unique levels of cooperation because, notwithstanding the bounded nature of the physical self, our psychological self-concept is a boundless and amazingly flexible structure. Based on the broad public support for sustainable solutions, we have a genuine opportunity for sustainable changes to the way we live and want to be, if we can give the self-concept a foundation for change in the direction we have identified in this chapter.

REFERENCES

Bliuc, A. M., McGarty, C., Reynolds, K., & Muntele, D. (2007). Opinion-based group membership as a predictor of commitment to political action. *European Journal of Social Psychology, 37*, 19–32.

Cialdini, R. B., & Goldstein, N. J. (2004). Social influence: Compliance and conformity. *Annual Review of Psychology, 55*, 591–621.

De Cremer, D., & van Vugt, M. (1999). Social identification effects in social dilemmas: A transformation of motives. *European Journal of Social Psychology, 29*, 871–893.

Doosje, B., Branscombe, N. R., Spears, R., & Manstead, A. S. R. (1998). Guilty by association: When one's group has a negative history. *Journal of Personality and Social Psychology, 75*, 872–886.

Henrich, J., Heine, S. J., & Norenzayan, A. (2010). The weirdest people in the world? *Behavioral and Brain Sciences, 33*(2–3), 61–135.

Jetten, J., Postmes, T., & McAuliffe, B. J. (2002). "We're all individuals": Group norms of individualism and collectivism, levels of identification and identity threat. *European Journal of Social Psychology, 32*, 189–207.

Keizer, K., Lindenberg, S., & Steg, L. (2008). The spreading of disorder. *Science, 322*, 1681–1685.

Kramer, R., & Brewer, M. (1984). Effects of group identity on resource use in a simulated commons dilemma. *Journal of Personality and Social Psychology, 46*, 1044–1057.

Lewin, K. (1947). Group decision and social change. In T. M. Newcomb & E. L. Hartley (Eds.), *Readings in social psychology* (pp. 330-344). New York: Holt, Rinehart & Winston.

Liu, J. H., & Hilton, D. J. (2005). How the past weighs on the present: Social representations of history and their role in identity politics. *British Journal of Social Psychology, 44*, 537–556.

Lorenzoni, I., Leiserowitz, A., Doria, M., Poortinga, W., & Pidgeon, N. (2006). Cross-national comparisons of image associations with "global warming" and "climate change" among laypeople in the United States of America and Great Britain. *Journal of Risk Research, 9*, 265–281.

Lorenzoni, I., & Pidgeon, N. (2006). Public views on climate change: European and USA perspectives. *Climatic Change, 77*, 73–95.

McGarty, C., Bliuc, A. M., Thomas, E. F., & Bongiorno, R. (2009). Collective action as the material expression of opinion-based group membership. *Journal of Social Issues, 65*, 839–857.

Morris, C. (1973). *The discovery of the individual, 1050–1200*. New York: Harper & Row.

Morton T. A., & Duck, J. M. (2001). Communication and health beliefs: Mass and interpersonal influences on perceptions of risk to self and others. *Communication Research, 28*, 602–626.

Morton, T. A., & Duck, J. M. (2006). Enlisting the influence of others: Alternative strategies for persuasive media campaigns. *Journal of Applied Social Psychology, 36*, 269–296.

Morton, T. A., & Sonnenberg, S. J. (2011). When history constrains identity: Expressing the self to others against the backdrop of a problematic past. *European Journal of Social Psychology, 41*(2), 232–240.

Ostrom, E. (2000). Collective action and the evolution of social norms. *The Journal of Economic Perspectives, 14*, 137–158.

Postmes, T., Baray, G., Haslam, S. A., Morton, T., & Swaab, R. I. (2006). The dynamics of personal and social identity formation. In T. Postmes & J. Jetten (Eds.), *Individuality and the group: Advances in social identity* (pp. 215–236). London: Sage.

Postmes, T., & Branscombe, N. R. (Eds.). (2010). *Rediscovering social identity: Core sources*. New York: Psychology Press.

Postmes, T., Haslam, S. A., & Swaab, R. I. (2005). Social influence in small groups: An interactive model of social identity formation. *European Review of Social Psychology, 16*, 1–42.

Postmes, T., Spears, R., Lee, A. T., & Novak, R. J. (2005). Individuality and social influence in groups: Inductive and deductive routes to group identity. *Journal of Personality and Social Psychology, 89,* 747–763.

Pronin, E., Berger, J., & Molouki, S. (2007). Alone in a crowd of sheep: Asymmetric perceptions of conformity and their roots in an introspection illusion. *Journal of Personality and Social Psychology, 92,* 585–595.

Rabinovich, A., & Morton, T. A. (2010a). *The effects of comparative focus on assimilation and contrast processes in intergroup context.* Unpublished manuscript.

Rabinovich, A., & Morton, T. A. (2010b). Who says we are bad people? The impact of criticism source and attributional content on responses to group-based criticism. *Personality and Social Psychology Bulletin, 36,* 524–536.

Rabinovich, A., Morton, T., & Postmes, T. (2010). Time perspective and attitude–behaviour consistency in future-oriented behaviours. *British Journal of Social Psychology, 49,* 69–89.

Rabinovich, A., Morton, T. A., Postmes, T., & Verplanken, B. (2009). Think global, act local: The effect of goal and mindset specificity on willingness to donate to an environmental organization. *Journal of Environmental Psychology, 29,* 391–399.

Rabinovich, A., Morton, T. A., Postmes, T., & Verplanken, B. (2012). Collective self and individual choice: The effects of inter-group comparative context on environmental values and behaviour. *British Journal of Social Psychology, 51,* 551–569.

Reicher, S. (2000). Social identity definition and enactment: A broad SIDE against irrationalism and relativism. In T. Postmes, R. Spears, M. Lea, & S. Reicher (Eds.), *SIDE issues centre stage: Recent developments in studies of de-individuation in groups* (pp. 175–190). Amsterdam, the Netherlands: North Holland Elsevier.

Sani, F., Bowe, M., Herrera, M., Manna, C., Cossa, T., Miao, X., et al. (2007). Perceived collective continuity: Seeing groups as entities that move through time. *European Journal of Social Psychology, 37,* 1118–1134.

Simon, B., & Klandermans, B. (2001). Politicized collective identity: A social psychological analysis. *American Psychologist, 56,* 319–331.

Sindic, D., & Reicher, S. D. (2008). The instrumental use of group prototypicality judgments. *Journal of Experimental Social Psychology, 44,* 1425–1435.

Skitka, L., Bauman, C., & Sargis, E. (2005). Moral conviction: Another contributor to attitude strength or something more? *Journal of Personality and Social Psychology, 88,* 895–917.

Smith, E., Seger, C., & Mackie, D. (2007). Can emotions be truly group level? Evidence regarding four conceptual criteria. *Journal of Personality and Social Psychology, 93,* 431–446.

Strathman, A., Gleicher, F., Boninger, D. S., & Edwards, C. S. (1994). The consideration of future consequences: Weighing immediate and distant outcomes of behavior. *Journal of Personality and Social Psychology, 66*(4), 742–754.

Swaab, R. I., Postmes, T., van Beest, I., & Spears, R. (2007). Shared cognition as a product of, and precursor to, shared identity in negotiations. *Personality and Social Psychology Bulletin, 33*(2), 187–199.

Swaab, R. I., Postmes, T., & Spears, R. (2008). Identity formation in multiparty negotiations. *British Journal of Social Psychology, 47,* 167–187.

Swim, J., Clayton, S., Doherty, T., Self, P., Gifford, L., Howard, G., et al. (2009). *Psychology and global climate change: Addressing a multi-faceted phenomenon and set of challenges. A report by the American Psychological Association's task force on the interface between psychology and global climate change members.* Washington, DC: American Psychological Association.

Tajfel, H. (1974). Social identity and intergroup behaviour. *Social Science Information Sur Les Sciences Sociales, 13,* 65–93.

Tajfel, H. (1978). Interindividual behaviour and intergroup behaviour. In H. Tajfel (Ed.), *Differentiation between groups: Studies in the social psychology of intergroup relations* (pp. 27–60). London: Academic Press.

Taylor, C. (2007). *A secular age.* Cambridge, MA: Harvard University Press.

Thomas, E. F., & McGarty, C. A. (2009). The role of efficacy and moral outrage norms in creating the potential for international development activism through group-based interaction. *The British Journal of Social Psychology/The British Psychological Society, 48,* 115–131.

Thomas, E. F., McGarty, C., & Mavor, K. I. (2009). Aligning identities, emotions, and beliefs to create commitment to sustainable social and political action. *Personality and Social Psychology Review, 13,* 194–218.

Turner, J. C. (1987). The analysis of social influence. In J. C. Turner, M. A. Hogg, P. J. Oakes, S. Reicher, & M. S. Wetherell (Eds.), *Rediscovering the social group: A self-categorization theory* (pp. 68–89). Oxford, UK: Basil Blackwell.

Turner, J. C. (1991). *Social influence.* Pacific Grove, CA: Brooks/Cole.

Turner, J. C., Hogg, M. A., Oakes, P. J., Reicher, S., & Wetherell, M. S. (1987). *Rediscovering the social group: A self-categorization theory.* Oxford, UK: Basil Blackwell.

Turner, J. C., & Oakes, P. J. (1986). The significance of the social identity concept for social psychology with reference to individualism, interactionism and social influence. *British Journal of Social Psychology, 25,* 237–252.

Van Zomeren, M., Spears, R., Fischer, A., & Leach, C. (2004). Put your money where your mouth is! Explaining collective action tendencies through group-based anger and group efficacy. *Journal of Personality and Social Psychology, 87,* 649–664.

Van Zomeren, M., Postmes, T., & Spears, R. (2008). Toward an integrative social identity model of collective action: A quantitative research synthesis of three socio-psychological perspectives. [Review]. *Psychological Bulletin, 134,* 504–535.

Van Zomeren, M., Postmes, T., & Spears, R. (2012). On conviction's collective consequences: Integrating moral conviction with a social identity model of collective action. *British Journal of Social Psychology, 51,* 52–71.

Van Zomeren, M., Postmes, T., Spears, R., & Bettache, K. (2011). Can moral convictions motivate the advantaged to challenge social inequality? Extending the social identity model of collective action. *Group Processes & Intergroup Relations, 14*(5), 735–753.

Van Zomeren, M., Spears, R., & Leach, C. W. (2010). Experimental evidence for a dual pathway model analysis of coping with the climate crisis. *Journal of Environmental Psychology, 30*(4), 339–346.

Walker, I., & Smith, H. J. (2002). *Relative deprivation: Specification, development, and integration.* Cambridge: Cambridge University Press.

Yuki, M. (2003). Intergroup comparison versus intragroup relationships: A cross-cultural examination of social identity theory in North American and East Asian cultural contexts. *Social Psychology Quarterly, 66,* 166–183.

Zimbardo, P. G., & Boyd, J. N. (1999). Putting time in perspective: A valid, reliable individual–differences metric. *Journal of Personality and Social Psychology, 77*(6), 1271–1288.

15

The Use of Hypocrisy for Promoting Environmentally Sustainable Behaviors

ELIZABETH S. FOCELLA and JEFF STONE

The human race is challenged more than ever before to demonstrate our mastery—not over nature but of ourselves.

—Rachel Carson

Recent scientific discourse about the dangers of global warming, shortages of major natural resources like clean water, and the disastrous effects of marine pollution has awakened the public to the need for more sustainable consumption of the world's resources (Griskevicius, Tybur, & Van den Bergh, 2010). Nevertheless, most people's pro-environmental attitudes and beliefs are not reflected in their actual behavior; their beliefs about what they should do are discrepant from their actions (Thøgersen, 2004; Diekmann & Preisendorfer, 1998). As Rachel Carson noted in 1962, to preserve our natural resources and avoid the dire consequences of overuse for our planet, human beings must bring their behavior into line with their pro-environmental attitudes and beliefs. Identifying and investigating new strategies that can motivate environmental behavior change is critical for getting people to stop and perhaps reverse the damage they cause to the global environment.

One way to motivate people to reduce the discrepancy between their pro-environmental attitudes and anti-environmental behavior is to make them feel hypocritical. Hypocrisy occurs when people publicly advocate a prosocial course of action and then are reminded of times when they failed to perform the proposed course of action in the past. When made aware of their past lapses to "practice what they preach," people become motivated to bring their future behavior in line with their advocated attitudes and beliefs. By changing their behavior to make it consistent with their prosocial attitudes and beliefs, hypocrites restore their sense of self-integrity and also take the steps that reduce their contribution to the problem.

The purpose of this chapter is to describe how hypocrisy can be used as an effective strategy to motivate people to adopt environmentally sustainable behaviors including those related to the conservation and consumption of natural resources. The specific goals are (1) to describe the theoretical assumptions that guide the use of hypocrisy for behavior change, (2) to review the laboratory and field evidence showing that hypocrisy motivates a wide variety of prosocial behavior changes including those related to sustainability, (3) to describe critical considerations when delivering hypocrisy in a behavior change campaign, and (4) to discuss the implications of hypocrisy for modifying the consumption and conservation behaviors that may stave off environmental catastrophe.

THE PSYCHOLOGY OF HYPOCRISY

The use of hypocrisy to motivate behavior change banks on the fundamental assumption that people are motivated to maintain consistency among their attitudes, beliefs, and actions. In his seminal book published in 1957, Leon Festinger proposed that inconsistency between people's beliefs and actions causes them to experience a state of discomfort, similar to the state of hunger or thirst. Festinger argued that this discomfort, which he called *cognitive dissonance*, would motivate people to restore consistency between the relevant cognitions by either changing their attitudes or their behavior, or by recruiting new cognitions. According to Festinger, the need to restore consistency could lead to meaningful changes in behavior.

Hypocrisy represents one way to induce the dissonance that motivates change (Stone & Fernandez, 2008). In the hypocrisy paradigm, participants are made aware of the inconsistency between their actions and their beliefs by completing two carefully constructed tasks. First, participants are asked to publicly advocate a course of action that they personally believe to be important. For example, someone who believes strongly in reducing carbon emissions would be asked to write an essay or deliver a speech advocating the importance of riding public transportation to work instead of taking a car. This serves to commit the participants to their stance on the issue, and since they are advocating for something that is consistent with their beliefs, they should not experience dissonance. Dissonance is then induced when people are asked to complete the second task, in which they are made mindful of past failures to engage in the advocated behavior. People are made mindful when they are asked to generate reasons why they failed to perform the behavior when they had the opportunity. The subsequent awareness of the inconsistency between their recently espoused beliefs and their actions induces a state of dissonance. When people experience dissonance as a result of the knowledge of their hypocritical behavior, they should be motivated to reduce their dissonance by bringing their future behavior in line with their recently espoused beliefs. By making an attempt to practice what they preach, people can restore the consistency between their beliefs and their actions.

A key element of hypocrisy is that it focuses people on changing their behavior to reduce their discomfort. The vast majority of dissonance studies, beginning with Festinger and Carlsmith (1959), show that when behavior is inconsistent with attitudes and beliefs, people can reduce dissonance by changing their attitudes to be consistent with the discrepant behavior (Cooper, 2008). In other words, they justify the discrepant act in order to reduce their discomfort and the perception that they did anything wrong (Tavris and Aronson, 2007). In contrast, a hypocritical discrepancy motivates people to literally practice what they preach; hypocrisy focuses people on taking the steps that are necessary to make their behavior consistent with the proscribed standards that they advocate to others. Thus, an act of hypocrisy arouses a form of dissonance that drives people to take action.

Two features of the hypocrisy paradigm make it especially likely that people will opt to change their behavior as opposed to change their attitudes in an attempt to justify their actions. The first is that when people advocate a prosocial course of action that promotes health or environmental conservation, they take a position that is highly supported by the prevailing injunctive norms, which are difficult for them to distort in order to reduce their discomfort. Second, when made mindful of failures to uphold the advocated norms for behavior, the discrepancy activates highly important cognitions linked to perceptions of self-integrity. An act of hypocrisy presents a threat to core self-beliefs about honesty and sincerity, and to the degree that advocates care about being honest and sincere about the behavior they advocated in others, a hypocritical act motivates them to restore the specific self-beliefs that underlie their self-integrity. The most direct way for hypocrites to restore their self-integrity is to bring their behavior into line with the course of action they proposed for others.

USING HYPOCRISY TO MOTIVATE PROSOCIAL BEHAVIOR CHANGE

There are over 20 published studies showing the power of hypocrisy for motivating prosocial behavior change (Stone & Fernandez, 2008). The initial studies showed that hypocrisy could motivate sexually active college students to adopt the use of condoms to reduce their risk for sexually transmitted diseases like acquired immune deficiency syndrome (AIDS) (Aronson, Fried, & Stone, 1991; Stone et al., 1994). In the first experiment (Aronson et al., 1991), sexually active male and female college students were targeted to help develop an AIDS prevention and education program. Through random assignment, participants in the *advocacy* condition were asked to make a brief speech about the importance of practicing safer sex through condom use (all agreed). To help them construct the speech, they were supplied with information about the risks of unsafe sex and the benefits of using condoms. They then delivered their speech to a video camera. In order to manipulate their level of mindfulness for past failures to practice safe sex, some of the students were then asked to reflect on and describe the circumstances that led them to have unprotected sex (e.g., they forgot to acquire condoms). They then wrote down examples of when they failed to use a condom during intercourse.

The effectiveness of the hypocrisy procedure was measured via self-report responses collected during an interview with the experimenter. The results showed that hypocrisy about practicing safer sex motivated the students to increase their intention to use condoms over control conditions (Aronson, Fried, & Stone, 1991). In a follow-up study designed to measure whether those in the hypocrisy condition were serious about their intentions to use condoms, participants were provided with an opportunity to purchase condoms after the study was over (Stone et al., 1994). The results showed that more students in the hypocrisy condition (83%) were motivated to purchase condoms when the opportunity was present compared to students who only advocated the importance of condom use (33%), were only made mindful of past failures (50%), or who were only exposed to information about the importance of condom use (44%). Thus, hypocrisy motivated the target audience to purchase the products they needed to perform the target health behavior.

There is also evidence that hypocrisy can be an effective strategy for motivating people to engage in behaviors that contribute to environmental sustainability. Importantly, many of the supporting studies were conducted in nonlaboratory, real-world settings to affect change in people's daily lives. In a field study aimed at using hypocrisy to promote water conservation (Dickerson, Thibodeau, Aronson, & Miller, 1992), female swimmers at a campus gym were approached by a female experimenter as they left the pool area. Before entering the locker room showers, the swimmers were asked by the experimenter, who presented herself as a member of a campus water conservation office, if they could spare a minute of their time by assisting with a water conservation project. Each swimmer was asked if she was on her way to shower and if she was in favor of water conservation. If the swimmer answered affirmatively to both questions, the experimenter introduced the experimental manipulations.

In the mindfulness-only condition, the experimenter verbally delivered a survey to participants, including questions such as "When showering, do you always turn off the water while soaping up or shampooing?" and "When you take showers, do you always make them as short as possible or do you sometimes linger longer than necessary?" The purpose of these questions was to serve as a way to remind participants of their past failures to conserve water. In the commitment-only condition, the experimenter asked the subject if she would be willing to print her name, with a thick black marker, on a flyer, reading "Please conserve water. Take shorter showers. Turn off showers while soaping up. IF I CAN DO IT SO CAN YOU!" The experimenter informed the subject that the flyer would be attached to posters that would be distributed on campus as part of a project meant to encourage people on campus to conserve water. In the hypocrisy condition, participants first received the mindfulness manipulation described previously, in which they were reminded of their past failures to conserve water, and then received the commitment manipulation described previously, in which they were asked to sign the flyer, advocating for water conservation. A fourth no-treatment condition was also included in this study in which the subsequent behavior of the participants was recorded to serve as a baseline measure of water use among students at the university.

Participants then proceeded to the locker room showers. To measure their subsequent water usage, a second experimenter, who remained unaware of the participants' experimental condition, used a waterproof stopwatch to record how long the participants spent showering, and if they turned off the water during their shower (presumably to apply soap and/or shampoo).

Dickerson and colleagues (1992) found that compared to participants in the three control conditions, those in the hypocrisy condition took significantly shorter showers. This study provides evidence that hypocrisy can be used to promote an environmentally friendly behavior outside of the laboratory setting on a college campus, but what about when people are in their homes?

In a dissonance study with methods similar to that of the hypocrisy paradigm, Kantola, Syme, and Campbell (1984) encouraged people to conserve energy by making them feel dissonance about their energy consumption. The researchers recruited homeowners in Perth, Western Australia, whose houses were equipped with ducted air conditioning, and who consumed average (compared to other homeowners in the area) amounts of energy. Using a mailed pretest survey, they selected potential participants whose survey responses indicated they were pro-attitudinal toward energy conservation.

All participants received a letter, a pamphlet about ways to conserve electricity, and a postage-paid postcard, upon which they could indicate if they wanted more information about ways to conserve electricity. The letter randomly assigned participants to one of four experimental groups. In the dissonance condition, the letter stated that participants were high consumers of electricity and that they had previously stated the importance of conserving electricity, thereby making them mindful of a discrepancy between their attitudes and their behavior. In a feedback-only condition, participants were given a letter stating that they were high consumers of electricity. In a tips-only group, participants were given a pamphlet and card about ways to conserve electricity. Finally, in a control group, participants received a letter thanking them for being a customer. The primary measure of the intervention was the home's consumption of electricity over two sequential two-week periods. The researchers found that the consumption of electricity for those in the dissonance group was significantly lower than the electricity consumption of those in all other conditions in the first two-week measurement period of the study, after the full four-week period of the study.

Using a similar procedure, Aitken, McMahon, Wearing, and Finlayson (1994) made residents of Melbourne, Australia, feel dissonance about their water consumption. Researchers recorded the water consumption of 226 residents and surveyed their positive attitudes toward water conservation. Similar to the Kantola et al. study, the interventions occurred via hand-delivered postcards. In the dissonance condition, participants were reminded of their positive attitudes toward water conservation, and then informed that their water consumption for the past week was above the average consumption for a similar household. In a feedback-only group, participants were informed that their water consumption for the past week was above the average consumption for a similar household. A control group did not receive a card. The primary measure was the household's consumption of water over a seven-week period. The data showed that residents who were reminded of their positive attitudes toward water conservation and were then made mindful of their failures to conserve water showed significantly more reduction in their use of water during the follow-up period, compared to those in either the feedback-only or the control condition. Taken together with the Dickerson et al. (1992) and Kantola et al. (1984) findings, these studies indicate that making people mindful of a discrepancy between their attitudes toward a target pro-environmental behavior, and their performance of the target pro-environmental behavior, can motivate them to practice the target pro-environmental behavior in the future.

Whereas these findings are consistent with the hypocrisy prediction, none provide direct evidence that the behavior changes were motivated by the presence of dissonance arousal. To investigate the presence of dissonance following hypocrisy, Fried and Aronson (1995) directly manipulated the influence of negative arousal by introducing a misattribution cue during the procedure. Based on previous research showing that when made salient, people can misattribute dissonance arousal to external sources (Zanna & Cooper, 1974), the authors reasoned that if the behavior change that follows hypocrisy is caused by the motivation to reduce the discomfort associated with dissonance, then if provided with another explanation for their discomfort, participants in the hypocrisy condition should exhibit less motivation to alter their behavior compared to when no misattribution cue is present.

College student participants in this study were asked to videotape a speech to encourage another sustainable behavior: recycling. Half were then exposed to a misattribution cue via a letter from a campus committee requesting that they report about how the lighting, noise, and temperature in the newly "renovated" lab space impacted them during the study. The other half were not provided with the letter or asked to report their perceptions of the lab. After all delivered their speech, half of the participants completed a measure designed to make them mindful of past failures to recycle, while half did not complete this task. Those in the misattribution condition completed the misattribution survey, after which it was announced that the study was complete. The experimenter then informed participants that the campus recycling center was looking for volunteers to make telephone calls for them. The number of participants who volunteered to make phone calls and the number of calls they volunteered to make for the recycling center served as the dependent measures.

The results showed clear support for the dissonance account of the hypocrisy effect: 68% of participants who made the pro-recycling speech and were reminded of past failures to recycle (hypocrisy) volunteered to make phone calls compared to only 16% of those who made the pro-recycling speech but were not reminded of past failures. However, the presence of a misattribution cue significantly reduced the percentage of people who volunteered in the hypocrisy condition to only 32%. Like other dissonance paradigms, these data indicate that the hypocrisy procedure induces a state of negative arousal that people are motivated to reduce. Other processes, such as attitude accessibility or self-perception, are less parsimonious with these findings.

Nevertheless, the findings of Fried and Aronson (1995), as well as research on self-affirmation processes (Steele, 1988), raise an important question for the hypocrisy effect: If people can avoid changing their behavior by misattributing their arousal, or by affirming an important but unrelated aspect of the self, then perhaps a hypocritical discrepancy does not assure that people will resolve the discrepancy by changing their behavior. Like counterattitudinal behavior, an act of hypocrisy may induce negative arousal that people are motivated to reduce by any means possible, even if the reduction strategy does nothing to resolve the discrepancy between attitudes and behavior. If this were the case, it would be difficult to predict when and how people would alter their behavior following an act of hypocrisy.

Stone, Wiegand, Cooper, and Aronson (1997) directly tested the self-integrity hypothesis by inducing hypocrisy about condom use and then simultaneously offering more than one behavioral option for dissonance reduction. It was predicted that after an act of hypocrisy, if people have an opportunity to affirm the self by performing an unrelated positive behavior, they might use that strategy as a means to reduce their discomfort, even if it does not address the discrepancy. However, if an act of hypocrisy arouses dissonance because the behavior threatens self-beliefs about honesty and sincerity, then in order to restore their self-integrity, participants should be motivated to change the discrepant behavior. Thus, when provided with a choice between performing the behavior that would reduce the hypocrisy directly and restore their self-integrity, or performing a behavior that will leave the discrepancy intact but reduce their discomfort by affirming an unrelated positive self-attribute, most people would choose to perform the behavior that most directly reduces the hypocritical discrepancy.

To test this prediction, after they made a pro-condom speech and were made mindful of past failures to practice safer sex, some participants were provided with the opportunity to donate to support a homeless shelter—a behavior that would reduce their dissonance via self-affirmation, but would not resolve hypocritical discrepancy directly. In another condition, some participants were offered the opportunity to donate to the homeless, but were then also offered the opportunity to directly resolve the hypocritical discrepancy by purchasing condoms. The results supported the self-integrity hypothesis: when offered only the affirmation option (donation), 83% of those in the hypocrisy condition used it. However, when the affirmation strategy was offered alongside the opportunity to restore self-integrity (condom purchase), 78% chose the direct option whereas only 13% chose the affirmation option. Experiment 2 replicated the choice for directly resolving the hypocritical discrepancy even when the indirect affirmation strategy held more importance for self-worth than the direct behavioral option. Together, the results indicate that when the only dissonance-reduction opportunity available to a hypocrite is a behavior that reduces their discomfort but not the discrepancy, they will take advantage of it. After all, people sometimes do want to feel good about themselves. Nevertheless, when a behavior is available that directly resolves the hypocrisy, most people would rather restore their perception of self-integrity by performing the target behavior (see also Fointiat, 2004).

These lines of research suggest that hypocrisy motivates a specific form of dissonance arousal and reduction that directs people toward changing their behavior. Once they advocate the prosocial standards and are then made mindful of past failures to uphold the standards, the threat to self-integrity motivates a desire to resolve the discrepancy by bringing the discrepant behavior into line with the advocated beliefs. Addressing the discrepancy directly appears to be the preferred mode of dissonance reduction even when other options for dissonance reduction are present. Research shows that hypocrisy can not only motivate people to change their behavior in the direction of increased environmental sustainability, but that this can be accomplished in a variety of settings, including one's own home, with a variety of behaviors, including water conservation, recycling, and electricity conservation.

OPTIMIZING THE EFFECTS OF HYPOCRISY ON BEHAVIOR CHANGE

Across a variety of topics and settings, hypocrisy is an effective approach for motivating people to prepare for and perform behaviors that contribute to sustainability, good health, and improved interpersonal relationships (Stone and Fernandez, 2008). The research examining when and how hypocrisy motivates behavior change reveals important parameters for using the procedure to motivate the target response. The next section describes factors in the delivery that moderate the influence of hypocrisy on behavior change.

The first step in the hypocrisy paradigm occurs when people who hold positive attitudes toward a target behavior advocate the importance of the behavior to others. For example, a person who believes in reducing energy consumption might write an essay advocating that everyone take steps to conserve energy in their homes. The research indicates that the effect of hypocrisy on behavior change is greatest when people construct and deliver, either in writing or through a recording, a persuasive message about the importance of performing the target behavior. Simply learning about the behavior, either by reading about the importance of performing it (Aronson et al., 1991; Stone et al., 1994) or constructing a speech but not delivering it (Stone et al., 1997) does not cause the same level of dissonance and behavior change as does the act of delivering the statement to an "audience," and then being made mindful of past failures. Advocating the importance of the target behavior to other people appears to be a necessary condition in the hypocrisy effect.

The second task in the hypocrisy paradigm is to make people mindful of past failures to engage in their previously advocated behavior. Research indicates that in order to maximize the effect of hypocrisy on behavior change, it is necessary to make recall of past failures personal, private, and easy. For example, in the research by Stone and colleagues (1997), students who recalled personal reasons for their failures to use condoms were significantly more likely to perform the target behavior compared to students who recalled reasons why other people fail to use condoms. This suggests that the most effective way to induce mindfulness for past failures is to have participants recall their own personal failures to perform the target behavior.

The hypocrisy effect is also most effective in encouraging behavior change when people privately recall their past failures to perform the target behavior. In another set of studies designed to encourage recycling behavior, Fried (1998) had participants make public speeches (Study 1) or write persuasive essays (Study 2) about the importance of recycling. To manipulate the level of publicity for past failures, participants in an anonymous condition completed the list but did not put their name on it; they were told to place their list in an envelope ostensibly full of lists completed by other participants. Participants in an identified condition completed the list but were asked to include their name and phone number and then sign it in front of the experimenter. Participants in a control condition worked on a recycling word scramble task for an equal amount of time. All then completed the behavioral-dependent measures including the number of telephone calls they would make for a recycling center (Study 1) and the amount of money they would donate to a recycling program (Study 2).

The results showed that hypocrisy participants who felt anonymous about their recycling failures donated more time to the recycling efforts in Study 1 and donated more money to the recycling program in Study 2 than participants who were also induced to feel hypocritical about their recycling habits but were publicly identified with their past failures to recycle. Moreover, in Study 2, participants were given the opportunity to report their attitude toward recycling prior to the request to donate money to recycling programs. The results showed that participants who were publicly identified with their past failures reported significantly more negative attitudes toward recycling than participants in the anonymous failure or control conditions. The publicity of their transgressions apparently pushed them to justify their past failures by changing their attitudes to be more negative toward recycling.

Research also suggests that past failures should be relatively easy for people to generate, because if people have difficulty bringing to mind their past failures to perform the target behavior, they may conclude that they have not behaved hypocritically. For example, in a study designed to use hypocrisy to reduce discrimination, Son Hing, Li, and Zanna (2002) identified college students with explicit positive but implicit negative attitudes toward Asian Canadians (i.e., aversive racists). Son Hing and colleagues predicted that when made mindful of past failures, aversive racists would have an easier time recalling past failures to be fair compared to low-prejudice individuals, and as a result would feel more hypocritical and be more motivated to perform an egalitarian act if provided with the opportunity.

To test this prediction, all participants wrote a persuasive egalitarian essay about the importance of the fair treatment of minority students ostensibly for use in a campus race equality pamphlet. Next, participants in the hypocrisy condition were made mindful about past failures to be fair by writing about a situation in which they personally reacted more negatively to an Asian person than they should have. Participants in the control condition were not made mindful, and all participants then completed a measure of negative affect. After the experimenter announced that the study was complete, all were asked to help a committee to make a decision about how to cut next year's budget for student organizations on campus. The main dependent variable was the percentage of budget cuts recommended for the Asian Students Association (ASA).

As predicted, the results showed that the aversive racists in the hypocrisy condition recommended a significantly lower budget cut for the ASA compared to aversive racists in the control condition and low-prejudice individuals in the hypocrisy condition. Aversive racists in the hypocrisy condition also reported higher levels of guilt compared to the other groups, although guilt was not significantly related to the level of budget cuts recommended. Importantly, independent coders reported that whereas truly low-prejudice and aversive racists both wrote equally strong essays and recalled equally severe examples of biased responses toward Asians in the past, aversive racists tended to recall more recent examples of biased behavior compared to low-prejudice individuals. The temporal difference supports the idea that if they have trouble coming up with recent examples, people may conclude that their past failures do not represent a meaningful or important discrepancy from their prosocial standards. If recalling past failures is easy, in part because they represent recent examples, then people may be more likely to perceive that their past behavior is discrepant from their advocated standards and be motivated to bring their actions into line with their beliefs.

Finally, recent research on hypocrisy indicates that not only is the ease of recalling past failures important, but also that the amount of elaboration people undergo when recalling those failures influences behavior change after an act of hypocrisy. Stone and Fernandez (2011) hypothesized that the amount of elaboration people were prompted to undergo when recalling their failures to engage in a particular behavior would determine under what conditions recalling many failures would motivate more behavior change and under what conditions recalling many failures would motivate less behavior change. To test their predictions, participants, all of whom reported in a pretest that they believe in the importance of sunscreen use, were randomly assigned to one of four conditions. All participants wrote an essay advocating for the use of sunscreen and were then asked to fill out a survey about their past failures to use sunscreen, ostensibly for the National Cancer Institute. As part of the survey, participants were induced to think of either two or eight personal failures to use sunscreen (recall manipulation) and were either told that they were one of thousands of people to take the survey (low elaboration), or that they were one of few (high elaboration). Finally, participants were given an opportunity to take a free sample of sunscreen as thanks for participation in the study. Findings show that under low elaboration, significantly more participants who recalled eight failures requested a sample of sunscreen (68%) than those who recalled two failures (39%). Interestingly, under high elaboration, significantly more participants who recalled two failures requested sunscreen (82%) than participants who recalled eight failures (52%). These findings indicate that the effect of recalling many past failures is dependent upon how carefully people think about their past behavior. Recalling many failures is only effective when people don't contemplate their past behavior too heavily.

In sum, hypocrisy is most effective for changing behavior when certain parameters are considered. Specifically, hypocrisy is most effective when people publicly advocate for a target behavior and then easily and privately recall past instances in which they personally failed to perform the advocated behavior. Recalling fewer past failures appears to be most effective when people are motivated and have the ability to think carefully about their past. But when motivation or ability to carefully consider past failures is low, then having people generate many past examples may be the most effective way to induce dissonance and the need to adopt the target behavior.

MASS MEDIA APPROACHES

Several of the studies reviewed in this chapter suggest that hypocrisy can motivate people to adopt the target behavior when implemented in the hustle and bustle of their everyday lives. Nevertheless, the studies reviewed up to this point also rely heavily on a "personal selling channel" to achieve their behavior change goals. Whereas the face-to-face or personal delivery of hypocrisy is effective, it also requires a somewhat costly level of time and effort for target individuals as they complete the activities that produce dissonance. Such costs may not be feasible or desirable, especially when the goal of a sustainability campaign is to influence a large audience quickly and at a low cost.

One potential mass media approach under investigation in our lab exposes a target audience to the hypocritical behavior of another person. Focella and colleagues (2013) proposed that people could be motivated to adopt a new course of action by witnessing the hypocrisy of someone with whom they share a strong social identity. Specifically, when observers perceive that a hypocrite shares an important group identity with them, it will cause dissonance because the in-group member's hypocrisy challenges the observers' positive view of the group as having integrity—as being honest, principled, and sincere about important issues (Stone et al., 1997). Consequently, the threat to the group's integrity will motivate highly identified in-group perceivers to reduce their vicarious dissonance by seeking a way to maintain their positive image of the group's integrity. The most direct way to accomplish this goal is for in-group members to bolster attitudes and behavior to support the hypocrite's proposed course of action.

To test the effect of vicarious hypocrisy, Focella and colleagues targeted female college students who held positive attitudes toward the use of sunscreen and were highly identified with their university campus. They then evaluated a recorded message by another female student about the importance of using sunscreen to reduce skin cancer. The speaker was portrayed as either an in-group (same university) or an out-group member (rival university). Perceived hypocrisy was created when the speaker admitted to previous failures to use sunscreen. The results showed that as predicted, female students who shared a strong social identity with the female hypocritical speaker became significantly more favorable toward the regular use of sunscreen than female students exposed to an out-group speaker, and compared to male students who did not share the same level of similarity to the female speaker. A second study replicated the effect of vicarious hypocrisy on the bolstering of attitudes toward sunscreen among highly identified females compared to control conditions in which their group identity was affirmed prior to exposure to the in-group hypocrite.

These findings indicate that exposure to the hypocritical behavior of another person can motivate those who share an important social identity with the speaker to bolster their support for the cause. They also suggest that hypocrisy can be implemented to change attitudes and behavior through channels, like broadcast mass media, which can be less costly and more efficient to implement. For example, the target audience could be exposed to a public service announcement or advertisement in which an in-group member advocates the importance of sustainable behaviors, such as electricity conservation or recycling. The in-group member could be a well-known person, like a celebrity or political figure, to whom the audience feels a strong social identity connection. Like many mass media campaigns, the most effective approach requires careful attention to the targeting of the audience, to ensure that they share an important social identity with the hypocritical advocate.

After listening to or reading about the in-group member's pro-sustainability message, the target audience could then learn of the in-group member's failure to practice the proposed set of behaviors. For example, they could read about or listen to a news report about how the advocate took a private jet to a conference on sustainability. Research by Focella and colleagues (2013) indicates that witnessing the in-group member's hypocrisy should cause feelings of dissonance among the audience and motivate them to reduce dissonance by behaving in ways that are consistent with the in-group member's advocacy.

CONCLUSION

With the growing need for environmental sustainability, research that encourages people to practice sustainability in their own lives can prove to be a useful tool to address the environmental problems facing the planet. Research on using hypocrisy to motivate a variety of sustainable behaviors indicates that making people mindful of the discrepancy between their pro-environmental attitudes and their lapses to behave in ways that protect the environment can cause significant changes in behaviors that reduce consumption and promote the conservation of valuable natural resources.

REFERENCES

Aitken, C., McMahon, T., Wearing, A., & Finlayson, B. (1994). Residential water use: Predicting and reducing consumption. *Journal of Applied Social Psychology, 24*(2), 136–158.

Aronson, E., Fried, C., & Stone, J. (1991). Overcoming denial and increasing the intention to use condoms through the induction of hypocrisy. *American Journal of Public Health, 81*(12), 1636–1638.

Carson, R. (1962). *Silent spring*. Boston: Houghton Mifflin.

Cooper, J. (2008). *Cognitive dissonance: Fifty years of a classic theory*. Thousand Oaks, CA: Sage Publications.

Dickerson, C. A., Thibodeau, R., Aronson, E., & Miller, D. (1992). Using cognitive dissonance to encourage water conservation. *Journal of Applied Social Psychology, 22*(11), 841–854.

Diekmann, A., & Preisendorfer, P. (1998). Environmental behavior: Discrepancies between aspirations and reality. *Rationality and Society, 10*(1), 79–102.

Festinger, L. (1957). *A theory of cognitive dissonance*. Stanford, CA: Stanford University Press.

Festinger, L., & Carlsmith, J. M. (1959). Cognitive consequences of forced compliance. *Journal of Abnormal and Social Psychology, 58*(2), 203–210.

Focella, E. S., Stone, J., Fernandez, N.C., Cooper, J., & Hogg, M. (2013). *Vicarious hypocrisy: Bolstering attitudes and taking action after exposure to a hypocritical in-group member*. Manuscript in preparation, University of Arizona.

Fointiat, V. (2004). "I know what I have to do, but …" When hypocrisy leads to behavioral change. *Social Behavior and Personality*, 32(8), 741–746.

Fried, C. B. (1998). Hypocrisy and identification with transgressions: A case of undetected dissonance. *Basic and Applied Social Psychology*, 20(2), 145–154.

Fried, C. B., & Aronson, E. (1995). Hypocrisy, misattribution, and dissonance reduction. *Personality and Social Psychology Bulletin*, 21(9), 925–933.

Griskevicius, V., Tybur, J. M., & Van den Bergh, B. (2010). Going green to be seen: Status, reputation, and conspicuous conservation. *Journal of Personality and Social Psychology*, 98(3), 393–404.

Kantola, S., Syme, G., & Campbell, N. (1984). Cognitive dissonance and energy conservation. *Journal of Applied Psychology*, 69(3), 416–421.

Son Hing, L. S., Li, W., & Zanna, M. P. (2002). Inducing hypocrisy to reduce prejudicial responses among aversive racists. *Journal of Experimental Social Psychology*, 38(1), 71–78.

Steele, C. M. (1988). The psychology of self-affirmation: Sustaining the integrity of the self. In L. Berkowitz (Ed.) *Advances in experimental social psychology* (Vol. 21, pp. 261–302). New York: Academic Press.

Stone, J., Aronson, E., Crain, A. L., Winslow, M. P., & Fried, C. B. (1994). Inducing hypocrisy as a means for encouraging young adults to use condoms. *Personality and Social Psychology Bulletin*, 20(1), 116–128.

Stone, J., & Fernandez, N. (2008). To practice what we preach: The use of hypocrisy and cognitive dissonance to motivate behavior change. *Social and Personality Psychology Compass*, 2(2), 1024–1051.

Stone, J., & Fernandez, N.C. (2011). When less failure causes more dissonance: The role of elaboration and recall in behavior change following hypocrisy. *Social Influence*, 6(4), 199–211.

Stone, J., Wiegand, A., Cooper, J., & Aronson, E. (1997). When exemplification fails: Hypocrisy and the motive for self-integrity. *Journal of Personality and Social Psychology*, 72(1), 54–65.

Tavris, C., & Aronson, E. (2007). *Mistakes were made (but not by me): Why we justify foolish beliefs, bad decisions, and hurtful acts*. New York: Harcourt.

Thøgersen, J. (2004). A cognitive dissonance interpretation of consistencies and inconsistencies in environmentally responsible behavior. *Journal of Environmental Psychology*, 24(1), 93–103.

Zanna, M. P., & Cooper, J. (1974). Dissonance and the pill: An attribution approach to studying the arousal properties of dissonance. *Journal of Personality and Social Psychology*, 29(5), 703–709.

Section 6

Enhancing Sustainable Behavior in Practice

16

This Was All Very Interesting, But How Can We Use It?
A Practitioner's Guide to Sustainable Behavior

SASKIA A. SCHWINGHAMMER

THREE-STAGE APPROACH TO BEHAVIOR CHANGE

*M*any communication professionals and health psychologists conceptualize the process of behavior change as proceeding through several phases or stages. The basic assumption underlying these working models is that in order for people to change their behavior or habits, certain universal stages in which different psychological processes operate need to be progressed. In the literature, several stage models have been proposed (e.g., the Precaution Adoption Process Model (Weinstein, Rothman, & Sutton, 1998); the Transtheoretical Model (Prochaska & DiClemente, 1982). The various theoretical and working models of such stages of behavior change concepts might differ in the number of stages that are distinguished and the way they phrase these stages, but there is broad consensus about at least three stages that are believed to lead up to successful behavior change.

Stage 1: Problem recognition. Before people contemplate changing their behavior, they need to have at least a sense of urgency, or some awareness that there is a problem or a hazard and that something needs to be changed. After all, if people do not know that unsustainable consumption patterns threaten the environment and might induce climate change, then they will not feel the urgency to start behaving in a more sustainable way.

Stage 2: Motivation to act. Once there is some basic level of problem recognition, people can progress from a state in which they first don't think the problem applies to them to a stage in which they feel engaged by the problem or situation. Importantly, for this involvement to lead to behavior change, people must be motivated to change their own behavior. Factors that influence whether one progresses from a state of simple awareness to a state into which one is motivated to act are, among others, perceptions of severity, susceptibility, control (self-efficacy), and social norms. Specifically, a person who is aware that the environment is threatened by unsustainable consumption patterns and does not regard this as a severe problem does not see how this affects her negatively, or does not feel that she can personally do something to counteract the process by changing her consumption pattern, will most likely not consider changing her behavior.

Stage 3: Regulation and execution of action. Once people feel motivated to change their behavior, they can progress to a state in which they actually regulate and change their behavior and habits, and act accordingly. In this stage, behavior change is facilitated by *cues to action* that can emerge both from within a person (e.g., emotions, goals) and the environment (e.g., nudges, primes, social cues). Specifically, someone whose social environment is crafted around sustainability (i.e., friends that are vegetarians, supermarkets that sell predominantly seasonal vegetables and fruits) will experience fewer difficulties when making her eating behavior more sustainable compared to someone whose environment is less "green."

The stage approach to behavior change can be used to nicely synthesize the theoretical perspectives and insights on how to stimulate consumers to behave more sustainably, which have been presented in the previous chapters. More specifically, close examination of the various theoretical perspectives shows that they all can be incorporated into the different stages of behavior change, so that together they form a useful and practical framework that provides starting points to stimulate sustainable behavior in every stage of the behavior change process.

UNINTENTIONAL BEHAVIOR CHANGE

At this point it is important to stress that the stage approach of behavior change does not necessarily mean that awareness, motivation to act, and the deliberate planning and execution of behavior are necessary to change behavior. Or, in other words, it does not contend that behavior change needs to be intentional. Rather, the stage approach to behavior change posits that these stadia and factors are needed if one aims to change behavior in a rational and contemplative manner that is driven and monitored by the person itself. However, if a change agent's intention is to change behavior in a more unobtrusive or automatic way, such that people need not be aware of the problem or be motivated to act, one would find oneself focusing solely on the third stage of behavior change—the regulation and execution of the (new) behavior. Taking this approach entails a person not actively regulating her behavior and that the external and internal cues to action will influence her more or less unconsciously.

Stage 1: Problem Recognition

When focusing on this first stage in more detail, it becomes evident that problem recognition entails two components. In other words, to create a state of problem recognition in consumers, two conditions must be met. The first is awareness: consumers need to have knowledge about the problematic character of current unsustainable consumption and production patterns and the dramatic consequences that will likely be the result of these patterns. Second, there has to be a sense of urgency: consumers need to be convinced that a shift toward more sustainable consumption and production is needed in order to accommodate the increasing world population's needs and to prevent environmental damage. Several of the previous chapters provide theoretical insights on how to increase consumers' awareness and/or how to instill a sense of urgency in consumers. This will be discussed in the following text; a more detailed elaboration of these theories can be found in the corresponding chapters.

Social marketing insights (see Chapter 2) can be applied when designing (mass media) informational campaigns that heighten consumers' awareness levels and that activate a sense of urgency in them. However, since the problem of (un)sustainable consumption and resulting environmental damage is rather abstract and psychologically distant to most consumers, various insights can be used to craft messages in such a way that the communication effects will be maximized.

First, construal level theory (Chapter 7) explains that there is a relation between psychological distance and how abstract an object is represented in people's minds. The general idea is that the more distant an object is from the individual the more abstract it will be thought of, while the opposite applies to the relation between closeness and concreteness. Moreover, the way people subjectively construe events influences the relative weight they place on more abstract versus concrete issues. So, when they construe events in a more abstract and distant manner more weight is given to abstract and distant issues, and vice versa (e.g., when someone is planning a vacation for the end of the year, the focus will probably be on relatively abstract issues like time planning and means of traveling, while a vacation that will begin in one to two weeks will usually elicit more practical thoughts about what clothes to pack and whether one's travel documents are still valid). This has important implications for the way messages about the current problem need to be designed. Specifically, if your message is to be about the abstract problem of unsustainable consumption and production patterns that will unfold in the future, and big abstract changes that are urgently needed, it would be advisable to construct the message in such a way that it is likely to instigate high construal levels in consumers. Higher construal levels are more likely when the focus is on core and primary properties, so in this case a rather abstract and psychologically distant message and tone of voice will make consumers see these issues as more important. On the other hand, if your goal is to inform consumers about more concrete effects the current problem has at this moment (or will have in the foreseeable future) on their daily lives and specific changes that are needed, it would be advisable to construct the message in such a way that it is likely to instigate low construal levels in consumers. Lower construal levels are more likely when the focus is on secondary and peripheral properties, so in this case a rather concrete and psychologically engaging message with practical and engaging examples will make consumers see the issue as more important and urgent. Naturally, the underlying and logical assumption here is that when consumers perceive an issue as more important, this will most probably make them more attuned to the message itself and its content, which will result in higher awareness of the problem and a stronger sense of urgency.

In addition, from social identity theory (Chapter 14) it follows that (Western) consumers are often guided by egocentric concerns and have individualistic short-term goals. This may make them hard to reach with messages about unsustainable consumption and environmental damage, because these problems will not impact them directly in the foreseeable future. However, this individualistic short-term view, which hinders problem recognition, can be changed into a more collectivistic and socially concerned mindset by stressing similarities between the own group and other people. From this it follows that if you would like to get consumers to recognize that unsustainable consumption and its environmental consequences are problematic, inducing a *we* feeling might be very helpful in creating more engagement with the problem and instigating a feeling that something needs to be done. Technically, this means that in your message you should use words that create a feeling of group membership (e.g., *we, unite, together*) and frame your message in a way that activates their interdependent and shared social identities.

Also, existentialist theory (Chapter 8) offers an explanation of why the environmental problem might not be a top-of-mind-issue for consumers. Specifically, it is suggested that an impending long-term catastrophe (such as the current environmental issue) is not as tangible, motivating, and engaging as a real, short-term catastrophe that has immediate consequences (such as the economic crisis). This implies that if the environmental threat can in some way be made more tangible and real (e.g., by giving concrete and moving examples of how the environment is already suffering and how this might impact people), consumers might be more likely to be concerned with regard to environmentalist issues and more likely to acknowledge that something needs to be changed.

In line with the existentialist approach, taking a social neuroscience perspective (Chapter 11) also teaches us that unsustainability and environmental issues fail to elicit strong basic emotional and empathic reactions because these are abstract matters that fall outside the interpersonal realm, and thus leave consumers without a sense of urgency that something needs to be done. Because feelings of empathy may be (at least partly) necessary for consumers to feel concerned about the damage that the environment suffers from their unsustainable consumption patterns, and in their brains these empathic feelings are not aroused for out-group members (or other objects that are not included in one's personal circle, like the environment), it is important to find a way to increase empathic reactions toward damage done to the environment. Neuroimaging research suggests that one way to accomplish this is to *personalize* the environment. More specifically, inducing a *we are all connected* feeling while communicating to consumers about environmental problems could help to draw attention to this matter and increase feelings that some action needs to be taken to change the status quo. Phrases like "You are a part of the environment" or "You depend on the environment to survive" might be effective in inducing such feelings of connectedness. Another approach that could be successful from a neuroscience perspective is to reframe the environmental issue in terms of purist and sanctity values. Stressing that the Earth and nature are pure and possess a certain holiness increases the likelihood that strong moral reactions are evoked in consumers, which can stimulate their recognition of the environmental problem.

A similar approach that focuses on the aforementioned notion of interconnectedness also surfaces in Chapter 13 (attitudes). Here it is explained that the issue of sustainability and environmentalism is a rather distant topic for most consumers, because there is less obvious involvement of personal outcomes. As a result, there may be a weak relationship between consumers' consumption patterns and their (pro)environmental attitudes. One way to make consumers act more in line with their environmental attitudes could therefore be to induce in consumers a feeling of *global citizenship*, or environmental citizenship. In this notion it is emphasized that each of us is an integral part of a larger ecosystem, and that our collective future is dependent on this ecosystem. Inducing such a feeling of interconnectedness might make the sustainability issue more personally relevant and involving, thereby increasing consumers' involvement with the problem of unsustainability.

Finally, system justification theory (Chapter 9) provides valuable insights in how to raise consumers' awareness of the current problem and to convince them that something needs to be changed. It posits that people have a basic motivation to maintain a certain feeling of (personal) control and that reminders of the unsustainability of their consumption and resulting environmental damage can pose a threat to their control beliefs. As a result, people might start to defend the status quo in order to eliminate the threat and bolster their feelings of control. Specifically, the processes of *system justification* and compensatory control mechanisms may lead people to defensively avoid learning about environmental problems and can even lead them to deny environmental issues. So the challenge here is to prevent these defensive processes from occurring. Luckily, system justification theory provides some insights on how to do this. First, to prevent system justification and defensive avoidance from happening, you should provide consumers with sufficient knowledge about the problem of unsustainable consumption and present it in an understandable way. You could do this by presenting information in easily digestible formats and by using simple and clear language. Second, you should be careful to frame the problem in such a way that it is not presented as unsolvable or uncontrollable, since these notions will immediately trigger consumers' defensive denial processes. Finally, presenting the current problem of unsustainable consumption as leading to and increasing chaos (and therefore resulting in the loss of control) might also be effective in getting them to acknowledge that something needs to change.

Stage 2: Motivation to Act

Once consumers not only acknowledge that the unsustainability of Western consumption and production patterns is problematic and that a change toward more sustainable consumption and production is needed, but also feel *personally* responsible for this change to occur, they progress into the second stage of the behavioral change process. In this stage, the experience of a motivation to act is the central psychological process in consumers' minds; they feel that they can contribute to solving the problem of unsustainability by changing their own consumption patterns. Several of the previous chapters provide theoretical insights on how to increase consumers' motivation to act. This will be discussed in the following text; a more detailed elaboration of these theories can be found in the corresponding chapters.

As mentioned before, perceptions of severity, susceptibility, and control are important factors that can impact consumers' motivation to act. By using social marketing insights (Chapter 2), informational campaigns can be launched to influence consumers' perceptions regarding these factors. For example, you could design campaigns aimed at (1) providing consumers with information and facts on the severity of the sustainability problem;* (2) increasing the personal relevance of the problem of unsustainability by providing consumers with tangible and emotional examples and arguments of how they could personally suffer the consequences of long-term unsustainable consumption, hereby making the problem *real* and self-relevant; and (3) increasing consumers' feelings of personal control regarding the problem of unsustainability by showing them that each individual is able to contribute in their own way to the solution of the problem by substituting personal unsustainable consumption habits and behaviors with sustainable ones.

In addition to social marketing, cognitive sociology (Chapter 4) provides valuable insights on how to increase consumers' motivation to act. This approach postulates that activated goals set people's minds and direct their energy. For example, if someone has a goal to act sustainably because she finds this important, this will bring her into a mindset that directs her attention, the decision-making process, and her energy toward sustainability. In other words, this goal would increase her motivation to behave sustainably. Because sustainability and pro-environmental issues fall within the scope of normative goals and normative goals are relatively weak compared to other goals, it is important to find ways to strengthen these normative goals, or to make them more salient in a given situation so that a consumer's motivation to behave accordingly will increase. There are several ways to achieve this. First, you could make sustainable goals more compatible with other competing goals, like hedonistic and gain-oriented goals. For example, if pro-sustainable behaviors and options are facilitated, made less costly, more fun, and the perceived status of these options and behaviors is increased, behaving sustainably will be more in line with these other goals that might be activated in consumers' minds. In this case, the different motivations of wanting to gain something, feel good, and act sustainably will not conflict but add up, and will steer motivation and behavior in a single direction—sustainable options.

Second, you could show that other people also behave sustainably and value sustainable behavior. Demonstrating or communicating this kind of normative support from other people can be very effective in motivating consumers to behave

---

* But beware of overscaring them or presenting the problem as too severe and therefore uncontrollable (see the insights from system justification theory described in the previous stage).

in a sustainable way. You could, for example, design (social) marketing campaigns or appeals that communicate certain pro-environmental or pro-sustainable social norms. When communicating about desirable sustainable behavior, descriptive norms (conveying information about what most people in a similar situation would do) will likely be most effective.* It is important to note that the effects of such descriptive norms are maximized when they describe behavior from other people that occurred in a setting that most closely matches the consumers' immediate social environment. So, for example, messages in hotel rooms as part of an energy conservation program telling consumers that the majority of guests who stayed in their room used their towels more than once, or messages telling people that the majority of neighbors are saving energy are most likely to be effective in motivating consumers to behave more sustainably themselves.

In addition to communicating social norms, you could craft the social environment of consumers in such a way that it signals that other people also behave sustainably; that is, that sustainable behavior is the norm. In line with this, various studies have demonstrated that minor changes in the surroundings or a situation that implicitly conveys a social norm (e.g., donating money to a street singer, the presence of graffiti, illegally parked bikes) can motivate people to behave consonantly with that social norm. This insight translates into straightforward recommendations for the current sustainability issue: Use the social environment to increase consumers' motivation to behave pro-environmentally and sustainably by minimizing (the visibility of) signs or traces of unsustainable or anti-environmental behavior as much as possible, while at the same time maximizing the visibility of sustainable and pro-environmental behavior. When the desirable sustainable behavior is not salient or does not stand out (because not many consumers display such behavior yet), you could try to create an illusion of sustainability. For example, an in-store promotional offer for a sustainable product could be accompanied with a sign reading "offer prolonged due to great demand," signaling that the product is immensely popular and that sustainable behavior is the norm.

The theoretical paradigm underlying most research on attitudes (Chapter 13) is also relevant in this light because it elaborates on why this approach could be successful. Specifically, it explains that in the environmental domain the actions and welfare of others are a predominant theme, more so than, for example, in the personal health domain. As a result, moral demands will be present to a higher degree than in most other areas and moral and social considerations (as expressed in social norms) are likely to be highly influential motivators and determinants of consumers' intentions to act, and their behavior.

Evolutionary psychology (Chapter 3) proposes a different approach to the current problem of unsustainable consumption. This paradigm claims that one of the most important human drives is to attract desirable mates. People try to do this by signaling and displaying that they possess several traits that are attractive to the other sex, for example, intelligence, openness, and agreeableness. According to evolutionary psychology, an effective way to make consumers more motivated to

---

* When communicating about undesirable behavior, the use of descriptive norms is most likely to work counterproductively.

behave more sustainably would be to harness this drive to attract desirable mates to promote sustainable behavior. Specifically, if you could provide them with the opportunity to signal their desirability to the other sex by behaving sustainably, this might fuel their motivation to choose sustainable options. This could be achieved by making sustainable (or green) behavior more costly, more elite, and harder to achieve. After all, when sustainable behavior is framed as *high status* and more scarce and costly, its signaling function will become more prominent, so that it helps consumers to display their desirable traits to the other sex. For example, a man who can afford to buy very expensive and scarce sustainable products shows women that he has the resources (e.g., money, time, and social connections) to obtain these, and thus signals that he has attractive traits, such as intelligence and agreeableness, that make him a desirable mate. Thus, consumers' motivation to behave more sustainably can be increased if sustainable behavior gives them the opportunity to signal and display desirable traits. Please note that these recommendations are derived from evolutionary theory and have not been empirically tested so far. Nevertheless, they might prove useful in situations in which sustainable behavior cannot be made less costly and easier; in these kinds of situations, framing sustainable options as being high status, for the elite, and sexy, might be an effective way to get at least a specific group of consumers motivated to behave more sustainably.

Another theoretical perspective that provides valuable insights on how to increase consumers' motivation to act sustainably focuses on psychological consistency (Chapter 15). This perspective is based on the notion that people have a basic need to be consistent in their cognitions, attitudes, and actions. If a situation arises in which a person's behavior is not in line with her attitudes, this need for consistency and the self-image is threatened, resulting in a drive to maintain or restore consistency. One area *par excellence* in which a person's actions might be dissonant with her attitudes is sustainability. Specifically, many consumers will hold pro-environmental attitudes, but actually endorsing a sustainable lifestyle at all times is much more difficult (not to say, next to impossible) to uphold. One day or another, the typical pro-environmental consumer will find herself in a situation in which she fails to act consistently with her pro-environmental attitudes, and feels like a hypocrite (e.g., when taking the car instead of the bike to work, or when buying a delicious steak instead of a protein-rich meat substitute). This is the bad news. The good news is that this failure of acting in accordance with one's pro-environmental attitudes and the resulting feelings of hypocrisy might actually increase one's motivation to act sustainably in future situations. Specifically, a consumer who just feels like a hypocrite because she failed to act upon her pro-environmental attitudes is likely to be motivated to restore consistency between her behavior and attitudes. One way of doing this is to behave more sustainably (e.g., choosing more sustainable products when shopping, trying harder to save energy at home). Research shows that chances of such changing of behavior to match pro-environmental attitudes are higher if one has recently expressed pro-environmental attitudes to others or in public. In this case, the drive for consistency, or the (anticipated) feeling of hypocrisy will more likely result in sustainable behavior.

There are several ways in which these findings can be used to increase sustainable behavior. First, make use of the public advocacy principle: one should try to induce consumers to publicly express or advocate their pro-environmental attitudes. You could accomplish this by having them sign (online) public petitions on pro-environmental issues, or find other ways to make their pro-environmental attitudes more visible (e.g., identify consumers who have donated money to a pro-environmental cause by means of stickers on doorposts or publishing lists of contributors in daily papers). Consumers who are committed to their pro-environmental attitudes will be more motivated to behave accordingly. Second, you could use hypocrisy experienced by others to motivate consumers to behave sustainably. Specifically, one could use a prototypical actor—who is similar to consumers in several ways and with whom consumers can identify (an in-group member)—to experience hypocrisy because he failed to behave consistently with his pro-environmental attitudes. Such a *vicarious hypocrisy experience* may be quite effective in motivating consumers to act more sustainably Eisenhowerian themselves. Television and online clips or radio spots in which an actor experiences humiliating hypocrisy might well serve this purpose. Third, you could also remind consumers of their own previous hypocrisy experiences in the realm of sustainability and pro-environmentalism. These reminders can reinstate a feeling of hypocrisy or cognitive dissonance, thereby motivating consumers to restore consistency between their attitudes and behavior by acting more sustainably and in line with their pro-environmental attitudes. Effective reminders can be phrased in the form of questions like, "When was the last time you …?" and can be embedded in various kinds of social marketing campaigns using social norms (e.g., "Of course, we are all concerned about the environment, and we want to stop environmental pollution. But when was the last time you …? Stop dreaming, start acting. You can make the difference. Start today!").

At this point it needs to be stressed that hypocrisy induction is only recommended to be used with consumers who have relatively strong pro-environmental and/or pro-sustainability attitudes; otherwise, inducing hypocrisy could probably lead to changing those attitudes (instead of the unsustainable behavior), and this is not desirable.

System justification theory (Chapter 9) also provides valuable insights on how to increase consumers' motivation to change their own unsustainable consumption patterns. It posits that people are motivated to maintain feelings of (personal) control. Whenever personal feelings of control are threatened, people start to compensate for that and increase their belief in, and reliance on, external systems of control. The operation of such defensive compensatory control mechanisms entails that people place the locus of control outside of themselves, attribute it to external systems like a government or a religious entity (e.g., God), and their feelings of personal agency decrease. In other words, people feel out of control and depend on external systems to address emerging problems. The parallel with the current situation of unsustainable consumption is apparent: the problem of unsustainable consumption and resulting environmental damage can be so complex, chaotic, and overwhelming that it may pose a threat to consumers' feelings of personal control. This will in turn instigate compensatory control mechanisms in which consumers place the locus of control and responsibility outside of themselves, eliminating or decreasing the feeling that they can personally contribute to solving the problem, or in other words, their motivation to act. As was explained in the first stage, the challenge here again is to prevent these defensive processes from occurring.

In addition to the tactics presented previously, which were aimed at increasing problem recognition, system justification theory proposes insights on how to increase consumers' motivation to act. First, you could frame the solution to the problem (i.e., behave more sustainably) as a means to satisfy consumers' need for control. For example, by explaining that recycling (sorting paper, glass, and plastic) or energy conservation brings order to the chaos of pollution and unsustainability, you appeal to consumers' motivation to maintain a sense of control thereby motivating them to perform these kinds of behaviors. Second, you could emphasize an individual consumer's ability to effect change. Specifically, if you communicate that each consumer can, in her own way, contribute to the solution of the problem, hereby giving her a sense of control, this might diminish belief in, and reliance on, external control systems and restore her sense of agency and control. With this restoration of personal control, consumers' motivation to act will automatically increase. Importantly, for this strategy to be effective it is crucial to actually provide consumers with concrete and practical tips on how they can behave more sustainably. In other words, a vital part of increasing consumers' motivation to act is to enhance their feelings of self-efficacy.

Finally, the theoretical perspective that focuses on emotions (Chapter 12) also provides us with some helpful insights on how to increase consumers' motivation to behave more sustainably. This theoretical paradigm postulates that emotions not only have an informational past-oriented function ("How do I feel about what I have done?"), but also a more future-oriented motivational function ("What do my feelings tell me to do next?"). In other words, emotions can be the starting points for behavior and motivate or mobilize a person to take action. The exact motivational nature of emotions varies from one specific emotion to another. For example, experiencing regret involves feeling that one should have known better, and a tendency to blame oneself, correct one's mistake, and undo what happened. The experience of disappointment, in contrast, involves feeling powerless, and a tendency to do nothing and to turn away from the event. When we apply these notions to the present situation of motivating consumers to behave more sustainably, it follows that consumers who experience regret will be more inclined to take action to undo something negative than consumers who experience disappointment. In line with this, research has demonstrated that regretful consumers are more likely to switch to alternative options and behaviors than disappointed consumers. Therefore, if you plan to communicate with consumers through emotional appeals or messages, it would be advisable to evoke feelings of regret instead of disappointment. So you should not tell consumers that their unsustainable consumption is very disappointing, because this will most likely evoke feelings of disappointment in them as well (which will probably make them feel bad and inert). Rather, you should communicate to them that not behaving sustainably is regrettable, and/or will make them regret their actions at a later moment when it is too late to undo the damage; these feelings of (anticipated) regret will probably evoke feelings of self-blame and increase their motivation to find more sustainable ways to behave (i.e., correct their mistakes). Again, it is recommended here to be specific in your communication: inform consumers concerning the kinds of behaviors that are unsustainable, and provide them with clear and practical alternative (sustainable) options.

Stage 3: Regulation and Execution of Action

When consumers recognize the problem of unsustainable consumption and production patterns and they feel personally motivated to act more sustainably, they can progress to a state in which they actually behave more sustainably. In this last stage, consumers might find it difficult to regulate their behavior; various goals, conflicting motivations, and situational and social cues might be influencing their behavior, both consciously and unconsciously. Fortunately, the previous chapters provide insights and tools that can both help consumers to act on their good (sustainable) intentions as well as nudge them toward more sustainable behavior.

From the chapter on social marketing (Chapter 2), some useful tips can be distilled on how to promote sustainable behavior. These are based on the underlying assumption that consumers must have both the opportunity and the ability to choose sustainable options. First of all, to give consumers the opportunity to behave more sustainably, sustainable products need to be available and accessible. Therefore, the first step would be to increase supermarkets' stocks and supplies of sustainable products. Moreover, these products should be presented in such a way that consumers will easily notice them. To increase chances that consumers will take sustainable products into consideration, these products should be presented prominently, for example, by placement on preferred shelf locations (at eye level, at the center of the shelves). In addition, to increase the accessibility of sustainable products for many consumers, sustainable products should be (made) available not only in the high-priced segments, but also in the mid-range price segments. If this is difficult to achieve, another option would be to create product lines that are not fully sustainable (but more sustainable than regular products) that fall in this mid-range segment. The advantage of this approach is that it gives many people the opportunity to take a small step toward sustainable consumption. In addition, to increase consumers' ability to behave more sustainably, a generic labeling system could be implemented on packaging that helps them to make sense of all the different products and information. Specifically, a comprehensible and easy-to-use system could help motivated consumers during their decision-making process to single out the most sustainable product (or the best product in terms of both sustainability and price concerns), and save them considerable time and confusion. It is important to note here that such a labeling system would also be sensible from a system justification perspective (Chapter 9), as it would help consumers to create meaning in the chaos of information and overload of choices, and provide them with a feeling of and means to exert personal control (see also Chapter 8 on existentialism, for the importance of creating meaning when communicating incentives for behavior chance).

Insights derived from cognitive sociology (Chapter 4) also argue in favor of implementation of a labeling system indicating the extent to which a product is sustainable, but from a different rationale. First, the existence of such a labeling system would serve as a signal that choosing sustainable products is considered important by many people, thereby crafting a social norm of sustainability. Given the fact that people usually conform to social norms, this will increase the likelihood that they will choose the more sustainable options. Second, this labeling system would give consumers instantaneous feedback on whether they are making a sustainable choice themselves, and as such provides them with an indication of whether they violate social norms regarding sustainability. When such continuous feedback is given to consumers on whether they behave in accordance with (or against) the existing norm, this facilitates regulation of their behavior in the direction of that norm. For this reason, other interventions that give consumers feedback on whether or not they adhere to social norms regarding sustainability could also prove successful in promoting sustainable behavior. For example, you could provide consumers with tailored information on their energy consumption (at household level) together with comparative information on other households. This type of feedback will tell them whether they are on pace with the rest of the neighborhood or need to lower their energy use in order to fit in.* It is advisable to accompany this comparative feedback to consumers who fall below the community average with a happy smiley face (a simple yet elegant way of expressing social approval) because this will eliminate the risk that these already green consumers will become more wasteful.

In addition, construal level theory (Chapter 7) explains that there is a relation between psychological distance and how abstractly an object is represented in people's minds. The general idea is that the more distant an object is perceived to be, the more abstract it will be thought of (an opposite relation exists between closeness and concreteness). As a rule, if people construe events in a more abstract and distant manner, more weight is given to abstract and distant issues, and vice versa. When we take into consideration that (1) a regular shopping experience usually focuses on instant gratification and feels psychologically close (because it is concrete, emotionally engaging, and absorbing) and is therefore likely to be accompanied by lower construal levels, and (2) unsustainable consumption and resulting environmental damage are for most people abstract and psychologically distant matters, it becomes clear that sustainability and pro-environmental concerns will probably not be top-of-mind when consumers are shopping and are therefore not given much weight during the decision-making process. Therefore, according to construal level theory, it would be advisable to induce higher construal levels in consumers when they are in the midst of buying something. Specifically, you could instruct consumers to "take a step back" when they find themselves in the heat of the decision-making process. The psychological and emotional distance that is created by stepping back will likely produce higher construal levels, which enables the more distant and abstract sustainability and environmental concerns to be brought (back) into focus (this strategy is comparable to taking a step back when in the heat of a fight with your spouse or partner: some distance often enables one to see

* You could also choose to include comparative figures of green households that use little energy in order to strengthen social norms with regard to sustainability.

the higher-order concerns and values of one's relationships (e.g., love, raising kids) more clearly.

Another tactic could be to make the abstract and distant issue of sustainability more concrete and salient during consumers' shopping experiences, so that it matches consumers' low construal levels. From this point of view, a labeling system that indicates the extent to which a product is sustainable would be recommended as well. After all, these labels will make the abstract and distant notion of sustainability more concrete and practical by showing consumers how they can behave more sustainably at that moment. It is important to note, however, that the previous recommendations regarding construal levels will only promote environmental and sustainability concerns and behavior in consumers who already value these issues or who have personal pro-environmental and sustainability goals.

The chapter on licensing (Chapter 6) also provides useful insights on how to promote sustainable behavior. This theoretical perspective puts forward that most consumer choices follow other choices or judgments, and that the nature of these earlier choices affects the present decision-making process. Specifically, a virtuous prior choice can boost a consumer's self-image so that it licenses a subsequent less virtuous or self-indulgent choice. When applied to the current context, this means that when a consumer has previously chosen a sustainable product or has acted sustainably, this might decrease the likelihood that she will display such virtuous behavior in subsequent situations or contexts. Fortunately, research shows that there are conditions under which this effect disappears. Specifically, when consumers have the mindset or an intrinsic motivation to behave sustainably, chances increase that they will continue to behave sustainably after engaging in sustainable behavior. In contrast, when consumers perceive sustainable behavior as a goal, behaving sustainably will fulfill that goal and decrease the motivation and likelihood of sustainable acts in subsequent situations. Similarly, when consumers perceive sustainable behavior as something that they are supposed or ought to do, this will also decrease the likelihood of future sustainable acts. Thus, if you want to minimize licensing effects, it is recommended to frame sustainable behavior as a way of living (a lifestyle) that is intrinsically rewarding, as opposed to framing it as an obligation or goal that consumers need to fulfill.

Subsequently, the paradigm that focuses on resource depletion and self-control (Chapter 10) offers useful starting points that may help to promote sustainable behavior. Simply stated, this line of research and theorizing postulates that exerting self-control consumes (cognitive) resources and that when these resources become depleted, people lose their ability to regulate their behavior. This may result in actions that one would generally want to avoid, like overeating, unwise spending, and procrastination. For example, a person who had to exert a considerable amount of self-control during work (e.g., by not interrupting and being polite to colleagues while he disagrees with them or because he has resisted the temptation to eat cake and snacks that were offered during meetings) might find himself in a depleted state on his way home, which may manifest itself in buying a snack at a kiosk or buying CDs he doesn't actually need. Luckily, this heightened tendency of depleted people to react on their impulses and situational cues can be pragmatically used to induce them to behave more sustainably. Specifically, research shows that being in a state of regulatory resource depletion fosters the use of heuristics present in the persuasion context, which increases the likelihood of compliance with the target request of an influence technique. This means that sustainable behavior can be increased in depleted consumers through the use of basic social influence tactics. You could, for example, draw on the following tactics: (a) use celebrity endorsers or spokespersons to increase the attractiveness of sustainable products, (b) provide consumers with immediate positive feedback when they behave sustainably (e.g., signs that say "Thank you for …" accompanied by a happy smiley face symbolizing social approval), and (c) create the impression that the majority of consumers display a particular sustainable behavior (e.g., construct an everybody-is-doing-it feeling).

And last but not least, another potentially effective technique to increase sustainable behavior emerges from the chapter on decision making (Chapter 5). Particularly, research on default effects has important implications for the current issue. Defaults are settings or choices that apply to consumers who do not take active steps to change them (e.g., the amount of time that is set on electronic devices like computers, coffee machines, or cell phones before a low energy mode is turned on while they are not being used; the wattage level on the quick-start mode of microwaves; organ donation programs for which people either have to opt in or opt out, etc.). Of importance here is that whatever these default choices are, many consumers stick with them. They do so because actively making a decision often involves effort (whereas accepting the default is effortless), and because they might believe that defaults are suggestions by the policy maker, which implies a recommended action. From this it follows that changes in defaults are likely to result in a change of choice. This technique of *nudging* consumers' behavior toward desirable default options or settings is often regarded as the prototypical instrument of libertarian paternalism because it guides choice while at the same time preserving the freedom to choose (Thaler & Sunstein, 2010). The usefulness for the present issue of unsustainable consumption is straightforward: if policy makers or communication professionals think that a particular default produces more sustainable outcomes, they can greatly influence the outcomes by choosing or presenting it as the default. For example, time settings for energy-saving modes on electronic devises could be adjusted so that more energy is saved, or sustainable options or choices can be presented as opt-outs instead of opt-ins (e.g., on dinner registration forms the choice for a sustainable vegetarian menu is already selected; if people want meat they should indicate so explicitly by deselecting the vegetarian option).

Producing Effective Change

Now that the theoretical perspectives have been fitted into a stage model of behavior change, it is important to stress that this classification has not been executed solely for the sake of providing order in the myriad theoretical perspectives that are offered in previous chapters. Rather, using the framework of a stage model enables one to match persuasive strategies to the particular stage of change in which a target group is. So, when you craft your influence techniques in such a way that they are in accordance with consumers' state of mind, this optimizes chances of producing effectual change. After all, providing, for example, a labeling system that indicates which products score high on sustainability and which ones do not, is not likely to change the behavior of consumers who are not aware that their consumption patterns are unsustainable and are not contemplating change in this domain. However, it can be a useful way to assist or nudge consumers who do realize that their lifestyle is unsustainable and are motivated to change to actually choose more sustainable options. Thus, tailoring persuasive techniques in such a way that they match consumers' stages of change increases the likelihood that your efforts will be effective.[*]

Hopefully, this synopsis in which the wealth of theoretical perspectives presented in the previous chapters is organized in a three-stage model of behavior change provides a starting point for selecting appropriate theoretical approaches and insights to start tackling the problem of unsustainable behavior. Moreover, I hope that the present chapter will help policy workers, communication professionals, and other practitioners to better translate these insights into practical tools and interventions, and inspires them to embark upon the challenge of stimulating more sustainable consumption patterns.

REFERENCES

Prochaska, J. O., & DiClemente, C. C. (1983). Stages and processes of self-change of smoking: Toward an integrative model of change. *Journal of Consulting and Clinical Psychology, 51*, 390–395.

Thaler, R. H., & Sunstein, C. R. (2008). *Nudge: Improving decisions about health, wealth, and happiness*. New Haven, CT: Yale University Press.

Weinstein, N. D., Rothman, A. J., & Sutton, S. R. (1998). Stage theories of health behavior: Conceptual and methodological issues. *Health Psychology, 17*, 290–299.

---

[*] In a given population, consumers will likely differ in their particular stage of change. When this is the case, one could decide to launch different campaigns matching the various consumer stages of change simultaneously, or choose instead to focus on one group of consumers and their particular stage of change.

Section 7

Concluding Remarks

17

Recurring Themes on Sustainable Behavior and Their Implications for Intervention

HANS C.M. VAN TRIJP

RECURRING THEMES ON SUSTAINABLE BEHAVIOR

*F*irst, several of the contributions emphasized that as a cognitive motivation, *sustainability* is probably not very strong as a driver of consumption behavior. Chapter 3, which takes an evolutionary psychology approach, is probably most outspoken on this. Miller brings up the point that there is no evolutionary meaning or value in the selection of products that would favor sustainability per se. From an evolutionary perspective, there is much more adaptive value in products that serve instant gratification, rather than the delayed and more socially remote rewards from sustainable consumption. Social marketing approaches (discussed in Chapter 2) similarly emphasize the importance of self-interest as a basis for the value exchange process. These self-interests need to be overruled for sustainability motivations to win people's favor.

In addition to added value of product choices in terms of direct gratification, social norms may also support levels of perceived self-interest. This point is at the center of the Lindenberg and Steg chapter, in which three types of consumer goals are discussed: hedonic, gain, and normative goals. Strengthening the normative goal inherent in sustainable consumption is crucial in their view and can be supported only through consistent social support. Without social support and constant scaffolding, people will fall back from normative to hedonic and gain motivations. The relative importance of normative goals can be enhanced by reducing the impact of hedonic and/or gain goals that are contrary to pro-environmental behavior (making them compatible rather than competitive) or by activating and strengthening the normative goal per se. In other words, by moving beyond the perceived trade-off (sustainability at the expense of gratification of the hedonic and gain goals) to develop propositions where the sustainable option is the hedonically and functionally more gratifying alternative, sustainable behavior may become a more attractive alternative to people. In addition, the authors present convincing evidence that norm-guided behavior can also be promoted through low-level priming of subtle changes in people's choice architecture.

Whereas social norms approaches emphasize compliance with the (perceived) group norm arguing for conformity with the behavior of relevant others, Miller, from his evolutionary psychological perspective, takes exactly the opposite line of reasoning, emphasizing distinctiveness and display value. He argues that green behavior is most likely to be promoted if it can travel on the trait-signaling instincts of people. He argues that sustainable behavior is most likely to be engaged in when it provides people with an opportunity to show off their superiority to others or when it is seen as a possession of highly valued fundamental traits such as high intelligence, agreeableness, conscientiousness, and so on.

The existentialism perspective, central to Chapter 8, relates the relatively low level of concern with sustainable development to the fact that sustainability issues lack a high level of immediate, concrete, and visible impact, compared to other issues (such as the current economic crisis) and current concerns. Proulx argues that positioning sustainable development as an urgent threat is most likely to be counterproductive as it will more likely strengthen a preference for the familiar, the certain, and the status quo. After all, what studies in existential psychology show is that when people are confronted with threats (such as an environmental crisis), the need for meaning, structure, consistency, and thus for conservatism and traditionalism goes up. The chapter by Banfield et al. on social justification and compensatory control similarly emphasizes the importance of perceptions of agency and control. If sustainability issues are positioned as overwhelming, and beyond personal control, it is likely to reduce the sense of personal responsibility and hence will lead to less, rather than more, action and behavior change.

Although the cognitive motivation for sustainability per se is not a particularly strong motivation for most of the people most of the time, several chapters emphasize that the attention to and focus on sustainability issues might be temporally and situationally enhanced as a result of shifting foci. This is most explicitly articulated in the chapter on construal level theory. How consumers psychologically construe choice and consumption events has a considerable and systematic impact on the role that more abstract sustainability considerations play in actual choice. Fit between the motivational mindset and the psychological positioning of the choice events selectively favors a focus on more abstract (*should-type*) considerations or more concrete (*ought-type*) considerations. The specific communication implication is that there are essentially two routes to take. The first would be that at the moment of actual choice, a more abstract construal is induced in individuals. Alternatively, (re-)positioning of sustainable options at a more concrete level might put them at an advantage in actual choice behavior. Focella and Stone provide an interesting perspective in that precommitment to good intentions may be exploited in relation to feelings of hypocrisy, which in turn may stimulate sustainable consumption.

Several chapters emphasize the importance of a focus on sustained sustainable behavior rather than one-off choices in favor of sustainable development. This is best articulated in the chapter by Meijers et al. who discuss carry-over and balancing effects from one sustainable behavior onto the next. Balancing effects (i.e., the higher probability of an unsustainable act to follow an initial sustainable act) may be the result of moral licensing and/or the fact that goal fulfillment through the initial sustainable act may (temporarily) decrease the motivational strength and accessibility of the sustainability goal. In stimulating carry-over rather than balancing effects, Meijers et al. argue for a central role of self view which can effectively be stimulated through the social labeling technique. Focella and Stone similarly argue that the most appropriate intervention strategies may depend on the consumer's stage of change, reflecting motivational priority in relation to (partial) fulfillment of the sustainability goal.

Other chapters focus on the implicit and explicit barriers that consumers may experience in moving toward sustainable behavior. In the social marketing approach (Chapter 2), this is reflected in the opportunity component of behavioral change. This perspective emphasizes that sustainable behavior is more likely to occur when the environment selectively makes the sustainable behavior as the easily available and easily accessible option. In other words, making the sustainable behavioral option the easy, low-effort option is an effective way of inducing sustainable behavior. This point is also central to the chapter on defaults, where Goldstein and Dinner argue for subtle changes in the choice environment that make the sustainable option the default option, implying that consumers would have to invest effort in diverging from the sustainable option, rather than the sustainable choice requiring extra time, effort, and additional cognitive resources. Goldstein and Dinner provide numerous examples of how different types of defaults could contribute to sustainable development. Lindenberg and Steg relate the use of defaults and subtle social cues to the issue of the self-regulatory capacity necessary for norm-based behavior.

Self-control is also central to two other chapters that discuss it as an effective approach to closing the attitude–behavior gap in sustainable development (Chapters 10 and 11). As Vohs and Fennis show, in the context of competing pressures to give up temporary temptations of short-term gains for long-term goals, self-regulatory resources are necessary to translate good intentions into sustainable behavior but may easily fall short. Gutsell and Inzlicht, taking a neuroscience perspective, argue that emphasizing prosocial value inherent in prosocial behavior may be too weak a signal to shift the balance in monitoring one's goal progress away from more immediately rewarding temptations. He argues that strategies aimed at promoting sustainable behavior will probably be more effective if the sustainable goals are made salient (e.g., through product labeling) and if stronger negative emotions are induced after self-control failure. Emphasizing the moral dimension of sustainable consumption by linking it to sanctity and purity of nature may be routes to achieve this. Vohs and Fennis similarly emphasize self-control and build on previous research that shows that people who are chronically or temporarily low in self-control are actually more compliant with social norms and persuasion tactics. In other words, this segment of consumers with depleted self-regulatory resources may be a good target when they are approached with the appropriate social influence techniques.

The role of identity in promoting sustainable behavior is a central theme in the chapters by Sparks and Postmes et al. Sparks argues that sustainable consumption can more fruitfully be considered at the level of interpersonal and intergroup relations rather than in intrapersonal terms as these, if appropriately operationalized, are already adequately covered in existing attitudinal theories. Sparks thus argues for a role of identity within those attitudinal representations of the sustainable consumption domain. Postmes et al. go deeper into the issue of the relation between sustainability and social identities as they argue that in-group–out-group comparisons may actually backfire in the ambition to promote sustainable consumption. Sustainable identities are not easy to bring about, because of the high level of psychological disjuncture between individual and environmental problems: Environmental problems are almost never related to people's core social identities. The problem of sustainability is a problem that we inherited from generations before us and the effects are much more relevant for the generations after us. In other words, it is hard to see it as a problem we can identify with, as *our* problem. Postmes and co-authors propose the Social Identity Model of Collective Action as a theoretical framework to inform sustainable efforts. It combines several elements such as moral convictions, a sense of efficacy, and emotions.

Emotions as a tool in promoting sustainable consumption are central in Zeelenberg and Van Doorn's contribution, adopting a *feeling-is-for-doing* perspective on the motivational functions of emotions. Inducing feelings such as regret and guilt can strengthen feelings of personal responsibility and thus motivate personal efforts toward sustainable behavior.

IMPLICATIONS OF INTERVENTIONS TO PROMOTE SUSTAINABLE DEVELOPMENT

Where does all this leave us in terms of informing interventions aimed at promoting sustainable development? Without repeating the specific suggestions that have appeared in each of the chapters, we extract a number of key implications for intervention strategies.

Make the ambitious issue of sustainable development "manageable" to consumers: It is obvious that sustainable development is a massive threat to future generations and the world as a whole. Few consumers can see the gigantic impact it can have and mixed messages from experts and politicians create confusion and at the same time provide a justification for consumers to opt out and not take personal responsibility. Lack of awareness of consequences and lack of ascription of personal responsibility are perhaps two of the biggest barriers to sustainable development. Consumers can be easily overwhelmed with the massiveness of the problem, causing lethargy and regression to the status quo, rather than inducing concern and action. Although media efforts such as *The Inconvenient Truth* may play an important role in enhancing attention and putting sustainability issues on the agenda, it is yet to be seen whether such *overwhelming* positioning of the problem actually promotes actions at the individual consumer level.

The perspective implies that positioning and communication efforts should aim at making the sustainability problem manageable to consumers. Rather than framing it as a global threat, it would be better to provide concrete action perspectives in terms of small steps that can cumulatively make a big difference. In terms of framing, this would imply that in communication efforts one should emphasize the achievements (the glass is half full) rather than inadequacies (the glass is half empty) of sustainability-inspired efforts.

Develop and communicate concrete representations of the abstract issue: Sustainable development is at a disadvantage in many concrete consumer decisions, simply because the abstract nature of it is likely to receive a lower weight when people are making concrete, real-time decisions. When making decisions, consumers tend to focus on concrete construals and, unless sustainable issues can be translated to that specific level, they are unlikely to drive actual consumption decisions.

The implication would be that sustainability issues would need to be brought to life in concrete terms. Following this line of reasoning, rather than emphasizing the abstract operationalization of Fair Trade products enhancing the livelihood of smallholders in developing countries, it should be made visible and concrete in terms of actually showing the livelihood conditions at the point of sale. And rather than communicating animal welfare as an abstract issue, it might be preferable to make this concrete as, for example, in terms of "never in life has this chicken had more living space than tonight in your microwave."

Do not over-rely on the rational cognitive motivation for doing good: Although it is tempting to rely heavily on the common sense that doing good is an important social motivation, many of the chapters argue that this cognitive motivation is effective in shaping good intentions, but generally too weak to induce sustainable consumption. This does not discredit the importance of cognitive–rational motivations, but it attests to the notion that these motivations need to be augmented with concrete action perspectives. Communication campaigns can be effective in agenda setting but probably less so in inducing behavior, on which sustainable development ultimately relies.

This notion implies that many of the government campaigns on raising awareness of the urgency of the problem and the moral obligation to take one's part are likely to be insufficient to really make the difference in promoting sustainable behavior in the general population. They are most likely to appeal to the (front-runner) segment of well-informed consumers, thereby missing the point for the majority of less informed and less motivated consumers who are likely to make the difference.

Appreciate differences among consumer segments: One of the key messages from the various chapters in this book is that there is "more than one road leading to Rome". Different theoretical perspectives suggest different and sometimes opposing intervention strategies and tactics to promote sustainable consumption. This is at least partly due to different consumer segments existing in the marketplace. Short of such a one-size-fits-all approach to promoting sustainable consumption, it seems that understanding the diversity in consumers' status quo is one of the crucial factors for developing and inducing effective sustainable behavior. This is because different key barriers may be experienced in the effective change of behavior and, as a result, different intervention strategies might apply to each of these segments.

The implication is that, rather than one golden bullet approach, a portfolio of different intervention strategies and tactics will be required to do justice to the diversity of sensitivity of different consumer segments toward specific intervention strategies and tactics. A key challenge will be to identify these segments at a level sufficiently actionable for the delivery of customized interventions.

Enhance the perceived self-interest inherent in sustainable consumption: Many sustainable decisions can be thought of as a classical social dilemma, where the short-term self-interest is perceived as being at odds with long-term societal benefits. In many instances, (perceived) self-interest takes priority in actual choice behavior.

The implication is that ways should be found in product development and product communication, where hedonics and gains at the personal level are not perceived as contrary to pro-environmental behaviors. One way to achieve this is by communicating that pro-environmental behavior may also carry a number of personal benefits. This can be achieved by emphasizing the monetary gains (as in the case of energy consumption) and higher product quality (e.g., superior taste) of sustainable options. Alternatively, the social norm that "pro-environmental is good" may be strengthened by education programs on biospheric and altruistic values, and by (mass) media campaigns that communicate sustainable consumption as the group norm. The idea is that deviation from the group norm is a costly process that is not in the interest of self-interest. For specific subgroups of consumers (e.g., youngsters), self-interest may also be increased through social distinctiveness on the basis of sustainable consumption ("It is cool to be green"), which in turn may in the longer run change the norm of larger groups. Finally, self-interest may be enhanced through the reduced cognitive effort in product choice by making the sustainable choice the low-effort choice. This can be done through processes related to default setting and other forms of nudging.

Enhance sustainable identity and status quo in sustainable consumption: Rather than positioning sustainability as an external goal (something one ought to pursue), efforts could be undertaken to make it part of the consumers' social identity. Social identity formation can develop from top-down processes where inferences about social identity (as advocated through thought leaders) are internalized as personal values, and/or from bottom-up processes where shared norms and values are induced from the observations of the actions of individuals, largely through in-group dynamics. Both of these routes, and particularly that of in-group dynamics, can lead members to induce a shared identity revolving around a common opinion. The aim would be to induce social norms, values, and self-stereotypes that define groups or *cultures* at a level of social categorization. The content of this inclusive social identity should be future oriented (motives, goals, etc.). The object would be to redefine and reinvent what humans *are*, by redefining a common consensual understanding of what we want humans to *become*, namely a species that can live sustainably, preserving available resources for future generations.

The implications are manyfold. Clearly this approach would involve a level of education and consistent communication and framing by opinion leaders ("yes you can"), as well as the facilitation of debate and discussion platforms between group members. Social media can play a crucial role in this process.

Exploit emotions as a driver for sustainable consumption: Finally, the relevance of sustainable consumption can be enhanced by strengthening its emotional elements. Several emotions have been proposed as guides to sustainable behavior. Guilt, shame, regret are all well known as powerful moral emotions and behavioral guides. In a complementary fashion, positive emotions such as pride and happiness may be associated with inducing sustainable behaviors. Whatever the specific emotion one focuses on, strengthening the emotional valence of sustainable consumption (or deviations thereof) may provide a more urgent and self-relevant dimension to it, and thus put it higher on the consumer's agenda.

CONCLUSION

Altogether this book has brought together a large number of theory-based suggestions for intervention aimed at promoting sustainable behavior. These suggestions converge in several directions, but at times also seem to contradict each other. However, we believe that they provide an important starting point for future research at the interface of psychology and sustainable development.

Names Index

A

Aarts, H., 42, 72
Abrahamse, W., 45, 46, 48, 74
Aglioti, S. M., 144–145
Aitken, C., 207–208
Ajzen, I., 170, 171
Albarracín, D., 75
Alexander, G., 139
Allcott, H., 47
Allen, C. T., 72, 76, 77, 78
Alony, R., 83
Amir, O., 41
Andersen, L. M., 16
Anderson, A. K., 147
Anderson, S. M., 113
Andreoni, J., 38
Angus, K., 20
Anton, J. L., 144
Antonenko, O., 141
Appiah, K. A., 176–177, 179
Aquino, K., 43, 46
Ariely, D., 38, 41
Armitage, C. J., 172
Aronson, E., 205, 206–207, 208, 209, 210
Arps, K., 84
Atkinson, J. W., 74, 113
Attari, S., 56
Attfield, R., 176
Auger, P., 18, 22
Avenanti, A., 144–145
Averill, J. R., 159
Avramova, Y. R., 3–10, 6, 71–80, 239
Ayal, S., 38
Ayduk, O., 84

B

Babcock, L., 48
Bagozzi, R. P., 159
Baldwin, M. W., 106
Banaji, M. R., 105, 113, 115

Banfield, J. C., 7, 111–123, 120, 238
Bar-Anan, Y., 83
Baray, G., 193
Barch, D. M., 139
Bargh, J. A., 40, 72, 74, 78, 95, 177
Barkley, R. A., 128
Barndollar, K., 40, 74
Barret, H. C., 39
Barton, M. A., 169
Basil, D. Z., 164
Basil, M. D., 164
Bateson, M., 42
Batson, C. D., 39, 141, 146
Bauman, C. W., 174, 197
Baumeister, R. F., 44, 88, 105, 128, 130, 133, 137, 155, 157
Baumgartner, H., 159
Bazerman, M. H., 94
Bechara, A., 139
Beck, L., 171
Becker, L. J., 74
Becker-Olsen, K. L., 21
Behne, T., 41, 42
Bekkering, H., 42
Belman, S., 55
Belyavsky Bayuk, J., 175
Bem, D. J., 72, 75, 76
Berenguer, J., 146
Berger, J., 196
Beshears, J., 55
Bettache, K., 197, 198
Bettman, J. R., 155
Beukeboom, C. J., 84, 93
Bhattacharya, C. B., 21
Biener, L., 20
Biga, C. F., 179
Biglan, A., 15
Bink, M. L., 40
Binney, W., 17
Birch, D., 74
Blanke, L., 140
Bliuc, A. M., 194

Subject Index

A

Ability, 4, 18, 19, 21, 229

Abstraction
abstract versus concrete goals, 86–87
construals, 82–84, 91–92, 93, 95, 221, 230, 238
developing concrete representations, 96, 241
problem, 186, 187, 197
social, 186, 187, 197
the Absurd, 104–105, 106–107, 108

Accessibility
cognitive, 89
of sustainable options, 19, 20, 21, 229

Action-perception model of empathy, 143–144

Action readiness, 157–158

Action tendencies, 157

Actions, 157

Adaptive defaults, 59

Advertising, 177

Affect, 174, *see also* emotions

Agreeableness, 30

AIDS prevention, 205–206

Anger, 158, 159, 160, 198

Animal welfare, 22, 241

Anterior cingulate cortex (ACC), 139, 140, 142

AOL, 63

Appointment options, 62–63, 64

Appraisals, 157, 158

Archetypes, Jungian, 28

Attention, 90

Attention deficit and hyperactivity disorder (ADHD), 128

Attitudes
attitude-behavior discrepancy, 4, 8, 14, 169–172, 178–179, 203, 205
consistency, 9, 226
green consumerism, 30
hypocrisy, 210, 211, 226–227
moralization, 196
motivation to change, 225, 226–227
time perspective, 190

TPB studies, 173

Australia, 207–208

Authority, 146

B

Balance effects, 6, 71–75, 76, 78, 239

Behavior
attitude-behavior discrepancy, 4, 8, 14, 169–172, 178–179, 203, 205
boosting pro-environmental, 44–49
changing, 7, 16, 111, 112–113, 119, 185, 205–212, 219–233
compensatory control, 114–115
construals, 82–83, 84
consumer segments, 241–242
continued sustainable, 6, 71–80, 231, 239
hypocrisy, 9, 203–215
impact of emotions on, 156, 158–159, 160, 161–164, 228–229
moral values, 141–142
motivating sustainable, 120–121
neuroscientific perspective, 7–8
norm-guided, 37–39, 238
self-control, 132–133, 134
short-term needs, 186
social marketing, 17, 18–20, 239
system justification, 113–114, 115, 227–228
value-behavior correspondence, 87

Beliefs, 6, 7, 29
hypocrisy, 203, 204
pro-environmental behavior, 45
social labeling, 76
threats to belief systems, 103–104, 223

Ben & Jerry's, 14

Benign defaults, 58

Biospheric values, 45–46, 48, 49, 242

Bounded rationality, 155

Brain, 138–140, 141, 143–145, 161, 222

Branding, 30

British Petroleum (BP), 111–112